Bill 'Swampy' Marsh—Chris Carter

Bill 'Swampy' Marsh is an award-winning writer/performer of stories, songs and plays. He spent most of his youth in rural south-western New South Wales. Bill was forced to give up any idea he had of a 'career' as a cricketer when a stint at agricultural college was curtailed because of illness, and so began his hobby of writing. After backpacking through three continents and working in the wine industry, his writing hobby blossomed into a career.

His first collection of short stories, *Beckom Pop. 64*, was published in 1988, his second, *Old Yanconian Daze*, in 1995 and his third, *Looking for Dad*, in 1998. During 1999 Bill released *Australia*, a CD of his songs and stories. That was followed in 2002 by *A Drover's Wife*. He has written soundtrack songs and music for the television documentaries, *The Last Mail from Birdsville—The Story of Tom Kruse*, *Source to Sea—The Story of the Murray Riverboats* and the German travel documentary, *Traumzeit auf dem Stuart Highway*.

Bill runs writing workshops in schools and communities and is employed part-time at the Adelaide Institute of TAFE's Professional Writing Unit. He has won and judged many nationwide short story writing and songwriting competitions and short film awards.

More Great Australian Flying Doctor Stories is a follow-on from his very successful first collection of *Great Flying Doctor Stories* (1999) and is part of his 'Great' series: *Great Australian Railway*

Stories (2005), *Great Australian Droving Stories* (2003) and *Great Australian Shearing Stories* (2001).

Bill performs his stories and songs regularly on radio, television and stage, and his plays have been performed across Australia.

More information about the author can be found at:
www.billswampymarsh.com

More
Great Australian
Flying Doctor
Stories

BILL 'SWAMPY' MARSH

ABC
Books

The ABC 'Wave' device is a trademark of the
Australian Broadcasting Corporation and is used
under licence by HarperCollins*Publishers* Australia.

First published in Australia in 2007 by ABC Books
for the Australian Broadcasting Corporation
Reprinted by HarperCollins*Publishers* Australia Pty Limited
ABN 36 009 913 517
harpercollins.com.au

HarperCollins*Publishers*
25 Ryde Road, Pymble, Sydney, NSW 2073, Australia
31 View Road, Glenfield, Auckland 0627, New Zealand
A 53, Sector 57, Noida, UP, India
77–85 Fulham Palace Road, London W6 8JB, United Kingdom
2 Bloor Street East, 20th floor, Toronto, Ontario M4W 1A8, Canada
10 East 53rd Street, New York NY 10022, USA

ISBN: 978 0 7333 2237 2

Cover designed by Design by Committee
Typeset in 10/15pt Bookman by Kirby Jones
70gsm Classic used by HarperCollins*Publishers* is a natural, recyclable product made from wood
grown in sustainable forests. The manufacturing processes conform to the environmental
regulations in the country of origin, Finland.

6 5 4 3 2   10 11 12 13

For 'the lady down the road'—Lyn Shea—with many, many thanks.

Contents

Acknowledgements

In memory of previous contributors and supporters: Gordon Beetham, Chris Cochrane, Joe Daley, John Dohle, Slim Dusty, Doc. Gregory, Pro Hart, Bill Hay, Don Ketteringham, Mrs Luscombe, Pep Manthorpe, Clive McAdam, Neil McTaggart, Jack Pitman, Les Rourke, Mavis St Clair and John 'Spanner' Spencer.

Special thanks to: HG Nelson, Todd Abbott and the crew at Summer All Over 2006, Angie Nelson (Program Director, ABC Networked Local Radio), Perth contacts Jan and Penny Ende, RFDS—Gerri Christie (Vic), Sally Orr (Brisbane), Monique Ryan (NSW), John Tobin (SA), Stephen Penberthy (Qld), Lisa Van Oyen (Kalgoorlie), Cheryl Russ (Derby), Clyde Thomson, Barbara Ellis, Robin Taylor and Becky Blair (Broken Hill), Luke Fitzgerald (ABC Rural Radio, Port Pirie), Brian Tonkin (Broken Hill City Library).

Thanks to: Kerrie Tuckwell and Bill Rawson (Media Monitors).

Contributors

More Great Australian Flying Doctor Stories is based on stories told to Bill 'Swampy' Marsh by:

Rhonda Anstee	Jack Goldsmith	Emily Pankhurst
Laurel Anthony	Alex Hargans	Stephen Penberthy
Rod and Gail Baker	Judy Heindorff	Fred Peter
Bob Balmain	Bill Howlett	Peter Phillips
Peter Berry	Micky Hunter	Jacqui Plowman
Reverend John C Blair	Wayne and Robina Jeffs	Graeme Purvis
Colin Bornholm	Ruth Ko	Kitty Powell
Etheen Burnett	John Lynch	Charlie Rayner
Donna Cattanach	Lady Ena Macpherson	Sharon Reddicliffe
Jane Clemson	Susan Markwell	Cheryl Russ
Ruth Cook	Neil McDougall	Monique Ryan
Graham Cowell	Michael McInerney	Chris Smith
Jack Cunningham	David McInnes	'Myf' Spencer-Smith
Dave Crommelin	Noel McIntyre	Graham Townsend
Heather Curtin	Anne McLennan	Kim Tyrie
Phil and Sue Darby	Rod McClure	Esther Veldstra
Bill Day	Norm Meehan	Dr Rob Visser
Rick Davies	Laurie and Coral Nicholls	Nick Watling
Jan and Penny Ende	Barry O'Connor	Margaret Wheatley
Lionel Ferris		Graham Winterflood
Norton Gill		

... plus many, many more.

Introduction

The early 1970s was a time of turmoil, not only for this country but also for many of us who lived here. The Vietnam War was coming to an end, the political climate was heading for a huge shift and a large section of my generation felt a sense of loss of 'self' and 'self-identity'. Along with many others, I felt that Australia had little to offer so I decided to travel the world with my then girlfriend. We sought solace amid the tumult of India. We visited a war-torn Kashmir, climbed to the heights of Nepal. We lived on a Greek island. We worked through a freezing winter in London. We drove through Europe, crammed up, along with two Australian friends and all our gear in what must've been the smallest Fiat ever manufactured. We travelled in the bilge of a Portuguese immigrant ship down the coast of Africa. We lived and worked amid the Apartheid regime of South Africa and drove through troubled Rhodesia (Zimbabwe) to view the well patrolled Victoria Falls. In many ways those couple of years were my life's education and I came to realise just how lucky we really are in this country and what huge potential we have.

I remember the day of our return: we were picked up from Fremantle docks by some people we'd never met before and, as the sun set on that warm night, we were welcomed into their house. Neighbours arrived from far and wide, the barbecue was lit, the outside beer fridge received a hammering—and for what seemed the first time in ages—I felt completely comfortable among people. What's more, they understood my humour—those one-liners, those small turns of phrase that we Australians, and virtually only we, can fully understand. Then as we all stood around an old upright piano singing out of tune, it suddenly struck me that I was home, and just what a precious place this 'home' is. As I said in the Introduction to *Great Australian Railway Stories*:

> ... after returning from that two-year trip overseas, Shirley and I travelled on the Indian Pacific from Perth, across the Nullarbor Plain, where just outside the window lay so many of the answers to the questions I'd spent the previous couple of years wandering around the world trying to sort out.

Since then, I've tried to write and collect as many Australian stories and songs as I can in the hope of saving them before they disappear. Because these are 'our' stories; the ones that belong to all of us; the ones that 'glue' us together as a reminder of who we are; the ones that this nation was built on regardless of colour, race or creed. To that end they should be taught in our schools, sung about in songs, shown in our cinemas, performed on our stages. Yes, we must remain open and learn from others— and we have a lot to learn—but if we allow our stories, songs, films and plays to be overshadowed by those from different countries then we'll be the lesser for it. We'll lose that all important sense of 'self'.

So, after many of life's twists and turns, I began my series of 'Great' books, which includes my first collection of *Great Flying Doctor Stories* plus *Great Australian Shearing Stories*, *Great Australian Droving Stories*, *Great Australian Railway Stories* and now *More Great Australian Flying Doctor Stories*.

Before beginning each book I try and contact as many of my previous contributors and supporters as possible, just to see if they have a yarn to tell or perhaps they might know of someone who has. Sadly, many of those great, old and not so old characters have passed on. I have given those people a mention under 'In memory of'.

Still and all, the support continued and *More Great Australian Flying Doctor Stories* grew out of the efforts of many, many, like-minded, people. It's impossible for me to get to all the little far-out places to meet and interview people, so it was with much appreciation that HG Nelson and his Summer All Over team found the time for an interview on ABC National and Local Radio to help get the word out there that I was looking for stories. The response to that interview was nothing short of fantastic. Also, many thanks for the support I've received from everyone in the Royal Flying Doctor Service (RFDS), especially to those wonderful people in Broken Hill who always give so freely of their time, encouragement and expertise. In addition, I'd like to thank those who helped so much when I was in Derby, where I was lucky enough to travel into the beautiful Kimberley area of Western Australia.

On a more personal level I'd like to thank my partner Margaret Worth for her continuing support, encouragement, patience and understanding, David Hansford, my musical mate—who can fix anything from a light bulb to a laptop, and has had to do so on many occasions—and Stuart Neal and his staff at ABC Books. Since my first publication, back in 1988, David and Christine Harris have given me a fifty-dollar emergency fund to take on each of my travels—'just in case'—and eight books later they're still doing it ... and it still gets spent along the way through one debacle or another. I'd like to thank my family: my dear little Mum who, as I write, is a 'healthy' ninety-three years of age, my 'big' sister, Barbara, who doesn't want her age published and my second 'biggest' sister, Margaret, who was such a support with transcribing my poorly recorded interviews. That also goes for Ian Bourne and Shannon Lore Blackman. I have two mates who are doing it a bit tough at the moment and I'd like to mention them, Shaw Hendry and Gerd Janssen. Their courage is inspirational.

My next venture is going to be 'Great Australian Stories from Little Outback Towns'. If you have a quirky, interesting, funny, sad, entertaining or dramatic story concerning an outback town with a population of less than two hundred, please feel free to contact me via my web site—www.billswampymarsh.com—before the cut-off date of July 2008.

Please don't send in any written material as all the stories in my books are adapted from recorded interviews.

I'm sure you'll enjoy this second book of great Flying Doctor stories as much as I have enjoyed collecting and writing them. The Royal Flying Doctor Service is an organisation quite unique to us and our environment. It was born out of Reverend John Flynn's dream to create a 'Mantle of Safety' for all remote and outback people. There're some great characters in here, some extremely humorous moments and there're some frighteningly dramatic ones—ones that had me on the edge of my seat as I was listening to them being told.

In conclusion, I'd like to acknowledge the staff of the RFDS. As one of my contributors said:

> On a daily basis they put their lives on the line for people who are complete strangers to them. They don't care who these people are, or what their nationality is, or what religion they are. And it doesn't matter ... how those very same people probably wouldn't take a similar risk for them. In fact, they wouldn't even realise the risk. What's more, the RFDS do it for free.

So I'm sure you'll appreciate that it wouldn't be possible to run an organisation which has 41 aircraft, 71 doctors, 115 nurses, one dentist plus a dedicated support staff without the public's help. If you wish to make a donation to the Royal Flying Doctor Service, you can call 1800 444 788.

My First Flight

I did my General Nurses' Training in Brisbane, then went to Sydney to do my Mid [Midwifery Training] before coming back to Queensland to do Child Health. In those days they used to say that you had to have your 'Mid' and your Child Health if you wanted to work in the bush. And I wanted to work in the bush. I'm from the country, anyway. I come from Mareeba, in far north Queensland.

After I'd done my General and Midwifery training I went to Thursday Island, which is just above the tip of Cape York. I was there getting experience in Midwifery and filling in time before I could do my Child Health in Brisbane. Then after completing my three certificates I went to the Northern Territory and worked in the Darwin Hospital for two years—this was before Cyclone Tracy.

I then left Darwin in 1974 and went to work in the Gulf of Carpentaria, in the Normanton Hospital. This hospital was serviced by a doctor from the Royal Flying Doctor Service on a weekly basis. I gathered lots of skills and a fair bit of experience while I was there and I think that this was where I got the idea of becoming a nurse with the RFDS. By then I'd also put a little money away so I decided to go overseas for a year, not working, just travelling around. And, as you do, when I came back home from my travels I had no money left. So, I looked in the paper and I saw that the RFDS in Western Australia was looking for a Flight Nurse, in Derby, up in the Kimberley. In those days Western Australia used to snap up all the nurses they could. So I applied for the job and they wrote back to say that the position had already been filled but they could offer me some Relief Community Health Work, out of Derby, and when a flying position became available I'd be given first option.

Good, I thought, that's what I'll do. So, I flew to Perth where I had three weeks' orientation—two weeks with Community Health

I really wanted to get in the air as a Flight Nurse—RFDS

and then a week out at Jandakot for the Air Medical part of it. After that I came to Derby to do Relief Community Health Work. And I remember that I wasn't all that long in Derby when they came to me and said, 'Here's a four-wheel drive vehicle. Go south to La Grange Aboriginal Mission. The nurse there has been by herself for three months and she needs a break.'

'Okay,' I replied, 'but where's La Grange Mission?'

'South of Broome,' they said.

Anyway, even though I'd never driven a four-wheel drive vehicle in my life before, they put me in this huge thing and said, 'You'll find the place easy enough. Just head south and turn left at the Roebuck Roadhouse, then right when you get to La Grange. There's no bitumen. It's all dirt. A distance of well over 300 kilometres.'

And, oddly enough, I found the place.

Of course, I was a little petrified at first but I got through it okay. I just ran the clinic down there for about ten days and the RFDS would fly in and do a doctor's clinic every week. Then after my relief at La Grange I came back to Derby and I did other small stints out at places like Looma, which is another Aboriginal Community about a hundred kilometres south of Derby.

But I'll always remember my first RFDS flight. At that stage I was still doing Relief Community Health Work but I was very keen because I really wanted to get in the air as a Flight Nurse. Anyhow, I was living next door to the normal Flight Nurse. Even though she was just about to leave she hadn't quite resigned as yet. And in those days, in Derby, there were only two Flight Nurses, one plane and one pilot and the nurses used to have alternate weekends on and the person who worked on the weekend had the Monday and Tuesday off. Also, with there being just the one pilot, he'd always use up his flying hours pretty quickly and when that happened the RFDS would charter a plane, if they thought it necessary.

Anyhow, this weekend the Flight Nurse who was on call wasn't feeling well, or so she told me, and she got asked to go out on this two-and-a-half-hour flight, down to Balgo Aboriginal Community

[Mission], to pick up an Aboriginal lady who was in labour. So then the nurse asked me if I'd like to go in her place and, of course, me being all green, I immediately said, 'Oh yes, I'll go.'

'Thanks,' she said. 'Our pilot's out of hours so it's going to be a charter flight.'

'That's fine by me,' I said.

Anyhow, the charter turned out to be the local Pest Controller who had a little one-propeller Cessna. He used to fly around the communities spraying for ants and termites and things like that. And I clearly remember that on the side of his little Cessna he had a sign that read 'Phantom Sprayer' along with a photo of The Phantom character, from the comic books.

When I saw that, my first thought was, Dear me, this looks a bit odd for a RFDS retrieval.

But it was still okay, just another part of the adventure. So then I worked out that, with this Aboriginal lady being in labour and with it being a two-and-a-half-hour flight out there to Balgo then two-and-a-half hours back to Derby, I really needed for her to be able to lie down in the aeroplane. My main concern was that if she had the baby while we were in the air, I wanted to be sure she could deliver safely and wasn't going to haemorrhage or whatever.

With all that in mind I rang the pilot and asked him, 'Can you take the seats out of the plane? You know, the back seats, because this lady will probably need to lie down.'

And his reply was, 'Gees, I wouldn't have a clue how to do that. I've never taken the seats out before.'

But in those days in Derby we had MMA (McRobinson Miller Airways) who I knew had an engineer. MMA had an Otter, which is a type of aircraft that they used to fly across to Koolan Island and back. But the thing was, they had an engineer who looked after all their aeroplanes so I said to the Phantom Sprayer, 'Look, how about we get the MMA guys to see if they can take the seats out.'

'Well,' he said, 'that'd be really good if we could.'

So, eventually he got the MMA guys to take the seats out and we put a mattress inside the little Cessna and then we loaded in all the emergency equipment and so forth. This was back in 1976 when we didn't have any telephone so it was all radio contact through the RFDS base. So there I was, out at the airport, all keen to go on this flight and we set off and because I'm as keen as anything I'm sitting up there and I'm checking a map to see where we're going.

Actually, at one stage, I thought I was looking at the map upside down. 'Oh, where are we now?' I said to the pilot, you know, wanting to get a bearing of where we were on the map.

'Well,' he said, and he pointed out the window, 'in about ten minutes, out on that side of the aircraft, you'll see Christmas Creek.'

On the map, Christmas Creek was about half way between Balgo and Derby. 'Oh, okay,' I said. 'Good.'

Anyhow, there I am, I'm peering out the window in the direction of where he said I'd see Christmas Creek. And after about another ten minutes had gone by and still nothing had appeared, I'm thinking, Well, surely we're going to get there sometime soon.

Then fifteen minutes went by and I'm thinking, Hey, what's going on here?

So I said to the Phantom Sprayer, 'Where's this Christmas Creek you said we were going to pass?

'Hang on,' he said, and he gazes up over his dashboard and he's looking over here and he's looking over there—like he's pretty lost—then he says, 'Oh, there it is, over there.'

So then he turns the plane and heads in the direction that we should be going. And I tell you, that didn't inspire confidence, not one little bit.

But we eventually found Balgo, much to my relief. At that stage I think it was the Saint John of God nuns who actually worked at the clinic out there, at Balgo Mission. So, we landed and a vehicle came out to meet the plane and they said, 'Oh sister, come into the hospital quick, we're having an emergency.'

Of course, my first thought was, Well, there's got to be trouble with the baby.

But, as it turned out, when we got in there everything was fine and the Aboriginal lady had just delivered her baby. Then, in those days, even though the baby was perfectly okay, as was the mother, you still had to bring them back. So we fixed her up and we got her in the plane and she had a comfortable ride back to Derby on the mattress.

And that was my introduction to flying with the Royal Flying Doctor Service, all the way with the Phantom Sprayer, and I'm thinking, Oh well, hopefully, if I ever do this again I'll go with a RFDS pilot so, at least, I'll have a proper aeroplane to fly around in.

But still, I wasn't all that daunted. I just so much wanted to be a Flight Nurse. Then not long after that first flight, the Flight Nurse who'd been 'sick' on that particular day, well, she resigned and I got the position.

So I was really pleased about that. I mean, I guess it's no big deal, really. There's no great fanfare where you get presented with wings or anything. It's just that my title then became Community Nurse with Flying Duties and that's because we were going out doing clinics, mostly. Oh, there was a bit of emergency work, retrievals from accidents and that, but mainly it was clinic flights. And all that happened not long after I first came to live in the Kimberley, back in 1976, and, except for holidays, I haven't been away since. So it's a sum total of thirty years now, that I've been living in Derby.

A Committed Team

I guess I should clear something up first. Initially it was John Flynn's idea to provide a Mantle of Safety, as he called it, for those living in outback and remote areas. To do that he established the Australian Inland Mission [AIM], which was part of the Presbyterian Church, and that organisation set up outback hospitals and sent out trained nurses and Patrol Padres, of which my father, Fred McKay, was one.

So, the AIM, as it became known, was instrumental in opening up a lot of the outback hospitals, which were staffed by trained nurses, who were recruited and sent out for two-year stints. Then the Flying Doctor Service was, in a way, established to work in conjunction with those services that the AIM and other outback-care organisations had set up. And those nurses relied on the Flying Doctor Service very heavily. Like the Flying Doctor would come and conduct medical clinics and everyone would turn up to see the doctor and, of course, the RFDS was available for emergency services like evacuations and so forth, as well. And, of course, that's developed on a very big scale now. So the AIM and the RFDS were both instigated by Flynn and, even though they were run as two separate organisations, they were inextricably linked.

John Flynn's title was Superintendent of the Australian Inland Mission and, though I was too young to remember him personally, I would've met him when I was an infant. Then, when he died at the end of 1951, Dad was appointed to take over. We were actually living in Brisbane at that stage so we shifted to Sydney, where the AIM's Head Office was, and we moved into a home that had been provided by them for the Superintendent.

We'd been in Sydney for about a year and, I guess, things within the AIM were getting a bit rocky. There were financial difficulties and there were also problems within the Board. That's no real secret there because it's all been well documented. Of course, being only seven or something, I was too young to be aware of what was going on. But, apparently, it was getting to the point where the future of the Australian Inland Mission was in doubt so, when they were having difficulties getting staff at the Bush Mothers' Hostel in Adelaide House, out at Alice Springs, Mum [Meg McKay] offered her services as Matron. And she offered to do that for gratis.

So, really, we'd just got established at school in Sydney and were beginning to make friends and then we were, sort of, uprooted to go out to live in Alice Springs. Adelaide House had originally been a hospital but then, when they built a new hospital in Alice Springs, the AIM took over Adelaide House and John Flynn redesigned it with the wide verandahs and the natural air-conditioning system that uses the soil temperature underneath the building. That was quite revolutionary back then. So Adelaide House became what was called the Bush Mother's Hostel and that was the place where mothers could come into Alice Springs before they had their babies at the local hospital. Then they could also convalesce there afterwards, before going back to their properties.

So, that was how we ended up in Alice Springs. I mean, we all thought it was a big adventure but, of course, Alice Springs wasn't the town it is now. There were only about two or three thousand people living there back then and we lived in a small, square upstairs room in Adelaide House, which is in the main street, Todd Street.

At that stage there were three of us kids in the family; my brother, my elder sister and myself. So when Mum and Dad were there, it got pretty crammed at times with the five of us, all living together at the top of the building where we also had to deal with the extreme heat in the summer and the bitter cold of the winter. But, of course, Dad was still going backwards and forwards to Sydney. So it was basically just the four of us upstairs, with the outback ladies living downstairs and the other staff members. Jean Flynn was there for the first few months also.

Fred McKay's plane naming with wife, Meg, and Barbara Ellis from RFDS Broken Hill—RFDS

But then, when they started building the John Flynn Church, on the vacant block next door, my father more or less returned to supervise that. So we watched the church being built, which was quite amazing because it also showed a lot of the Flying Doctor story. Out the front there's the two wings, which symbolise a Flying Doctor plane. I mean, they really did an amazing job in designing and incorporating the entire story of John Flynn's life and achievements into that building. So Dad was involved with the building of the church and I remember we had the architect staying with us a lot of the time, and what a very eccentric and funny man he was, too.

So we had two years in Alice Springs before we returned to Sydney. Then the following year, in 1956, the AIM started up a home in Adelaide at the seaside suburb of Grange, where outback children could come and stay while they were receiving specialist medical treatment. Once again, my mother offered her services as matron and my brother and I went to live with her in Adelaide, while my elder sister, who was doing her Leaving Certificate, stayed in Sydney.

I remember that as a difficult and emotional year for everybody because the family was, sort of, split in two. Dad was off everywhere, but mostly based in Sydney. Mum, my brother and I were in Adelaide and my eldest sister was boarding with the neighbours in Sydney. Then somewhere in amongst all that my youngest sister was born. So I got another sister, and then at the end of 1956 we returned to Sydney and we were based in Sydney from then on.

But Mum and Dad, they were a real team, and a very committed team. Mum wasn't nursing after we came back from Adelaide but, instead, she was going around and speaking to a lot of women's groups and other organisations. The term they gave it was 'Deputation Work'. It was more or less publicising the work of the AIM in conjunction with the Royal Flying Doctor Service and, I guess, seeking donations and support and manpower and just keeping the work in the minds of, mainly, the church people. So she was quite busy with her speaking engagements and what not.

And Dad, well, as Superintendent of the Australian Inland Mission, he spent a lot of time travelling around to the various outposts visiting the nursing staff and the various developments that were happening. Later on he'd do a lot of flying—some of it with the RFDS—but in the earlier days he still drove. Sometimes he'd be away for anything up to a month or six weeks. So, we saw little of him and there were even Christmases when we never thought he'd make it back home.

I recall one particular Christmas when he was driving his truck, an International. We were living in the Sydney suburb of Northbridge then and from our front windows we could look out over the gully and see the traffic approaching. And I remember all us kids, full of excitement and anticipation, sitting at the windows watching and waiting for him to come home for Christmas.

So, yes, they were a very committed couple, especially to the work they were doing and, I think my father, sort of, missed out on the family a lot. But at every opportunity they'd try and make up for it. I mean, we never felt deprived or unloved or anything like that. It was just the area of service they were involved in. And of course, being kids we didn't fully realise that we had to share our parents with a lot of other people and a very big space of country. So, yes, I guess, we felt that we didn't have them around enough. And also, with Dad not being there that much, it must've been hard for my mother. But when we did have time together, they both made a special effort. Holiday times were very memorable. Oh, we did some really wonderful things together as a family then.

Then, of course, they passed away pretty close to each other. We'd all grown up and had left home by then. But Dad passed away quite suddenly in 2000. It was unexpected. Our mother's health had been deteriorating for some time but, after Dad died, she sort of really went downhill. I think it was because they were such a team that, without him, she felt she really had very little more to offer. So she lost a lot of her sparkle, then she passed away in 2003.

A Great Big Adventure

Well, for a lot of years I'd been wanting to do a big trip because my grandfather had Clydesdales all his life. He did all the roads around Victoria, up around Kerang and that area. That was his lifetime job, and I sort of grew up with the horses there, and I thought, Well, I'm gonna do something one day. And I started thinking about it and I thought, Oh well, while I'm doing it, it'd be good to do something helpful for somebody.

Then, probably about ten years beforehand, I'd had a hernia after doing the Border Dash out on the Nullarbor. I was in a bit of a bad way there for a while and the RFDS flew out to the Nullarbor Roadhouse and they picked me up and they took me to Adelaide. Then they picked me up and flew me back again.

Now, with the Border Dash, I guess that I should explain that every year over on the Nullarbor they had, and still do have, I think, an event that they call the Border Dash. It's also a fundraiser for the Royal Flying Doctor Service. It started off as just a bit of an argument one night in the pub at Border Village when they reckoned one bloke couldn't run the 12 kilometres from Border Village Roadhouse in South Australia, to Eucla Roadhouse, which is in Western Australia. So he ran it. Then the next year they said, 'Oh well, you know, we might make this a yearly thing.'

So it became known as the Border Dash and, back when I got my hernia, it used to be a very friendly run. You know, you'd have a support vehicle driving along beside you and there'd be a stubby of beer passing hands, here and there. It was all very social, nice and casual. And Eucla's a little township and there're a few married women there and they'd come along and be pushing their kids in prams and all that and the women from the roadhouse staff, they'd join in, and so while most people ran, some people walked.

But everybody who went on the Border Dash had a sponsor and whatever amount they were sponsored for, it all went to the Royal Flying Doctor Service. Of course, it's all grown since then. Nowadays, they get professional runners from Adelaide, Perth and all sorts out there. Oh, they get big heaps of people. It's just before football season and a lot of the footy teams use it as a training run, plus it's also a bit of a bonding weekend for them.

Anyhow, about four days after I did the Border Run, I come down with this hernia. So when I started thinking about doing this big trip, I started thinking about how the RFDS helped me out back then and I thought, Why, can't I do it for them. They probably saved my life out there. So I said, 'Yeah, I will. I'll do it for the RFDS.'

So I went and saw the Flying Doctor people here in Rockhampton and I told them that I wanted to do a trip from Rocky, which is about 700 kilometres north of Brisbane, all the way down to Ceduna, which is out on the west coast of South Australia. And they gave me the addresses of who I should contact about it all and I wrote away and I told them what I was going to do and they sent me big heaps of pencils and stickers and stuff like that.

That's how it sort of first got going. Then I had to send away and get a letter that made it all legal for me to raise money for the RFDS. And I went to the Commonwealth Bank and opened a special account and they gave me a pay-in-book, with all the details, so that each time I got to a town I'd bank what I'd picked up along the road. That's where most of the money ended up coming from; people stopping along the road to have a yarn and to take a photo, then they'd put $2 or $5 or $10 in the Royal Flying Doctor Service collection tin I carried with me. Rotary Clubs along the way helped out as well.

While I was getting all that organised, I did a lot of test runs. You know, I'd go out for three or four days testing things. I had a covered wagon and one of me mates set up one of them things that the sun shines on—a solar panel—and that charged the battery I had on the side of the wagon. I ran lights and a little caravan fridge off that. Actually, this mate first set it up with a generator that he had running off the rear axle, but I couldn't keep the belts on it so we gave that away and we finished up settling for this solar panel. So that was good. It worked out well. And I just had a piece of flat timber going from one side of the wagon to the other and bunked down in there, in the swag. But a lot of nights it turned out to be so beautiful that I just threw the swag down by the camp fire. Fantastic.

So when everything was organised, I set out in the wagon from Rocky with two Clydesdales, Big Mac and Bill, and my little dog, Minnie, a fox terrier. And all along the way people helped with water and horse feed and a bit of food. It was really unbelievable, especially through outback New South Wales. There was an eight-year drought going on and nobody out there had anything. Oh, it was a terrible, terrible, drought. You know how the little bit of moisture runs off the edge of the road of a night, and so there's the tiny pickings there? Well, the drought was so bad that the kangaroos were coming into the edge of the road just to get what was left of that. And they were so weak from lack of food that they couldn't move. They didn't even bother to take any notice of me when I come along, and the horses didn't worry them either. And you'd see a vehicle go past and the driver would toot the horn to warn the roos and half of them would fall over dead. That's true. There was just no feed, no nothing. It was that bad, it was.

And a lot of the stations out there, they were still going but, they just had managers on them. You know, there's thousands and thousands of acres or whatever and these managers, all they did was go around the boundary fences. They had no stock or anything. I guess the properties were all owned by Sydney lawyers and doctors or what have you: probably tax dodgers or something. I don't know. But these people had nothing out there, you know, and they did everything in their power to help me. Absolutely everything.

Because, what you've got to realise here is that there wasn't just Minnie and me. The horses needed food and they needed water every night. Like a Clydesdale will drink 75 litres a day. You know, I did carry water but just emergency water and the New

South Wales Pastoral Protection Board supervisors helped with water drops along the way. But, oh, I would've never have been able to do it without the station owners or the station managers, that's for sure.

Well, there was one woman, she heard that I was coming through and she drove all the way out to the main road with some water and food for the horses, then she picked me up, took me back to her place where I had a shower and what-have-you and I had a beautiful tea with her and then she drove me all the way back to camp. And that was a 210 kilometre round trip she did. That was the sort of thing that was happening.

And a lot of these people I'd never even met before. Some I didn't even get to meet. Like, I'd just be driving along and there'd be a 44 gallon drum of water and a couple of bales of hay, sitting on the side of the road, with a sign on it saying, 'for the Royal Flying Doctor Service horse-drawn wagon trip.' And I didn't even have a clue who left these things.

Then, at one stage, I got bogged. That was near G4 Station, between Walgett and Brewarrina, in the central north of New South Wales. It's all black soil through there and we got this rain and the horses were slipping this way and that and the wheels on the wagon were sliding all over the place. Then the trailer wheels got clogged, and the horses just couldn't handle it. So we just could not move.

Anyway, I walked the horses into G4 Station and the people there came back out with a big four-wheel-drive tractor and towed the trailer in. Then we were there for about eight or ten days, waiting for everything to dry out enough to get out of the place. But they looked after us really well. They killed a sheep for us and everything. And those people had nothing, neither.

Then sometimes the news would get out that I was coming along and people would kill a sheep and they'd cut up half a side and put it in little bags for me. And here I am with a little caravan fridge, you know. The freezer was flat out holding six mutton chops and here they are hitting me with about thirty or more chops.

And another funny thing; everybody wanted to give me eggs and you can't say 'No' because they just won't take 'No' for an answer. Anyway, this particular day I had about six dozen eggs with me and this elderly couple pulled up. They were pensioners who were just touring around in their little caravan on holidays. So when they pulled up I asked them if they'd like to have a dozen eggs.

'Oh, lovely. Oh, lovely,' they said.

Anyway, there I am talking to the elderly lady and the old bloke's walking around and around and around the wagon. And he's looking under it here and over it there and all through it and then, after he'd searched all the wagon over, he comes back and he says, 'Where do yer keep yer chooks?'

And, oh, I had to laugh because he was thinking it was like in the olden days when they always had a cage of chooks underneath the wagon. That's what he was looking for. Yeah, 'Where do yer keep yer chooks?' he asked, and I didn't even need to have any chooks because everyone was giving me all these eggs.

Charlie Rayner, Big Mac and Bill arrive at Ceduna after travelling a distance of 3,200 kilometres, raising money for the Flying Doctor Service— Charlie Rayner

So, there was quite a few funny little things like that that happened. Another one was with two English girls. They were probably in their early twenties or something. They were travelling around Australia and they stopped for a chat because they'd never seen anything like a horse-drawn wagon in their lives before, and one of them asked if she could travel with me for three or four days.

I said, 'Yeah, that'll be fine.'

Then the other one says, 'No, you can't travel with him because we've got to get to such and such a place at such and such a time.'

Well I thought that was a bit rich, you know, but then there was nearly a blue. Oh yes, I thought there was going to be an all-out brawl between the two of them so I said, 'What about I make a compromise.' I said, 'I'll get the fire going and put the billy on and you can have tea with me then you can head off.'

'Oh, that'd be lovely,' they said.

So anyway, after tea they nuzzled off and away they went.

But I must say that I did have a couple of run-ins. See, I went through Bourke and followed the Darling River down to Wilcannia, then along the road to Broken Hill and down the Barrier Highway into South Australia. But Walgett, Brewarrina and Wilcannia, they were terrible. It's a shame. The police at Bourke weren't going to let me go through to Wilcannia. Apparently, not long beforehand two young couples had been driving along and they were forced out of their cars, then they were beaten up and the cars were hijacked and taken for joy-rides. So they were wary of me going down that way, because of the trouble. But I said, 'Well, what am I going to do. I've got no other way to go, you know.'

So, I went on and when I got to Wilcannia there was an old Aboriginal bloke, a full blood. He used to be a drover, and when he saw me coming past, oh, he run out and he waved me down and I probably spent a good hour and a half there with him while he was going on about the old droving days. Oh, he was showing me all his old photos and all that. And oh, it was fantastic. I enjoyed every minute of it.

Then a couple of hundred yards further down the road the kids started pinching gear. They'd just walk along beside the wagon and they'd grab something then they'd take off. And most of the time they were grabbing lumps of harness and stuff like that; stuff I needed, that was of no good to them. But they'd just take it anyway. It was really just a pain in the butt. That's what it was. And there was nothing I could do about it. But they're funny, kids, aye. It's sad, that's all you can say.

But you get all types, don't you, both black and white, because further down along the highway, over near Peterborough in South Australia, these two white blokes pulled up in a ute. One was a decent sort of a bloke, but the other one, I think he was on something already. Anyway, the decent bloke was talking to me and, just out of the blue, the other one said, 'So, where's yer drugs?'

'There's no drugs on this trip, mate,' I said. 'I don't believe in that sort of stuff.'

'Bullshit,' he said. 'Yer'd have ter be on drugs ter be doin' somethin' as mad as this.' Then he said, 'Anyway, I'm gonna have a look.'

'No, yer not, mate,' I said. 'You just don't walk into people's houses and do those sort of things.'

Anyway, I had a knife that one of me mates gave me, back here in Rocky. He'd made it out of a saw blade, so the blade was probably about 12 or 13 inches long, you know. I was using it for any dead kangaroos I came across; like cutting the roo meat for Minnie and what have you. Well, I had it behind the seat so I just pulled it out and started cleaning my fingernails with it. And this bloke, well, he did a bit of a double take when he saw the knife. So while he was goggling at me I said, 'I haven't got any drugs here, mate. I don't believe in 'em so I wouldn't have 'em here in the first place.'

Anyway, he went, 'Eh, we'll bloody see about that. We'll be back.'

They took off then and I was a bit concerned that they might come back, but they didn't.

But Minnie loved the journey. She was a little girl—elderly—but she just absolutely loved it. I thought I lost her one time. Did I tell you about that? Well, there was quite a few pig shooters of a night through some of those outback places in New South Wales. Anyway the sound of their guns must've frightened her and she took off. And, oh, I never had a clue where she was. I couldn't find her anywhere. There I was yelling out and yelling out and wandering around the place. But, no, nothing.

Anyway, I hung about till around ten o'clock the next morning before I left. And I was just about to hop into the wagon and drive off and here she comes. She's in a real lather and there was blood all over her feet. Red raw, they were. God knows how far she ran that night. But it was good to have her back, I can tell you, because she was great company and, as I said, she just loved the trip.

Then I guess the highlight of the great big adventure was my sixtieth birthday at the Tilpa Pub. That was unreal, that was. How it came about was that, well, the night before I was camped at a station property out of Tilpa and the people there, oh, they were fantastic. I've still got all their names and everything but they were having a barbecue there for their grandson's birthday. He was eight years old or something. Anyway, I was talking to the little feller and I just happened to say, 'You and I are nearly twins.'

And he said, 'Why?'

I said, 'Because it's your birthday today and it's my birthday tomorrow.'

Well, he got a bit of a giggle out of that. So, anyway, the elderly lady there—she must've been the grandmother—when she brought the birthday cake out she had two candles on it; one for the little feller and one for me. And it was a really lovely night with a good feed and what have you, plus a few yarns. Then the next morning I headed off and I got into Tilpa and I set up camp, probably about three or four hundred yards from the hotel. Then after I'd done that I thought I'd go over and see if they served a counter tea and, if they did, I'll shout myself a meal for me sixtieth birthday. So I went over to the pub and the publican there, he said, 'Have yer set up camp for the night?'

'Yeah.'

'Well, do yer reckon yer'd know your way there and back,' he said.

Of course, all this had me sort of intrigued, so I said, 'Yeah, why's that?'

And he said, 'Because yer probably mightn't be able to walk back to camp tonight.'

'Why?' I said.

He said, 'Because I believe it's yer sixtieth birthday.'

Well, within half an hour, I reckon there would've been, oh, I don't know, about sixty people came and went, you know. At any one time there was probably thirty people there, in the pub. And there were only about six people who actually lived in Tilpa. There was the publican and he had a barmaid and then there was a couple over at the little store. Well, that was about it. So there might've only been about four people, I guess, that lived in Tilpa. So, all these other people, I don't know where they come from. But I reckon there was a good number of ringers and fencers and shearers and all that amongst them so they must've come from off properties or something.

Now I think what must've happened was that the elderly woman where I stayed the night before—the grandmother—she must've rung the publican. And things travel fast in little places like that. But I never saw a penny go over the bar all night so I think the publican and this elderly lady must've paid for everything. I don't really know. And the next morning the publican handed over something like four hundred dollars, which was good money. And then, when I opened me little camping fridge that night, they'd also snuck a couple of fresh bunny rabbits in there. So that was Tilpa, yeah at the Tilpa pub.

And so I finally made it to Ceduna. I left Rockhampton on 9 April 2001 and finished up in Ceduna on 26 October 2001 and I travelled a distance of 3,200 kilometres. Seven months it took me, and I raised a total of $4,511 for the Flying Doctor Service.

But that's just what the typical Aussie is, isn't it: a giver. And since then I've been back and I've seen a lot of the people who looked after me and here they were, doing the same thing again. I mean, they weren't giving me donations but they were making me stay overnight and they were feeding me and all the rest of it. So it truly is an amazing country with some amazing people living in it. And what truly amazed me was how the isolation out there in the outback doesn't really isolate people, it brings them together, and the Royal Flying Doctor Service is a great part of that.

A True Legend

This is an interesting story about a fellow, a true legend, who was a pilot with the Royal Flying Doctor Service for I-don't-know-how-long. His name's Phil Darby.

At the time this particular incident happened I was Chief Pilot with the RFDS here in Cairns, in far north Queensland, and also their Senior Checking and Training Pilot. So, in that capacity, I quite often found myself out at different RFDS bases for a couple of weeks either checking and training pilots or doing relief work while one of our pilots went on holidays or something.

In this case it was one of my very early trips down to Charleville, in south-western Queensland, and while I was relatively new to that area Phil had previously been the pilot down there for—oh, for heaven's sake, I don't know—maybe ten years or more. Actually, Phil worked with the RFDS when it first opened down at Charleville so by then he'd had a chance to solidly cement his persona within the township and the surrounding countryside.

Anyway, by this stage, Phil had been posted over to Cairns and I was relieving out at Charleville and while I was there we were called out to this property—Thylungra—which was then owned by CSR [Colonial Sugar Refining Company]. It was also the place where they had a polocrosse weekend, you know, the polo they play on horseback. But Thylungra was run on behalf of CSR by a manager chappie whose surname was Green. Anyhow, this chappie's wife fell ill and we were called to go out there. So the doctor and I and a Nursing Sister, we climbed into—I'm not sure if it was a Queen Air or we took the King Air that time—but anyway, off we went out to this property.

When we landed, there was the truck waiting at the airstrip so we pulled up and we all got out of the aeroplane and the manager bloke, Green, was there with his wife, and she was looking very

'G'day,' I said, 'my name's Nick Watling. I'm flying the aeroplane today'—
Nick Watling

grey, indeed. She was not well at all. So the doctor went to have a closer look at the wife. Anyway, the manager, this chappie, Green, I could see that he was sort of eyeing me up and down in an extremely suspicious manner. And he was rolling a durry—a roll-your-own cigarette—in the fashion that they can only do in the outback. You know how they roll the durry, sort of nonchalantly while they're deep in thought about something or other, and in this particular case I had the strong feeling that it was me he was thinking about.

Well, I said to myself, this feller obviously doesn't know who or what I am. So I went up to introduce myself. 'G'day,' I said, 'my name's Nick Watling. I'm flying the aeroplane today.'

'Oh yeah,' he said, in a half-interested sort of way. 'So where's Phil?'

'Well,' I said, 'Phil's been posted. Phil and I are at the same base in Cairns these days.'

'Oh,' he grunted, sounding none too pleased with this turn of events.

Then he left it at that, but you could see that what I'd said wasn't really sinking through to this feller, Green. So there he is, he's still rolling his durry and he's deep in thought then he looks at me and says, 'But Phil's the pilot for Queensland, isn't he?'

And I thought what a brilliant job of PR Phil had done during the years he was out there, in the Charleville area. Because, this feller, Green, he just could not possibly imagine that anyone else other than Phil Darby flew aeroplanes for the RFDS. And the fact that Phil had gone to Cairns, you know, 800 nautical miles to the north-east didn't affect a thing. If anybody was flying out to pick up anybody's wife or anyone who was sick or injured, the pilot had to be Phil. Nobody else would do, and so who was this strange bugger by the name of Watling, and what right did he have to be out there flying 'Phil's aeroplane'? And that's the way it felt to me.

So that was Phil Darby, a wonderful feller, a brilliant bloke who was tremendously valued and loved as both a man and a pilot, particularly throughout the Charleville area, where they virtually looked upon him as a god. Oh, he'd give you the shirt off his back, Phil would, he was that generous. And if you ever wanted someone to fill in anywhere, there'd always be Phil. He'd be the first to put up his hand, every time.

But, on the other hand, if you wanted someone to obey the rules to the strict letter of the law, well then, perhaps not Phil. Of course, being Chief Pilot, I was responsible to the Civil Aviation Authority for the running of the place and Phil had to be reined in on occasions. So we had our moments together. But, in saying that, Phil went through his many, many years flying for the RFDS without having one accident relating to that sort of approach to life. In fact, I'd reckon that Phil could land the aeroplane on a postage stamp, in the middle of the night, you know, and there's not too many that could do that.

A True Privilege

Well, I suppose, something that pops straight into mind was my first lesson in cultural safety. To be more accurate, I guess I should say that it was a real lesson in how to work appropriately with an Aboriginal patient.

There was one old fella, he was into his seventies and it was the first time he'd ever been in an aeroplane. The only trouble was that I didn't speak his language and he didn't speak English so we had this real communication problem right from the start.

Anyhow, we got him into the aeroplane and I'm trying to tell him to put his seat belt on, but he couldn't understand what I was on about. So then thinking I was being helpful, I went over to show him how it was done. And, well, didn't he take exception to that. He got angry at me for trying to interfere with him. Obviously he didn't know what was going on because he got stuck into me. Oh yeah, he was hitting out at me and everything. Then finally I worked out how he must've been seeing the situation, from his point of view, what, with it being his first time in an aeroplane and then, to make matters worse, here was this white woman pushing and pulling him around.

'That's okay. Now I understand,' I said and I got one of the other patients to explain to him what he had to do, and he was alright after that.

Then I had another old patient who was incredibly incontinent in the aircraft, so then we had an overflow problem, out onto the floor, didn't we. And at the altitude we were flying, it was so cold that the urine froze. At the time I was unaware of what had happened, that was until I went to stand up and I felt this crack, crack, cracking. That's funny, I thought, and when

I looked down I saw that my shoes were stuck to the floor of the aeroplane.

And there was another old fella who obviously didn't understand the principals of aircraft safety because he decided to light a fire on the floor of the aeroplane. Oh, he just got cold so he started pulling old bits of rubbish and stuff out of his pockets and then he tried to light it with a match. Yeah, on the floor of the aeroplane, as we were flying along, because he was cold.

Of course, when we saw that we freaked out. 'No, no, you can't do that!'

'But I'm cold,' he said.

'I'll turn the heater up! I'll get you a blanket! I'll do anything, but don't light a fire on the floor of the aeroplane!'

So, yeah, I must say, it's a true privilege sometimes with these Aboriginal people, particularly with the real old traditional people, to see them when they're having a first-time-in-their-life experience. I remember when I took one old fella from here, in Alice Springs, down to Adelaide. Oh, he was a lovely man. I'd say he'd also have to be well into his seventies and, anyhow, he'd never seen the ocean before.

At first, I found it really hard to believe. But then, when I thought about it, I realised that he wouldn't even have come across an ocean on television or anything because he'd never even seen a television before, either. Maybe he'd seen a dam. I guess he'd seen a creek and probably a river, but it was obvious that he couldn't grasp the concept of what an ocean actually was. But you just think that everybody knows, don't you? We just sort of take it for granted.

Anyhow, I pointed out the window of the aeroplane and I said to him, 'Out there, that's the ocean.' And he gazed down upon that huge, vast expanse of water, spreading all the way out over the horizon, and he was so shocked. He just couldn't believe there could be so much water anywhere. Even the word 'ocean' was strange to him.

'Ocean?' he kept asking. 'What is ocean?'

I said, 'Water. Karpi.' Because karpi is the word for water in their language.

So he stared back out the window of the plane for a while, then he looked back at me and he said, 'No, no, not Karpi. Too much for Karpi.'

A Wife's Tale

I met my husband, Phil, in Cairns. He'd previously been a pilot with the RFDS out in south-western Queensland, at Charleville, and had come to fly with them in Cairns. That was around 1974. At that time I was working for the Queensland Education Department as a teacher at the School of the Air in Cairns, and, in a way, we shared the HF Radio because the School of the Air was in the same building as the RFDS.

It proved a very suitable accommodation for both organisations because the RFDS did medical calls before school started of a morning, then we took over. But just because School of the Air was using the radio, that wasn't to stop anyone from out bush, who had an emergency, to cut in and call on the same frequency. When that happened, someone from the School of the Air would go and get someone from the Flying Doctor side of things. So, yes, it worked quite well, really.

Back then, at the Cairns Base of the RFDS, I think they only had two pilots, two doctors and two nursing sisters. So staff wasn't all that plentiful and it was just in Phil's nature to be ready to go at a moment's notice. That's just the sort of person he was. So, you know, it was like he lived his life waiting on his next call. Of course, they didn't have mobile phones or anything back then. They just had, like a little beeper that they attached to their belt and when that went off it meant you had to ring up the base and see what was going on. Virtually, he was on call seven days a week, twenty-four hours a day; so your life was pretty governed by the beeper, and that placed huge restrictions on where we could go.

I can remember a time in the late 1970s when the other pilot went on holidays and that left Phil to hold the fort for about two weeks. And, as what usually happens, you know, that coincided

Main street Charleville—RFDS

with a very busy time and he was working for forty-eight hours straight or something. I mean, they just wouldn't allow those sorts of things to happen nowadays. In fact, I think it'd be illegal, even if it were in special circumstances.

But I suppose a lot of the flights Phil did perhaps mightn't have had that great twist in the tale for them to be good reading. Oh, I'm sure he made a lasting impression on the people or the patients who he flew out for and brought back to hospital or whatever. But I doubt he'd remember most of them because being a pilot for the RFDS was his job, and that was that.

Like, I was thinking the other day of an American lady who lived at an out-station of Wandovale, west of Charters Towers. She was a mum of five and an aeronautical engineer by profession who'd married an Australian stockman. I was quite friendly with them because I taught the kids through School of the Air. At one stage she purchased an ultralight aircraft and during clinic flights out there she and Phil used to talk flying.

But bringing up a family is tough at any time, let along doing it in a remote area like that where things can become even more difficult. Because, one day, in just a few unsupervised moments her second littlest child poured a whole packet of Rinso over the face of the littlest one—a babe who was probably only eight months old or something. Phil then got the call to say that a child was suffocating.

And that was really dramatic for the mother, as you might well be able to imagine, and Phil flew out there for that child and it all ended up happily ever after. But there were no difficulties with the weather or in landing the aeroplane on the dirt airstrip and there were no problems with the people getting the child to the airstrip or any of that stuff. You know, in a movie they'd make it much more dramatic. But in real life it was just a part of Phil's job, so to speak.

And I'll tell you a funny one. Phil hadn't been feeling too well with the flu one weekend and he was called to fly to Cooktown to pick up a lady who'd miscarried early in her pregnancy. No one was accompanying him so he asked me if I'd like to go along for the ride, which I did. It was a beautiful clear day and we arrived in Cooktown after a stunning flight up the coast. Being the only other person on board, after we landed I let down the door of the Queen Air and the young lady and her partner made their way over to the plane. Of course, they mistook me for a Nursing Sister and so the patient handed over a rather large specimen jar—it was bigger than a coffee bottle—that must've contained the miscarried material.

I'm a bit more hard-hearted now but, back then, blood didn't really grab me. So I was a bit taken aback, but I tried to take it in my stride. Anyhow, we flew the patient back to Cairns where an ambulance took her to hospital. But then, later on, and this is the funny bit, Phil told me that there was a further side to the story. Apparently, Phil had met the partner of the lady who'd had the miscarriage at a clinic, in another town, the year before and he'd shared with Phil the fact that he was organising a vasectomy for himself. Yes, a vasectomy. And that was always a bit of a joke between Phil and myself because it was obvious that this lass was, unfortunately, caught out in one way or another. So I guess if any story had a twist to it that one would have.

Accident Prone

This story goes back to about March '65, up at Bulloo Downs Station, and it's about an old Aboriginal mate of mine, a chap by the name of Rex Athol Yarnold. Oh, and there was also Lenny Brock—'Brockie' as we called him. We were all mates. I think the way we all first got caught up together was with this bloody speedway driving, you know. We were all speedway drivers. Anyhow, this story hasn't got anything to do with that except that that's where Rex, Brockie and me first teamed up, speedway driving.

But Rex and I had already been up to Bulloo Downs the previous year—that'd be in '64—to do a bit of shooting for a week or two and in the end it bloody flooded and the water went all grey so they put some lime in it and, the next day, we were drinking it. So there you go, the lime cleared it all up.

Bulloo Downs? It's in the far south-western corner of Queensland, tucked in there, near the New South Wales and South Australian borders. If you ever want to get there, you go up to Hungerford and, when you leave the Hungerford pub, you turn west and you run along the fence for 64 miles and you open and shut about ten gates and eventually you'll come to the Bulloo Downs boundary. From there you go off to the homestead where Bill Rinke lived. Bill was, like, the manager up there or some bloody thing, you know. Any rate, that's where the Flying Doctor had to come and pick up Rex.

So, as I said, Rex and me, we'd been up there to Bulloo Downs to do some shooting back when it flooded in '64 and then Brockie come with us when we went again in '65. Brockie was a speedway driver, too.

How we got to know about Bulloo Downs was that Rex had some relatives living up that way who were working rabbits. They were a couple of Aboriginal ladies by the name of Gene and Maude Glover and they had about a dozen kids or more, you know, from different relatives and that, all living there on Bulloo Downs. I reckon that both Gene and Maude would've been in their fifties at the time, and by working rabbits I mean they had all the rabbit traps and all the gear and they were trapping for Sydney Rabbit Supply. A chap called Pat Wade was running Sydney Rabbit Supply back then and he worked out of the Haymarket, in Sydney, and Pat was paying Gene and Maude.

But anyway, all over Bulloo Downs they had these chillas. A chilla is what you put the dead rabbits in so that they don't go off in the heat. And these chillas had a motor on them that you had to start so that the rabbits would be kept cold. Well, one day, when Rex, Brockie and me was up there, this bloody chilla was playing up so Rex goes over to see if he can get the bloody thing going. The only trouble was that when he tried to, his fingers went through the pulley thing that was attached to the motor of the chilla and it took the tops of his fingers off, on his left hand. Three fingers, just down to the first knuckle. Yeah, just up the top, up there, yeah, so he lost them.

So we took Rex up to the homestead where that Bill Rinke lived and they got in touch with the Flying Doctor Service, you know. Then the Flying Doctor flew out and they decided to take Rex back into Broken Hill with them so that they could sort out his fingers. So off they went and it looked like Rex was all okay then because they said they were taking him straight to Broken Hill.

That's the last I saw of Rex for a while but later on, when I caught up with him in Sydney, he was telling me that while they were flying him back to Broken Hill they got a call that someone else out that way was in trouble. I don't exactly remember what the problem was but I think some bloke's back went on him or something, you know, and so they decided to stop off to get this rooster. But when they landed, the ground was too soft and the plane got bogged and it wouldn't budge. So then the pilot told Rex that if he wanted to get to Broken Hill, he'd better get out and push the bloody plane to help get it going again.

So Rex says, 'Here I am, a bloody patient, who's lost me fingers and I'm out there on the wing of this aeroplane pushing the bloody thing along so we can take off.'

Then, when it got going, he had to jump back into the aeroplane real quick before it took off without him, you know. Anyway, in the end, he finished up in Broken Hill, and they'd have a record of it there about how Rex lost the tops of his fingers.

So that's the story about Rex and the Flying Doctor. But, oh, Rex was always in some sort of strife or other. There's something else that's interesting, if you want to hear it. This didn't have anything to do with the Flying Doctor because this was later on. But see, Rex and me, we had a bit of a falling out there for a little over ten years when he was living down at Ardlethan, in the south-west of New South Wales. So for ten odd years I didn't speak to him. Then right out of the blue, one time he come up to see me. I'm not exactly sure when it was right now but I remember it was just before Light Fingers won the Melbourne Cup. By then Rex'd already had a bloody stroke and he was telling me all about it, how he was stuck in a wheelchair for about four months and, oh, he reckoned he was dirty on the world and crooked on all the people in the hospital and then, one day, he just thought, Oh, I'd better get over this.

So he decided to get up out of that wheelchair and get on his way again. Oh, he was still a bit gimped up, like. You know, he just had a gimp on the leg and the arm, but he was mobile.

Anyhow, when Rex come up to see me that time, just before Light Fingers won the Cup, he had these bloody clippings from the local newspaper, down Ardlethan way, and it was all about him having a big run-in with a train. So he showed me these clippings and he said to me, 'Barry,' he said, 'I was just driving along in the station wagon, mindin' me own business and I looked up and there's this bloody train there, right in front of me, and by then it was too late to stop so I just drove straight into it.'

And when he drove into the train he reckoned he hit it so hard that he got pushed right from the front seat of his station wagon and he finished up stuck against the back window, you know, of

A rabbit trap—The Hansford Collection

the station wagon. And he reckoned that when they came to have a look at him, he could hear them saying, 'He's dead. He's dead.' And Rex's all squashed up at the back window, thinking to himself, I don't bloody think so.

So yeah, he walked away from that one, and soon after that he come up and he showed me the bloody things all about it in the paper. So yeah, he was pretty accident prone. Well, the whole lot of the Yarnold family was really, even his son, Henry. See, old Rex had a bit of a problem with Henry and Henry was up the Cross, in Sydney, one night and I don't know what was going on in his bloody head but he jumped off a four-storey building. The only thing was that instead of landing on the pavement like he planned, he landed in this bush. So he got up and walked away, and there was a chap there who had a camera and he won an award for taking photos of it, you know. So yeah, they were a pretty accident-prone family but they always seemed to survive, somehow.

Any rate, after Rex come up and seen me that time with the paper clippings of him having a prang with the train, not long after, he went back home to Ardlethan and he dropped dead from a heart attack. That was on 2 January, the year after Light Fingers won the Melbourne Cup.

Amazing

In about 1958 I was working at Alice Springs Hospital. Back then the RFDS didn't have their own specialised nursing staff so, if there was a call out, the Matron would come along and just grab whoever she could from the hospital's nursing staff. I actually worked in the Maternity Ward for white women, but it didn't matter what ward you worked in, you might even be lying in your bed—it could even be on your day off—and the Matron might come around and say, 'Hoy, Kitty, we've had a call from the Flying Doctor Service. Get on the plane, you're going out to where ever it was.' And you just had to jump to it, grab whatever medical supplies you thought you might need and get out to the airport as quick as possible to fly out to wherever, help stabilise them and then bring them back into Alice Springs.

Anyway, this time the Matron came along and she said that I had to go out to, I think it was, Areyonga Aboriginal Community. 'There's a demented Lubra out there who needs to be collected and brought back into Alice Springs,' she said.

Areyonga's south-west of Alice Springs and, as it turned out, she wasn't demented at all, just depressed. But anyway, off I go and I must've been a bit demented myself because I forgot to take any restraints or anything. All I grabbed was 10cc of a sedative called Paraldehyde, just in case.

Now, back then the Flying Doctor Service was using Connellan Airlines. Like, Eddie Connellan was quite a famous person and he owned an airline, and the RFDS chartered his planes for their flights. So we get out to Areyonga Aboriginal Community and the Manager there met us at the airstrip and he said to the young pilot, 'The Community vehicle's broken down. Can you taxi the plane up to wherever this woman was.'

That was something you couldn't really do, you know, just

'Can you taxi the plane down to where this lady is?'—RFDS

drive the plane off the airstrip and down a dirt track. But anyway, the young pilot did. Then there was some sort of delay while we waited for them to get the Aboriginal woman ready. Anyway, the Manager was very interested in planes so, while we were passing the time, the pilot took him for a bit of a flip around, which I'm sure he wasn't supposed to do either. But he did, anyway.

By the time they got back from their joy-flight the woman was ready and they carried her the short distance from the settlement to the plane, on a litter, which is like a type of stretcher. So, we load this Aboriginal lady, the one that was supposed to be demented, onto the plane. She was only quite young and, as I said, I think she was more depressed than demented because after she got in the plane she was as quiet as a mouse and didn't say anything.

So off we fly. Now, a lot of the pilots that used to go up to Alice Springs to work for Connellan's were young pilots who went up there to clock up their flight hours. Many were relatively new to the job so a lot of them weren't all that experienced. Anyway, we're flying along and this pilot somehow got lost and he turned around to me and said, 'Do you know where we are?'

I took a look outside and couldn't see any landmarks that I recognised. It was all the same, sort of, looking desert. 'No, I don't know where we are,' I told him.

'Oh,' he said.

Anyway, I wasn't too worried because that happened, at times, out in the middle of nowhere, and you'd just fly along looking for a road or the railway line and, when you found it, you took your directions from that. So there I was, looking out the window, hoping to see a road or something, when I happened to say to this young Aboriginal lass, I said, 'Do you know where we are?'

As I said, she hadn't said boo up till this stage, but she lifted her head, took a quick look out the window and she said, 'Jay Creek'.

That's all she said, Jay Creek. And she was right. She was spot on. We were at Jay Creek, and she was the only one who knew where we were. And I thought, How ironic was that. Because, you know, she'd never been in an aeroplane before. So she'd never looked down on the land from that height so how could she just glance out the window and pinpoint exactly where we were? Amazing, isn't it?

Ashes

This happened back in 1975 and there's no humour in this story because it was a fairly tragic event. At the time we were shearing up at Winning Station, which is about 150 miles north of Carnarvon, just inland from the central Western Australian coast. And the shearers' cook there, what he did with all his scraps and fat and bones and rubbish and things was, he used to burn them outside the shearers' quarters.

Anyhow, we were there for quite a few weeks and so there was just a heap of white ash. You know, if you looked at it, you wouldn't even know it was hot. But one of the shearers was there with his wife and two little kids and well, you know, we'd finished work that day and it was just on dark and one of the little kids— about two years old, he was—he didn't have any shoes on or anything and the next thing we heard him screaming.

The pedal radio—RFDS

So we rushed around and there he was, this little kid, standing in the middle of all this hot ash. I guess he'd run across it and got stuck, so panic set in and he just stood there, right in the middle of it, screaming and screaming. Actually, he was very lucky that he didn't fall over in the fire or anything because it was just red hot coals; well, just all white hot coals really, and you couldn't see them.

Anyway, myself and another chap, we ran over and we pulled him out of it. But all his feet were badly burnt. They were more or less cooked, really. Oh, he was in such agony the poor little feller. So we rushed around to the neighbouring station with this little kid and they gave him some pain-killers from the Flying Doctor medical kit that they always kept at the homestead. And they also had an airstrip. It was only a dirt one but it was still a usable strip. By this time it was about seven or eight o'clock in the evening and we got on to the Flying Doctor on the two-way radio. No, actually, I think it might've even been a pedal radio back in those days. But it was the Carnarvon base we got in touch with.

We told them what had happened and that it was an emergency and they said they'd fly straight out. Then, at the airstrip, being just dirt, there were no lights or anything and we had to get all the cars we could muster so that the Flying Doctor pilot could find out where to land by just using the car lights as his guide. So we had the cars lined up and down each side of the runway and then we had a couple up at the far end so that the pilot could see where to stop. I'd say there must've been about twenty cars. From memory they had them on low beam and the pilot, sort of, flew into the lights. I think it was a twin engine Beechcraft Baron or something like that. As I said, it was just a dirt strip, and it was in the dark and still this chap landed the RFDS plane perfectly, just by using the car lights as a guide. I tell you, you've got to marvel at those chaps.

Anyway, he had the doctor on board with him so the doctor treated the little boy on the plane and they flew him back into Carnarvon, then down to Princess Margaret Hospital in Perth.

But unfortunately, one of the little boy's feet finished up like a club foot and he lost the toes on both his feet. And, you know, even now, I can still see that little kid standing in that hot ash, just screaming and screaming.

So it's not a happy story, like I said, but still, it was a great thing that the Flying Doctor was able to fly out and get him because otherwise, I wouldn't even want to contemplate what the end result for that little boy might've been.

Been Around, Done a Thing or Two

I'm 70 years old actually, and I've retired. I was in the car game for forty-five years but, oh, back a while now, I had a bit of a heart turn and I was in Chinchilla Hospital. Chinchilla's west of Brisbane, between Dalby and Roma. Anyway, after four days, the Flying Doctors came out and they flew me to Brisbane. So really, I just wanted to say an extra thank you to the Royal Flying Doctor Service, you know, not only for how they helped me but, for all us bush people, especially those that live out in the real remote areas. They'd be done without them.

So that's all I was going to say and then I was going to tell you a little story about my dad. Dad used to be a drover. Out through the west of Queensland he was commonly known as 'Flash Jack McIntyre'. You might've heard of him. I used to go out droving with him too, right out Charleville way, all around throughout that district; Tambo, Augathella, Cunnamulla, Eulo and all them places. One of my brothers also used to be out that way. He was a Senior Sergeant of Police; Neil McIntyre.

But long before he joined the police force, Neil and my other brother, Duncan, and myself—my name's Noel—we all done a stint or three out the west, droving with Dad and other fellers. It was an experience, I can tell you. As a matter of fact, do you know Howard Hobbs? From memory he's the Local Member for Maranoa. Well, we used to do a lot of droving for his father. I think his name was also Howard Hobbs, and they lived at Tambo.

Oh, there's stacks of stories I could tell. It just goes on and on. But see, if someone asked me to go camping today, I'd say, 'No thank you, very much.' Because, you know, when you were out droving, it was a tough old life. You hardly saw anyone and you didn't eat very well and you only had a wash every time you got to a creek or a bore drain. Don't get me wrong, it was good experience but it certainly made me realise the good things in life.

Anyhow, see, Dad was out droving one time and, back in those days, the telephone lines they had were only bush telephone lines. You know, they were just a length of old wire cable that ran between properties and properties, and they were only strung up loosely between one old rickety wooden pole to another or, if they could find a tree, it was hung from one tree to another tree, that sort of thing; pretty rough. Anyhow, Dad used to hang a leading-line between the horse he was riding and the pack-saddle horse. So he was going along, nice and steady, when a telephone line got caught in the pack-saddle and the packhorse shied and it threw the pack-saddle back and it hit Dad fair on the mouth. Then, as Dad got hit, he flinched and his spurs dug into his horse and it leaped and bolted off. And that's how Dad ended up in Charleville Hospital, where he had quite a lot of stitches in his mouth and all that.

Now, what you've got to understand is that this was fifty odd years ago and, back then, there were lots of people who were living out in those real remote places who'd never even been into a big town. Like, they were born in the bush and that's where they stayed for the whole of their lives, out in the bush.

Anyhow, the nursing people in at the Charleville Hospital were telling dad about this old-timer who'd worked out on a remote station property. He'd never been out of the bush so he'd most certainly never seen a town as big as Charleville, which meant it was a dead-cert that he'd never been in a hospital before. Anyhow, he'd been pretty badly bunged up. I'm not real sure just why now. It might've even been a riding accident or something. But the thing was that it happened away out in one of the real remote areas and the Flying Doctors had to go out and bring him back into Charleville for treatment.

Well, this old-timer arrived at Charleville Hospital—as I said he was pretty bunged up—and the nurses said, 'We're going to have to take you for X-rays.'

Now, of course, this old-timer didn't have a clue what an X-ray was so he started to get real worried. 'Will it hurt?' he asked.

'No,' they said, 'You wont even know you've had one.'

But that didn't seem to ease this old-timer's worries. For starters, he was a bit suspicious about putting all his trust in these strange, city-type people. To his liking they talked too fast and, anyway, you'd have to be mad to want to live in a big place like Charleville. So he was really nervy. Then by the time they got him into a wheelchair, he was even more nervy. He'd never been in one of those neither. As they were wheeling him down the corridor, he was so bad that he was sweating.

By the time they pressed the button for the lift he was in a real panic. Then, while they were standing around, waiting for the lift to come, they noticed that the old-timer's knuckles had gone white from gripping so hard onto the wheelchair.

'It'll all be over very soon, sir,' they said, trying to reassure the old-timer.

So the lift arrived and they rolled this old feller into the lift and they pressed the button to take the lift to the second floor of the hospital, which was where the X-ray Department was. Then just

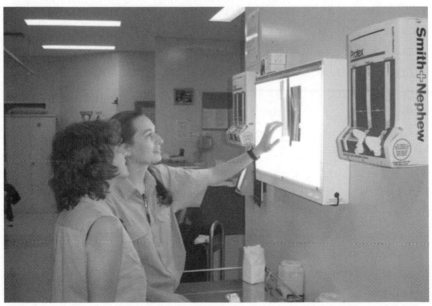

'Isn't it bloody marvellous how they do X-rays, eh? That didn't even hurt a bit'—RFDS

as they wheeled him out of the lift on the second floor, the old-timer let go a big sigh.

'Are you alright, mister so-and-so?' they asked.

'Well, you were right,' he replied. 'Isn't it bloody marvellous how they do X-rays, eh? That didn't even hurt a bit.'

And Dad was laughing his head off about this because, you know, Dad had lived. He'd been down to Brisbane and all those places, where they've got lifts and escalators and all that. So he'd been around, done a thing or two, as they say. But, you know, back fifty years or so a lot of those old-timers away out in the backblocks of Queensland, they'd never seen a lift, and there was this old-timer, who'd never been out of the bush, well, he thought that the lift was an X-ray machine, didn't he.

Black 'n' Decker

My name's Micky Hunter. I'm from out at Hillston, in the central west of New South Wales, just west of Griffith. I'm part Italian, part Aboriginal so, mate, that's why I tell everyone I'm from the 'Wog-Abo Tribe'. But I worked a long time as a stockman-ringer, all over the place, and a lot of that ringer stuff is what I'm writing in a book. I'm calling it 'Not Another Bloody Book' and it's stories of the incidents and the old fellers I met along me life and stuff like that.

Have you heard of Sir Sidney Kidman? Well, mate, Sir Sid is my top, number one, best Aussie. His fairness and everything is just one great thing about him and another is that the man never swore or drank or smoked cigarettes. But, yeah, I did all that. I still do but I don't drink now, but I did all that stuff. So there you go. But with my book, I've been working on it for a long while now, and talking to people all about it, and yeah, it's a good idea but I can't find a structure at all, you know.

Anyhow, here's a Flying Doctor story that's going to be in my book. It's probably one of the best of them really because it's fair dinkum. It really happened. Because, just between you and me, there's a lot of make-believe stories in my book so there's a few in there that are a bit 'stretchy', if you catch my drift. But this one's a true one, and it's about how a Flying Doctor helped a young ringer when his horse went over on him up in the Normanton area, in the north-west of Queensland.

What happened was that there was different mobs of us ringers, all over the place, mustering up there in the claypan country, and it happened around one of the mustering yards. I couldn't tell you the name of the property offhand because it was a long time ago now, mate, back in the mid-60s, before the boys went to 'Nam [Vietnam]. Anyhow, we'd been mustering, yeah, and

*We were all standing around the plane listening to the outcome as the pressure of the injured ringer's skull was being relieved by an electric drill—*RFDS

in our mob there was fifteen of us ringers and there was four or five thousand cattle.

See, with the mustering, you bring the cattle into the yard and you do various different things with them. Most of them was scrubbers that, you know, you hadn't seen for eighteen months or two years or something like that. So we'd brand them, de-horn them and de-knacker them. There was just five of us blokes who were in our contract team and the other ten we employed was mostly good Aboriginal fellas from around the country. Up there we sort of knew everyone around the place. It's a brotherhood, you know, all us ringers are, yeah.

Anyhow, our boss brought the plane down and he said he'd just heard over the radio that there'd been an accident over with another mustering team, a couple of hundred kilometres away. Now you know how you sort out strays? Well some men do it with vehicles and it's like a game, you know, they bellow and holler and they get the cattle extremely excited so when one takes off, one of the 'Yahoo-ringers' goes and chases it on a horse. And a boy was chasing some strays, like I said, and his horse went over on him and he was squashed by his beast.

So then we was listening to all what was going on over the boss's aeroplane radio. A young doctor was already there with the injured boy. He might've already been in the area doing clinics or something, so he touched down there pretty quick to check the boy out. Then he reported into Head Office, you know, because he didn't know what to do and he wanted to talk to an expert doctor.

Now, I'm not sure where he rung into but it might've been Cloncurry or one of them bigger Flying Doctor bases. And we could hear them talking through the airwaves to each other, so we could hear all what was going on, yeah, and it wasn't too good. From what the young doctor was telling the expert doctor, the young ringer, who'd got trampled on, well, he had real bad head injuries so there was a lot of pressure on the brain and it looked like he was going to die.

Well, the expert told the young doctor that the first thing he had to do was to try and relieve the pressure on the ringer's head. But then the young doctor said that he didn't know how to do that. Maybe he was either a young first-timer or maybe he hadn't done a lot, I don't know. Anyway, the expert doctor asked the young doctor if there was one of them home electric drills handy. You know, one of them Black 'n' Decker-type drills, the same as we was all using in the workshops. So it was one of those, and the expert doctor wanted a steel bit put into it. Yeah, a steel bit.

So they found an electric drill and the young doctor got someone to put the drill bit into the drill because he didn't know how to do that neither. Then after they done that, the expert started telling the young doctor how to operate on this young ringer; like, where to drill a hole in the boy's head to relieve the pressure.

And we could hear it all because, see, we was all standing around the boss's plane listening to the outcome of this young ringer being squashed by the horse. And we even heard the sound of the drill, because there was a big whirring sound when he first started it up and then, when the drill was going into the boy's head, the whirring sound slowed right down. And he done it. The young doctor done it. He drilled into this boy's head. I don't know what come out of the head, whether it was blood or whatever it was but the young doctor relieved the pressure alright because this young fella, they flew him out in an emergency plane and apparently everything turned out alright. So there you go.

Blown Away

In 1990 my wife and I and a small group of friends made plans to travel down the Canning Stock Route. There were four cars, three Land Rovers of varying vintages and us, with our Hilux. For my wife and I it was literally the start of five months travelling, which was fantastic. Actually, it was brilliant.

One of the blokes who was probably the key to putting the trip together was my mate, Murray. Murray's no longer with us I'm afraid but, to give you some idea as to what sort of character he was, some years ago Murray decided to tackle the Simpson Desert. And where everyone else drives it—and Murray had already driven it about five times—this time he decided to walk it. Yes, walk it. So he put together a bunch of people with camels and followed the route of Madigan the explorer across the Simpson.

One of the other guys who went with us on the Canning trip was a fellow called Vic Jaeger. Vic's Member Number 1 of the Victorian Land Rovers Owner's Club and what Vic doesn't know about four-wheel drives and travelling, probably isn't worth knowing. Now, Murray was the best mechanic I knew and he told me that Vic was the best mechanic he'd ever known. That's how good Vic was, so he was a handy sort of person to have along on a trip like that.

Anyway, my wife and I stayed back in Melbourne a little longer than the others because they wanted to take their time in getting to our rendezvous point of Halls Creek. Then my wife and I sprinted from Melbourne to Halls Creek, doing the trip in five days, which included having to fix a car problem along the way. When we got to Halls Creek we ended up waiting for three days before Murray, Vic and the others arrived. They got there a bit late.

Then we all headed off from Halls Creek and instead of going down the usual way, we thought we'd go off the main stock route. The track, if you could even describe it as that, proved to have been so little travelled that, when we got to one particular spot, a 20-foot tall sand dune had literally covered the track. There were no wheel tracks over it, either. Nothing. That's how much out of the way we were at that point. I'd even go as far to say that it was the most remote place I'd ever been in, in my whole life.

So, it took a bit of work for us to get our vehicles up and over this dune. Then, when we eventually got over, you wouldn't believe it, there, just on the other side of the dune, waiting to come up, was a fellow in a Nissan Patrol, with his wife and two kids. Now we didn't expect to see anyone away out there, let alone a fellow driving by himself with his wife and kids.

Given that we were in such a desolate place and we were there with four beautifully equipped cars, our instant thought was, This fellow must be nuts to be out here by himself.

But as it happened, that wasn't actually the case because the fellow told us that he and his family had left his travelling companions that morning, after there'd been an accident and the RFDS had come to the rescue. Apparently this fellow, his family and another couple and their children had been travelling together. They'd stopped overnight on a claypan, a bit further back down the track, and a little nine-year-old girl from the other family climbed the only tree out on this claypan. Then, as little girls sometimes do, she fell out of the tree and, unfortunately, when she landed she suffered a fracture of one thigh. So it was a fairly serious situation that they then found themselves in.

Luckily, they were well equipped with both their vehicles having radios and so forth. So they got onto the Royal Flying Doctor Service and the RFDS gave them directions to a disused airstrip, which was relatively close to where the young girl had fallen out of the tree. Then, after they'd arrived at the strip, the RFDS had asked them to call back and give them an estimate of the condition of the strip so they could get some idea as to the possibilities of landing an aeroplane.

So they did just that. These two families drove out to the

disused strip and had a look and, as anyone would do in an emergency like that, they called the RFDS back and told them that the strip would be safe enough for an aeroplane to land on. After they'd made the call, the two families then proceeded to get stuck in and clear the shrubbery and what have you off the strip, the best they could. When that was completed, they set up a smudge fire so that the pilot could gauge the wind direction when he came in to land. Then they waited.

While all this was going on, the RFDS pilot had taken off from Derby—I think it was Derby—in a King Air, with a doctor and nurse on board. And when they arrived, the pilot did a series of low overflights to check the condition of the strip for himself, before deciding whether it was safe to land or not. He then deemed it an emergency and he put the King Air down on this disused, freshly cleared strip. That, in itself, was an extraordinary effort because the King Air is a heavy plane and, what's more, it needs about 800 metres to take off, which was another concern they were yet to face.

In one particular spot, a 20-foot sand dune had literally covered the track— RFDS

Anyway, all went well and the injured girl was picked up and was, at the time we met the fellow, on her way to a hospital in Perth in the King Air and her parents had parted from the family in the Nissan Patrol to head off for the closest town, which was Newman. From there, their plan was to fly down to Perth and meet up with their daughter.

So that was what the fellow in his Nissan Patrol told us, when we met at the dune.

But when I got to thinking about it all, I was just blown away by the logistics of that particular RFDS operation, on many counts. Firstly, the pilot, when he arrived at that roughly cleared airstrip, way out in the middle of nowhere, he had to make an instant assessment of its condition, and he had to get it absolutely right. If he got it wrong, it'd spell disaster for everyone. Of course, he'd be fully aware that these people would've told him that this airstrip was safe enough to put the aeroplane down, even if it wasn't, because their assessment was that of desperate parents with a badly injured child. They'd just want somebody there who could save their child. Secondly, the pilot would know that the decision he was about to make was not only about the life of a little girl but that he was also responsible for six million dollars worth of aeroplane along with the lives of the doctor and the nurse he's got onboard.

Also, of course, the doctor and the nurse have to place their absolute faith in the pilot's assessment of the situation. Even if they're terrified about what he's about to do, all they can do is sit there. If you talk to some of the nurses, and I have asked this question, 'Don't you get scared when you go out on some of these tricky retrievals?'

They'll tell you that, 'Yeah, there are times when we're terrified, but we have complete confidence in the judgement of the pilots and the decisions they make.'

So there was all that to be taken into consideration before they even landed the King Air. But then, what also astounded me, in that situation, was the absolute remoteness of where the retrieval had taken place. We'd travelled south for a week, without seeing a soul, to reach that 20-foot dune along the Canning Stock Route and the other two families had travelled north for a week, without seeing anyone. Just to give you some idea, the closest town was Newman, which was a good three or four days' drive away—I repeat days—and when you have a little girl with a fractured femur, any sort of delay in getting treatment might mean she could suffer permanent damage or lose a leg or, possibly, even die.

And it was only thanks to the professionalism and the courage of the RFDS crew that, on the same day this little girl fell out of the tree, they flew out there and plucked her out of the most isolated place I'd ever been in my life and had delivered her to a major hospital in Perth. So quite possibly a little girl's life was saved. Well, her leg was saved and that's the next most important thing.

Now, this's going to sound terribly naive, I know, but for me, the pilots, the doctors and the nurses of the Royal Flying Doctor Service are my heroes because at any given time they display that same courage and competence as they did in that situation with the little girl. On a daily basis they put their lives on the line for people who are complete strangers to them. They don't care who these people are, or what their nationality is, or what religion they are. And it doesn't matter to those pilots, doctors and nurses how those very same people probably wouldn't take a similar risk for them. In fact, they wouldn't even realise the risk. What's more, the RFDS do it for free. How good is that?

Dirt to Dust

Right back in 1928, when the Flying Doctor Service first started in Cloncurry, Qantas used to supply planes for them. Then in about 1957, Qantas handed it over to TAA. So I became the third TAA pilot in Alice Springs, and that was in about 1965.

By that stage I was familiar with flying around in the dust because, prior to joining TAA, I'd flown light aircraft all over northern Australia. Then when I joined TAA, they based me in Charleville and I was flying DC3s down to Birdsville every Sunday night. That's when Birdsville was a scheduled service. We'd go as far as Adelaide one week, and Broken Hill the next week. I remember we also used to overnight in Windorah, where we'd stay at the local pub. Oh, we had some great times there until we inadvertently drove a Land Rover through the front fence of the pub. After that the publican wouldn't let us stay there. She wouldn't have a bar of us.

But that's another story, though it was ironical that about two years after going through the fence we had an engine failure out at Windorah and the plane needed an engine change. That meant we had to stay overnight so, naturally, I thought that the pub would be the place to go and get a room. And as soon as I walked in the front door, the woman who owned the pub, she took one look at me and she shouted, 'Hey, you, I told you before, get out and stay out!'

So that was that, and I had to find somewhere else to stay.

But anyway, because I was used to flying in the dirt and the dust, out around Birdsville and all those places, TAA management rang me up one day and said, 'How would you like to go to Alice Springs?'

'Okay,' I said and so I went to Alice Springs.

And there was certainly plenty of dust out that way because there was an eight-year drought going on. Even the gum trees were dying. That's true. You'd drive in from the airstrip, into Alice

Dust storm approaching Alice Springs—Neil McDougall

Springs, and there'd be no undergrowth at all, and even the big gum trees along the Todd River were dying.

Mine was supposed to be a two-year posting but I enjoyed myself so much, and I got on so well with everyone, that they left me there for three years roughly, up until 1968. It was during that time that I was seconded into the Royal Flying Doctor Service.

In Alice Springs, in those days, the Flying Doctor Service only ran the radio base, that's all, and the Commonwealth Government used to foot the bill for the doctor, the nursing sisters, the pilot and the aircraft. Then, as time went by, and the RFDS gradually started buying their own aircraft and using their own pilots, TAA bowed out of that operation.

But back in the mid-60s, they didn't have any of the fancy aircraft they have today. In Alice Springs, the plane we used was a twin engine De Havilland Dove. The Dove was the first civil aircraft built by the Poms after World War II and, for its time—1946—it was a remarkable aircraft. It had two 370 supercharged Gipsy Queen motors with fully feathering props, pneumatic undercarriage, flaps and brakes. It had a fuel system that came out, many years later, in the DC9, that you could operate manually or by booster pumps which, for its day, was an excellent system. We could put eight hours' fuel on, which gave us enormous range for a light aircraft of that era. They even had engine fire bottles, which was unheard of in light aircraft, back then. Plus the Dove was the only IFR [Instrument Flight Rules] aircraft in Alice Springs and I was the only instrument-rated pilot. So, naturally I got every dirty trip. And over the three years I was in the Alice I'd say I transported around 1500 patients and conducted near on 2000 medical clinics in small towns, Aboriginal communities and out on cattle properties. In fact, my area extended north to Newcastle Waters, west to the Western Australian border, east to the Queensland border and south over the South Australian border. To give you some idea just how vast the landmass was, someone once got a map and they superimposed England, Scotland and Wales into the area we—the Alice Springs RFDS—covered.

But, with the dust, as I said, there was an eight-year drought going on, and when I arrived in the Alice, they were keeping sand off the station homesteads and stockyards with bulldozers. All the grass and all the herbage had gone. There was nothing left but drifting sand and dirt. It was so bad that the blowing sand used to bury the runway markers, even in Alice Springs.

Now here's a very strange phenomena. I remember, one morning, I taxied out and there was unlimited visibility. It was as clear as a bell. I did an engine run and everything was right to go. Then, just as I was about to take off, I looked up and, to my amazement, the dust was rising up out of the ground, vertically. I repeat, vertically.

It was unbelievable. I'd never seen anything like that before I went to Alice Springs and I've never seen it since leaving Alice Springs. There was no wind. It was dead still, and this dust cloud just rose up, out of the ground. And I've got no solid explanation as to why that would've happened. I can only guess that, as the sun warmed up the earth, it created a vertical current which lifted the dust up. So from having unlimited visibility, by the time I took off, I only, probably, had less than 300 metres visibility. And that all happened within ten minutes.

Another time I was coming back into Alice Springs after I'd been on routine medical visits, right out near the Western Australian border. It was about a half hour before dark and when I was nearing Ayers Rock there was unlimited visibility. But my sixth sense kept saying, There's something wrong here.

We weren't in any dust or anything. There was no wind. I just had this feeling, you know, that conditions just seemed right for the dust to come.

Well, I had two doctors and two nursing sisters with me and one of the doctors was sitting in the cockpit, so I said, 'Do you mind if we stay at Ayers Rock. I don't like the weather very much.'

'What's wrong with it?' he said.

'I don't know,' I said. 'I've just got a feeling that there's some dust coming up.'

So I called up Alice Springs: 'What's your latest forecast regarding dust?'

'There's no dust to mention,' they said. 'It's fine. It's beaut. Unlimited visibility.'

Now you've got to remember that, in those days, the only radio aids and runway lights were in Alice Springs, Oodnadatta and Tennant Creek and, by that stage, we were still about 300 miles from Alice Springs. So we were due to arrive some forty-five minutes after last light. As it was, we could land at Ayers Rock and we had accommodation there. So we could stay there if we needed to, but Alice Springs said, 'No, it's fine in Alice Springs. You'll have no problems at all. It's beaut.'

We still had a cattle station to visit. That was our last chance to stop. But I still had the inkling that something wasn't quite right so, while we were at the cattle station, I called Alice again and I said, 'Are you sure there's no dust there?'

'Unlimited visibility,' they said.

'Okay,' I said, but I still wasn't convinced.

Anyhow, if I really needed an alternative I still had enough fuel to continue on to Tennant Creek. So we flew out and then, when I was about 30 miles out of Alice, I called up again and they said, 'Sorry, visibility's now down to zero in dust.'

'Well, thanks a million.'

Anyhow, I decided to do one instrument approach at Alice Springs, then divert to Tennant, if need be. And when I got down to minimum flying level I could just make out the lead-in lights. So I followed them in and, 'plonk', we landed safely on the ground. But honestly, the dust was so thick that I had trouble finding the taxiway to the hangers. And my wife was coming out to pick me up and, when she arrived, she said, 'Oh, that dust's terrible. I had to keep stopping the car on my way out because I couldn't see anything on the road.'

And that dust had come from nothing.

Then another time, see, we had to be checked every six months for our instrument rating renewal and, anyway, the bloke came up to check me and we flew out over the South Australian border to Ernabella Mission. Ernabella was, I suppose, about 250 nautical miles away. And it was a dusty trip; a very, very dusty trip.

Anyway, I finally found my way to Ernabella Mission and when we got on the ground, the bloke who was supposed to be checking me, he said, 'Well, I haven't seen anything since we left Alice Springs so it's got me absolutely rooted just how you found your way out here.' He said, 'I couldn't understand why you kept going. I was expecting you to turn around and go back to Alice Springs.'

Now I didn't tell him but, you know, because we were flying out in these areas all the time, you could just about find your way through anything. And what I'd done was, I knew that you'd have all the red of the soil and then there'd be the white of the salt lake, and just the other side of the salt lake there was a road that ran down to Ernabella.

So I just came down through all the red dust and, when I could just make out the white of the salt lake, I knew, exactly, where I had to turn right and follow the road to Ernabella. But I didn't tell him that because you don't give away your trade secrets, do you? And he said, 'Well, I'm rooted. I didn't see a thing the whole trip.'

And that just about covers some of the experiences I've had flying with dust and dust storms.

Dobbed In

Two things before we start. First, about the medical chests that all the station properties, and so forth, have. The Royal Flying Doctor Service provides those free of charge and there's about 800 of them throughout Western Australia and they're worth about $1200 each. Oh, I think that some of the bigger mining companies might pay for theirs.

A while ago I remember there was a doctor here in Derby, and he used to say, 'You could wait for up to five hours in a big city hospital to see an emergency doctor. Whereas, if you're in the bush, thanks to the Royal Flying Doctor Service, you can talk to a doctor within a minute on the radio or on a telephone. You've got over a thousand dollars worth of free drugs at your disposal and, within two hours, an aeroplane, which has all the equipment you're ever going to need, will be there to pick you up. And it's free of charge, not only in this state, but anywhere throughout Australia.'

The only people the RFDS actually charge for their services are workers compo cases and overseas insurance travellers. But the thing is, after the Flying Doctor Service gets you there, to wherever you're going, you do have to find your own way home. The RFDS doesn't bring you back. And when that happens you have the PAT [Patient Assisted Travel] Scheme to help you. I think there's a PAT Scheme in every state, though most probably it goes under a different name. Now I'm not sure, but I don't think you even have to pay for that service. You just go to the PAT clerk at the hospital and they'll organise everything for you.

The second thing I'd like to mention is just how strong the CWA [Country Women's Association] is here in Western Australia. We do a lot more than make scones and cakes and stuff and sell them at small street stalls, along with the occasional raffle ticket or two. Yes, we still do those types of things but, we're also an

The School of the Air sessions were hilarious, mainly because the teachers couldn't see what merry-hell the kids were getting up to—RFDS

extremely strong political lobby group. So much so that, these days, the government either run or they bow when they see the CWA coming. For example, it was through our efforts that the first remedial teacher and the School of the Air teachers were provided with a car. We also lobbied strongly for the Flying Doctor Service to employ their own doctors instead of using hospital doctors. By employing their own doctors you have greater continuity of service by properly trained people who are familiar with all facets of RFDS procedure. And that only happened five years ago, up here in Derby. So that's the strength of the CWA.

Now as for stories, most of what I remember happened during the Royal Flying Doctor radio sessions. How it all worked was that, just like in other states, we also had the infamous 'Galah Sessions' where everyone could get on the radio and chat with their neighbours and all that. They went from midday to one o'clock every day. The 'Galah Sessions' were really strong up here until about 20 years ago, which was when the telephones came through the Kimberley.

Prior to the arrival of the telephones, everything was organised through the RFDS radio. Not only were there the usual emergency calls and the medical sessions with the doctor but you also organised all your P and C meetings, all your CWA meetings, your Ag Department meetings over the RFDS radio. Plus, you ordered your cattle trucks, ordered your food through the RFDS radio system and, of course, everyone within cooee who was able to listened in.

How the day panned out was; there was a morning medical session at seven o'clock with a doctor on the other end of the radio. So if you were crook you told the doctor—along with the rest of the Kimberley—what was wrong with you or your family and, hopefully, the doctor could help treat you. If the doctor couldn't help you, it was more than likely that someone might chip in with some suggestions.

Then there were eight o'clock, 11 o'clock and three o'clock sessions where the telegrams were read out over the radio. These arrived from the post office and were read out from the RFDS base. Also, if you needed to send a message, you called in to the Base on your radio and that message was then phoned through to the post office where it was sent out as a telegram.

And, of course, the School of the Air also shared radio facilities with the RFDS. In fact, Port Hedland School of the Air still have their offices combined with the RFDS. And that service was just wonderful for our kids when we were out on Gibb River Station.

But the School of the Air sessions were hilarious, mainly because the teachers couldn't see what merry-hell the kids were getting up to. I remember that twice a year all us parents who were home tutors and their kids, and the governesses and teachers would get together and attend a seminar-meeting at the Broome Camp School. And at this camp us parents used to perform skits for the teachers, just to show them what the kids got up to behind the scenes, and you'd get these new teachers watching our performances and they'd go, 'Oh my god, is that what really goes on?'

One skit we did was about a session that was called 'M and M' [Music and Mayhem]. 'M and M' was held early in the morning and was designed for the kids to have some exercise. So you'd have your child sitting beside you and you'd go on the air and the teacher would tell the kid what exercise they were supposed to do, then they'd say, 'Okay, Johnny, are you jumping around there?'

And Johnny would be just sitting there looking completely bored with it all, and the teacher would say, 'Okay, then, how did you go, Johnny?'

And little Johnny would put on this huge act like he's completely exhausted and he'd huff and puff into the radio, 'Really well, Miss. That exercise was a tough one.'

Another skit we did was about when they'd send out Christmas recipes which showed the kids how to make like, you know, those milk-ball things made with apricot and coconut and all that stuff. So we'd act out how the kids would be mixing up all this squishy stuff and we'd have the 'teacher' pretend to come on the air and ask, 'Now, how are you doing out there, Jenny?'

Then we'd have the person who's playing the part of poor little Jenny, well, she'd be up to her elbows in this gooey stuff and, all of a sudden, she's expected to pick up a microphone, and say, 'I'm fine. Things are going real well, Miss.'

Of course, with the School of the Air sessions, you'd also get a very clear insight as to what was going on at all the other properties. We had one lady out on a station near Halls Creek. They were just starting up back then so things were pretty rough. You could imagine, at that early stage, they just had a shed and not much else to live in. But this lady was a real character and her boys were just so full-on, if you know what I mean. And one day this little boy who was in my daughter's class, you could hear him sounding really upset, so the teacher asked, 'Are you alright, Donald?'

'Sniff ... Sniff ... Yeah ... Sniff ... I guess so.'

'Are you sure you're alright?'

'Sniff ... Sniff ...' Then he bursts out crying, 'Wahhhh ... Wahhhh ... Mum's just hit me!'

Of course, all this is going out over the airwaves. Then another time his mother had obviously gone off to do something else and he was stuck with his school work and he got upset, so the teacher asked, 'Are you alright, Donald?'

And then you hear this little whimper, 'I need my Mum.'

Oh, he was a real little character, he was. But she was too, you know. Like, the teacher would say, 'Okay, Donald, you've finished your painting now. Put it down and maybe you should put a rock on it to hold it there until it dries.'

Then you'd hear the mother shouting in the background, 'Bloody hell. Nick off down the bloody creek and get a bloody rock to hold this bloody painting down.'

And the creek's like 200 yards away or something. So you could imagine everyone who's listening in is rolling around with laughter while all this stuff's going on.

Then—and this happened quite a few times—you'd hear this great big bang coming out over the radio and the teacher would come on air and ask some kid or other, 'What's going on there?'

'Oh, it's alright Miss, we just shot a snake in the corridor.'

And all those wonderful bits and pieces would be broadcast out over the Kimberley. There was another little boy. One day he's dreaming away. You know, boys can be terrible that way, and the teacher couldn't get his attention so she said, 'Are you alright, Andrew? What's going on there?'

'Oh, I'm just watchin' all the boys [Aboriginal stockmen]. They're outside there, sittin' 'round, havin' a beer and a smoko.'

'And is that more interesting than doing your school work?'

'Oh yeah, you bet!'

So you couldn't get away with anything. One of the big ones was when one of the kids told the teacher, 'Dad's not here today. He'll be back tomorra.'

'Oh, where'd he go?'

'He's just gone over to get a killer.'

A 'killer', of course, is an animal you kill for your own meat. And, I mean, it's a well-known rural joke that if you ever wanted to find out what your own beef tasted like, you just went over to your neighbour's place and had dinner there. So here's this kid broadcasting to everyone in the Kimberley that his dad wouldn't be back until tomorrow because he was on his way over to the cattle station next door to knock off one of his neighbour's cattle. So the kids were always dobbing you in, in one way or another, and the RFDS provided the radio.

Another one, and I'll make this the last little story; it's about a woman out at one of the stations who really got dobbed in. One time, the teacher wanted to speak to her so she said to the kid, 'Can I talk to your Mum, please?'

'Mum can't come. She's busy,' the kid replied.

'But I need to talk to her. Could you go and get her, please.'

'Mum can't come.'

'Look,' the teacher said, starting to get really frustrated with the kid, 'I really need to talk to your Mum.'

'Mum can't come.'

'And just why can't she come?'

Then the kid gathers up enough courage to shout back at the teacher, 'She can't come because ... SHE'S SITTING ON THE TOILET!'

Emergency!

Just a quick story and you may have already heard it. It's not my story. It was told by a well-known doctor-surgeon who used to be here in Dubbo, in central New South Wales. The doctor's name was Bob North. I think that's what his name was, anyway. Anyhow, Bob told this one at his farewell presentation, type of thing, about four years ago, when he was leaving or retiring or whatever he was doing.

Bob reckoned he was on duty in at Dubbo Hospital, one time, and there was this other doctor, a much younger feller, who'd just arrived from Sydney. I'd say he'd only been in Dubbo for a very short time. As far as I know he was straight out of university. The thing is, he was new at the job so he was pretty inexperienced as far as the more practical matters of doctoring go.

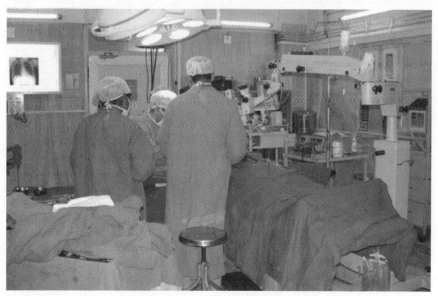

Bob was flat out in surgery, performing some extremely delicate operation—The Hansford Collection

Anyhow, Bob was working flat out in surgery, performing some extremely delicate operation. It was something very critical so he was very focused and very busy and this young doctor comes racing in to the surgery. 'There's an emergency,' he says. 'We've just taken a telephone call from the Flying Doctor base and they want a doctor to fly up to Lightning Ridge with them, immediately.'

'What's the problem?' Bob asked while still focusing on the job at hand.

'Well, they say that there's a bloke up there who's fallen down one of the mine shafts.'

'Doesn't sound too good,' Bob replied.

'No,' said the young doctor, 'apparently he's been stuck down the mine shaft for about a week, with nothing to eat and he's only been keeping himself alive by drinking his own urine.'

Anyway, Bob said, 'Well, son, as you can see, I'm flat out, so you'll have to go up to Lightning Ridge with the RFDS by yourself and see to the feller.'

Of course, this really threw the new doctor into a flap. Being just out of university this was something very different than what he'd ever been taught.

'Well,' the young doctor said, looking to Bob for some wise and worldly advice, 'what do I do when I get there? How do I go about treating him? What's the procedure?'

'Well, son,' Bob said, still concentrating on his patient, 'the first thing yer gonna have to try and do is to get the feller off the piss.'

First Drive

My first flight for the RFDS was as a freelance 'driver' out of Cairns. I describe myself as a driver because, basically, that's all a pilot is. The only difference between us and a bus driver is that we've got wings. Anyhow, that was back on 13 November 1982 and because all the aircraft were already busy, we did that flight in a non-RFDS aircraft, but with an RFDS doctor.

In fact, I've just got the old log book out and, before that first flight with the RFDS, already on that day, I'd been from Darwin to Groote Eylandt, Karumba and on to Cairns in a Shrike Commander. But what happened back in those days was that there was an operator out of Cairns called Outback Air, who was owned by Richard Murray-Prior, and Richard used to be the casual pilot for the Flying Doctor Service. So Richard must've been unavailable on this occasion because his wife, Ilma, rang around looking for somebody to fly an aeroplane and she got me and asked if I could go out somewhere with a doctor to evacuate someone.

It was dark by then and, as I said, I'd already been around the place a bit already so I said, 'Well, Ilma, I'm not long home from Darwin. But if you can't get anybody else just give me a call back.'

Of course, by my saying that, she had me then, didn't she? In actual fact, a few years later, when I was employed full-time with the RFDS, Ilma worked for us as a manager of the RFDS Visitors' Centre, here in Cairns, and I happened to ask her one day, 'Ilma,' I said, 'away back then, in '82, did you really ring around and look for anyone else to go out on that evacuation?'

And her reply was along the lines of, 'Don't be silly, of course I didn't.'

Anyway, it didn't take Ilma long to get back in touch with me to say that she's rung around all over the place—which, of course, she hadn't—and that she couldn't find anyone else.

So I said, 'Yes, okay, I'll do the trip.' And then I was told that the place I had to go out to was a small town called Mount Surprise, which is south-west of Cairns, east of Georgetown.

It was all quite an odd experience for me really because, for starters, I'd never been to Mount Surprise before and secondly, I'd never flown in the aeroplane I was going out in; a Piper Aztec. I mean, I was endorsed on it, but I'd never been in this particular one before so, as far as that goes, it was a strange aeroplane to me. Then the doctor that came out with me was a fellow by the name of Russell Findlay and along with his medical gear Russell also had a book which gave the details of where the Mount Surprise airstrip was and so forth.

Then we were on our way out there and when I looked at the book Russell had brought along, it placed the aerodrome—this is from memory because it's going back a while now—but it placed the aerodrome something like about 20 miles west from Mount Surprise.

And I said to Russell, 'Gee, it sounds pretty strange for them to have an airstrip that far out of such a little town like Mount Surprise.'

The cockpit—RFDS

'Oh well,' he said, 'that's what the book says.'

Anyway I was still a bit concerned about it so I checked in with Townsville Flight Service to see if they could verify where the airstrip actually was and they said, 'No, we can't tell you, but Phil Darby will probably know where it is.'

Phil was a very experienced pilot with the Royal Flying Doctor Service. He'd been everywhere and knew the area like the back of his hand. Anyhow, Phil was coming back from Weipa and the bloke in Townsville said, 'We'll have a talk to Phil.'

So, when Phil got into range they explained how we were on the way out to Mount Surprise but the information in the Aerodrome Book seemed a bit odd because it positioned the strip as being well west of the town.

'Yeah, that's where it'd be,' Phil told them. 'That'd be right.'

'Oh, okay then,' I said and that was that.

But luckily enough, Phil must've had a bit of a think about it and decided, Hang on, I don't know so much about that. So he looked it up in his aeroplane and he got back in radio contact and he said, 'The book you've got is wrong. The strip's actually closer to town.'

Then he asked if I'd ever been there.

'Well, no,' I said, 'I didn't even know that Mount Surprise existed until someone rang me up tonight.'

And he said, 'Well there's a big hill right next to the strip, be wary of that.'

'Thanks for the warning,' I replied.

Now, I'd flown a bit at night, of course, but when you're coming out of Cairns and those sort of bigger towns where there's plenty of lights around them it's fine, but, with a little place like Mount Surprise you know it's going to be quite a black spot. Anyway, they had flares out and so we found the place alright and I remember—and it still happens to this day—next to the hill you get what we call a katabatic wind, which is where the air cools down and rushes down the hill. So you get quite a wind off it and when you're going in to land there's quite a bit of drift. Still, we negotiated that and we landed okay and the doctor said, 'Do you want to come into town with me to see this patient.'

'No thanks,' I told him, 'I'd prefer to have a look around here.'

So the doctor went into town while I stayed out at the airstrip. But when my eyes started to get used to the dark and I got my bearings, I could see this hill right next to the strip. Anyway, I had a bit of a look around for future reference, just in case I came back again. Then before too much longer they returned with the patient. As it turned out it was a female school teacher who'd taken an overdose of drugs, so we loaded her up and tied her into the seat and we prepared to leave.

Now, you've got to take off at a certain speed so that, if you have an engine failure, you can still keep flying. And I remember that I got a little bit slow when we lifted off. And it's all in the mind, because it's very hard, you know, to lower the nose when you don't know the area and you don't know exactly where the hill is out there. Anyhow we made it. But I can remember still holding onto the aeroplane until we got to about 7000 feet and once we got to 7000 feet I put the autopilot on. But gosh, it was as dark as hell. I'd never had that experience before. It was certainly a real eye-opener for me.

So we arrived back at Cairns without any trouble and, yeah, the teacher would've survived okay. But whether she stayed off drugs is another thing. Who knows. I mean, I've since discovered that there's a lot of sad cases out there; people who just don't look after themselves.

Anyway, that was my first flight, 'driving' for the Flying Doctor Service. I'm now full-time with the RFDS here at the Cairns base and then, sometimes, I'll relieve drivers out at the RFDS bases in places like Mount Isa and Charleville.

But I learnt a lot from that first flight, because there's nothing worse than going out to some place where you've never been before, especially at night, and you don't know what obstacles there are, you know, if there's towers about or there's hills around the place. So it certainly got me going. And because of that experience, what I try to do now is that, on the days I go out to some of these more remote towns and properties, I take as many digital photographs of the area as I can and I put them on a disk and keep them in the hanger. Then, when a new driver comes along, someone who's unfamiliar with these areas, I can say, 'Before you go out there, have a look at these because they'll give you a bit of an idea as to the lay of the land.'

Gasping

Yeah, the RFDS did actually come out for me once. At the time my husband, Pad, and I were working at Mount House Station, up the Gibb River Road, here in the Kimberley. It was during the wet season and the Station Manager was away on holidays so there were only four of us in residence. Anyhow, all of a sudden my lips went blue and I began to really gasp for air. It was smoko time and everyone was sitting in the kitchen and I walked up to Pad and I said, 'Pad, I can't breathe.'

And he took one look at me and went, 'Oh, you're not doing too well, at all, are you?'

The Flying Doctor Service radio was down at the Station Manager's homestead so they took me down there and they did the emergency button thing on the radio to get in contact with Derby. You know what that is, don't you? It's when you press the emergency button and a light in at the RFDS base comes on to let them know there's an emergency.

Anyhow, by this stage I'm lying on my back. The girl who was with us, she was good. She'd rolled up a towel and put it behind my neck, you know, to support my neck and open up my airways. But even then I was still really gasping because I just couldn't get any air. Probably a little bit of panic had set in as well, which mightn't have helped things.

So, they answered the emergency in at the Derby RFDS base and they ask what's wrong and Pad gets on the radio and says, 'My wife can't breathe!'

Then they start asking him all these questions. 'Does she suffer from asthma?'

'No.'

'Has she done this?'

'No.'

'Has she done that?'

'Do you have any idea why she's not breathing?'

'No.'

'Is she pregnant?'

Pad had to think about that one. 'I don't think so,' he said. 'Not that I know of, anyway.'

Then he asks me. 'You're not pregnant, are you?'

'No,' I gasped.

'No, she says she's not pregnant,' Pad replied. 'She's just lying here, gasping. You know, like, what else can I say?'

And I'm thinking, Oh my god! Because I'm getting pretty frightened by now. Like I'd tried very hard to lie there and relax and just think of something else but when your husband's on the phone calling out, 'She's lying here gasping!' Well, it's a bit hard to relax.

Anyway, they said, 'Well, okay, we'd better come out then.'

And they did have to divert their flight. Apparently they were going to Fitzroy Crossing or somewhere, and it wasn't an emergency, and Mount House Station wasn't all that far out of their way, which was fortunate. So it was a relief to hear them say that they were actually going to come out.

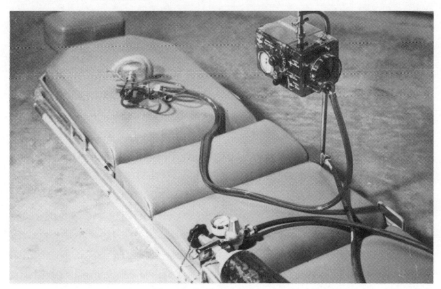

Respirator at the ready—RFDS

Still and all, they weren't able to arrive for about an hour so I just laid there on the floor trying to relax. Then about half an hour after we'd made the call to the Flying Doctor my breathing started to come good again, and my lips weren't quite as blue. But then I came out in this most hideous rash, mainly around my collar, round my socks, around the tops of my jeans. It was burning unbelievably and I started getting these great big welts.

When that happened we immediately figured out what was wrong. See, I must've walked under an itchy caterpillar nest and all the dust had fallen out onto my clothing. You know the little hairy caterpillars? It's their defence mechanism, you know, so that things won't touch them. Well, all their hair creates a dust that accumulates in their nest and if you get it on your clothes it rubs into your skin and you get this god-awful rash. So that's what happened. It was the itchy caterpillar.

Anyhow, once the rash came out, Pad was fine then. He started to relax when he realised what had happened. But, of course, the rash didn't come out until after I'd almost drawn my last breath, did it? Well, it certainly felt that way. I honestly thought I was going to stop breathing.

So then Pad stuck me under a nice cold shower and that got rid of most of the itchiness. But I was still having a bit of trouble breathing so, with the Flying Doctor already on his way, we went out to meet him. And that was a fair drive because the RFDS registered airstrip was about a 30-kilometre drive around the other side of the mountain. It's a big long, wide strip. So then I had to endure being bounced around in the front of the car.

Anyway, when we got there, we waited for another half an hour until they arrived and we were able to tell them that it was probably the itchy caterpillar that'd caused the reaction.

'That's unusual,' the doctor said, 'because normally it's the rash that hits you straight away and not the struggling for breath.'

He likened it to me having an enormous asthma attack and, had they known, they would've been able to tell Pad to give me a spoonful of liquid Ventolin that was in the RFDS medical kit in the homestead. And that would've reduced the reaction. Anyhow, they gave me some antihistamine shots to get rid of the welts and that and then they were off again. But they were really good about it. You know, they were glad to see I was alive. But, oh gee, it knocked me around for a few days, and I certainly did appreciate them coming out.

Gone with the Wind

It was around the beginning of 1969. The Flying Doctor base was about three or four miles out of Broken Hill, on the Wilcannia Road, and they had an auditorium there where they used to show a promotional film, for the tourists, about the RFDS and what they did.

Now, the actual RFDS doctor, at that particular time, was Doctor Graham Ambrose and the pilot was Vic Cover, or just 'Cove' as he was known amongst his friends and enemies. I knew both of them very well. Cove had a reputation as an incredible pilot, plus he was a bit of a larrikin, to boot. He had a weekender out at Menindee, along Sunset Strip. I went to a couple of his New Year's Eve parties there and they were events to remember, that's if you could, of course. Cove was well-known in the district and, as I said, a terrific pilot. Graham Ambrose was a young doctor, forty-ish, and a nice bloke. We were in Rotary together. He was President and I was Vice-President, and quite often he'd be away on Flying Doctor visits and so forth and I'd step in for him on Rotary nights.

Anyway, Graham said to me one day, 'Fred,' he said, 'the Stuyvesant cigarette company are keen to improve their corporate image so they want to make a film along the lines of a day in the life of the Flying Doctor.' He said, 'Fred, would you be willing to act as a patient?'

I'd done a bit of local repertory so I said, 'Yes, of course, I'll only be too willing to play the part of a patient.'

Well, out come this film crew from Sydney. Now I don't know whether it was because I'd built my expectations up too high or not but, I must say, I was a little surprised that there were only three in the film crew. Still, there you go. There was the director, who was quite well-known back in those days because he'd made a bit of a name for himself introducing 'This Day Tonight' or 'Today, Tonight'; you know, one of those television news-type shows in Sydney. He was a corker bloke and so was his crew. There was a cameraman. Now, the cameraman had recently broken his right leg, I think it was, in a motorbike accident and was in plaster from heel to hip. So he had a bit of trouble getting around. Then there was the sound man who had this big recording box and a microphone set up.

It was planned that we'd meet out at the RFDS base at a certain time and we'd fly out to Mooleulooloo Station to shoot the first part of this film. Anyhow, who should suddenly appear in Broken Hill, none other than some heavy in the Flying Doctor Service. He was either a Group Captain or a Chief Pilot or a Chief something-or-other. Now, whether he arrived in town on purpose or just by accident, I don't know. But he rocked up and, sort of, invited himself to come along with us.

Lights, camera, action—RFDS

So at the allotted time we all met up out at the RFDS base. The plane we were flying in was an old Drover. I think it was made by de Havilland. The Drover was originally a two-engined aeroplane that'd just been recommissioned and had a third engine put in it so that it now flew higher, faster and had shorter take-offs; something like that.

Anyway, before we even got to the stage of taking-off there was a brief debate between this Group Captain, or whatever he was, and Cove. The Group Captain wanted to fly the plane and Cove dug his heels in. 'No,' Cove said, 'I'm responsible for the aeroplane so I'm gonna fly the damn thing and that's all there is to it.'

So there was already some friction between this Group Captain feller and Cove. Anyway, Cove wouldn't budge on the matter and eventually the Group Captain gave in and Cove flew us out to Mooleulooloo Station, which was about 70 or 80 miles north-west of Broken Hill, over the border, into South Australia. I reckon the Treloar's had the place back then and probably still do.

Now, there was no script or anything. It was only while we were flying along that this director feller and Graham had a bit of a discussion, along with a few interruptions by the Group Captain. It came down to my problem being either a heart attack or a burst duodenum ulcer. So that was going to be my part, because I'm going to have to have something very dramatic that's going to cause an emergency call to the Flying Doctor. Anyway, they settled on a burst duodenum ulcer because they thought it best that a cigarette company, like Peter Stuyvesant, wasn't associated with a heart attack. Then they decided that I might be doing some welding on the front of a trailer and that's when I'd have this burst duodenum ulcer and it'd hurt very much and I'd fall down on the ground and roll around in agony and they'd call the Flying Doctor.

Anyway, we landed at Mooleulooloo Station and, first, they set me up in a room where I'm pretending to talk to a mate over the radio. This was all supposed to be taking place during one of the infamous 'Galah Sessions'. We were talking about stock prices or oil prices, or what have you, then I said, 'Look mate, I've gotta get off the air now because I've gotta go and weld this trailer up before we head off into town.' And I get up and out I go, outside. Cut. They were my major lines in the film.

Meantime, while they're doing all this filming, not only is Cove having continuing problems with the Group Captain, but the cameraman's also having trouble with him. Unfortunately the Group Captain somehow just happened to have brought his little camera along and each time they're about to do some filming, he's forever tapping the cameraman on the shoulder, checking the light reading or some such, and telling him where he's going wrong. So the Group Captain fancies himself with the camera as well as being an expert pilot.

So to the next scene and I'm welding this trailer. Well, I've never welded before, but I've got this mask on and I'm making lots of sparks and all of a sudden I'm hit by this burst duodenum ulcer. I fall down and I start rolling around on the ground in agony— gyrating and contortionising—because I'm supposed to be in such a bad way. Cove reckoned that Bert Lancaster couldn't have done it better.

Then it must've been the lady of the house who called the Flying Doctor because the next scene is where they're carting me out to the plane, which is conveniently parked nearby. I'm on a stretcher, Cove's in front and Graham's at the back. The Group Captain's offering advice. Now, I don't know if you've ever seen the old Drover but the aeroplane door's about six feet off the ground. So when they get to lifting me up into the plane, there's a problem in getting the stretcher so high up and then getting it in line with the door. You could liken the situation to a couple of heavy weight-lifters, where they have to lift the weight up to the waist then do a jig and push it right up and over their heads. But Cove and Graham were struggling and I was stuck there on the stretcher, halfway between a clean and jerk and a snatch and lift.

Anyway the director said, 'Hang on, we'll fix this.'

So, with a bit of mastery of filming, they managed to get one end of the stretcher balanced just inside the plane door. Then, while Cove's holding it up, with his arms outstretched, they cut the filming so that I can crawl out of the stretcher and lay down in the plane before they get the action going again. So that fixed that problem.

Then behind Mooleulooloo Station there's this monstrous hill—it's a tiny Ayers Rock—and they decide to go up there to film the Drover while it's taking-off, then as it's landing. The only trouble is that the cameraman's got his flipping leg wrapped in plaster. Anyhow, he declined the offer of the Group Captain to take over the filming and, with a lot of effort, the cameraman stumbles up the top of this hill. When he's settled, the director gives a wave of his arms to start filming and Cove takes off, does a couple of circuits, then he lands again. Cut. That shot's completed.

Anyway, after a quick lunch, we're on the plane and we're flying back to Broken Hill, over the border, into New South Wales. There we were, we're flying sedately at about 3000 feet, with the Group Captain keeping an eagle eye on Cove, just to make sure he's doing everything right when, all of a sudden, the plane rears up in the air and points skyward. It's vertical. And Vic's got the stick back like we're in big trouble. Oh, it was gut retching. Then just as suddenly, the nose drops and down we come again, then we flatten out again.

'Christ, what was that?' the Group Captain shouts.

And Vic says in that slow laconic voice of his, 'Oh, didn't you see it. We just flew over the border fence.'

So Cove got him in the end and the Group Captain shut up after that.

Anyhow, after we arrived back in Broken Hill we went up into Graham's house where they'd set up a little room to double as a single hospital ward, with all these electrical things around the place. So I'm lying in bed with all these ECG things stuck on me, left, right and centre, because I'm still supposed to be in bad shape. Graham's all professional in his white coat and he's got his stethoscope and he's telling me that I'm going to be alright, thanks to the Royal Flying Doctor Service getting out to Mooleulooloo Station, just in the nick of time, and that no permanent damage has been done, and I'm going to be safe. I'll live.

'Good,' I say. 'Thanks very much.'

And really, that was pretty much it. But I tell you, when the film come out, it wasn't actually too bad, even if I do say so myself. It went for about twenty minutes and, as Cove says, 'They ended up playing that film in the RFDS auditorium, three times a day, seven days a week, for about ten straight years.' And when you come to think of it, that's a pretty long run for a film, maybe even longer than *Gone with the Wind*.

Got the Scours

My father, Charlie Shultz, owned Humbert River Station, which was 32 miles west of Victoria River Downs Station, in the central-west of the Northern Territory. Humbert River runs into the Wickham River, which Vic. River Downs was on, and that ran into the Victoria River. My father sold the property in about 1972, and I grew up there and left when I was about twenty-five.

I'd surmise that, around the end of 1945, there was still no Flying Doctor Service in Wyndham because, when I was a baby I was quite ill and my mother had to take me on the mail plane from Vic. River Downs Station and I ended up in the Derby Hospital for a couple of weeks. We didn't have an airstrip at Humbert River and Vic. River Downs had a big landing strip. Back in those days, the mail run came out from Wyndham to the bigger stations like Vic. River Downs, then back to Halls Creek and on to Derby. That's why I ended up over in Derby rather than going to Katherine where they also had a larger hospital.

Humbert River was virtually at a dead end and, during the wet season we had to ride on horseback the 32 miles to Vic. River Downs to get our mail. Usually we'd head off early in the morning with a couple of changes of horses, along with a couple of packhorses, and you'd go over one day and come back the next. I mean, you didn't go over every week, you'd only do that once a month or something. In the dry season we could drive over but even then it took two-and-a-half hours just to get there, which might give you some idea as to just how bad the road was.

Then we only got in food supplies once a year. Those supplies would come up by boat to Wyndham and we'd pick them up in about August or September. My mother was the cook. We had about thirty to forty Aboriginals in all and of those only about ten actually worked for us and the others were their family members;

you know, the older people and young children who also stayed on our property and were kept by my family. That was in the days when a lot of the half-caste children were being taken away from their Aboriginal mothers and my parents took on about four part-Aboriginal children and schooled them on the station so that they weren't taken away. In fact, later on, my parents took on some more.

So, it must've been later in the 1940s before the Flying Doctor Service started coming out. Then we got a radio in about 1952, maybe '53, which was linked into the Royal Flying Doctor Service network out of Wyndham. And, oh, it was just like having a lifeline, you know, for all sorts of things. As you might imagine we were quite isolated and they were something that you were really in touch with.

I remember the RFDS radio contact sessions. The first one was at eight o'clock in the morning, which would've only been 6.30 a.m. in Western Australia. The doctor would be at the hospital, on a direct line and he'd come on air and say they were open for medical appointments. First, he'd ask if there were any emergencies and they'd be dealt with while everyone else waited their turn to have their questions answered.

Now, with the Wyndham RFDS base, the furthest easterly cattle station that they broadcast to was south of Katherine, in the Top End of the Northern Territory, just near Mataranka. Then the furthest south would've been, perhaps, Inverway Station, which is virtually on the Northern Territory–West Australian border plus, of course, there were a lot of places in West Australia.

We actually had a normal 12-volt car-battery operated wireless—it was a Traeger. All the two-way radios in the outback were Traeger. And we all had a different call sign. So you'd give your call sign and say who you were and tell them if the patient was a female or male and what their age was and so forth. Then you told them whatever was wrong or, you know, that somebody had fallen off a horse and what their injuries were.

After listening to all the information the doctor then had to try and judge what to do. If the patient was critical they'd fly out and

RFDS medical chest—RFDS

get them and if they weren't critical, the doctor would prescribe some treatment or medication from the cattle station's medical chest. Really, it must've been pretty hard to work out what medications they should take, especially if the person at the calling end wasn't trained or even educated in any medical sort of way.

All the medications came from the Royal Flying Doctor medical chest. It was quite big, probably about 4 foot wide by about 2 foot 6 high and 2 foot 6 deep. On the inside of the lid there was a plan to let you know what medicines, or what have you, all the trays in the chest contained. Originally the trays were named by their medical terminologies but because people didn't understand the medical names of the drugs they later numbered them, which made it much easier. If you could imagine, it was like ordering a Chinese meal where the numbers related to a specific medication. And when you ran out of anything you just wrote away and asked them to send you the refills.

Now, I don't think the RFDS medical chest was absolutely free. I think, back then, it was heavily subsidised because I do remember we paid a certain amount to be on the radio network and, obviously, we paid for telegrams and such. Then I have a vague memory of the medical chest rental being on the bill at the end of the year.

As far as the medications went, one of the favourite items in the medical chest most certainly would've been the sulphanilamide powder. This must've been before antibiotic or penicillin powders came out and the sulphanilamide powder was sprinkled like a talcum powder on open wounds and things like that. Of course, being in that sort of country, a lot of it was also used on the horses, which I don't think the Royal Flying Doctor Service would've been too happy about. We got it in big packets, like in two-kilogram bags. You know, we didn't waste it, but my father certainly used it on horses. It was very good, actually.

Then there was the Golden Eye ointment, which was also very good. I think it was another sulphur-based ointment, and that was used for all sorts of eye infections. The flies were really bad and the Aboriginal people always had sore eyes. You know, you'd try to teach them to chase the flies out of their eyes but you were still always using the eye ointment. Actually, the Golden Eye ointment seemed to fix most things, so, once again, it was also used on the horses.

But that was just the way it was and, of course, everybody listened in on these sessions so everybody knew everybody else's intimate business. I mean, the men in particular seemed extremely embarrassed if they had to get on the radio and talk about medical problems; you know, especially if they were talking about their wife. But that wasn't unusual because the men out there were far more comfortable describing what was wrong with a cow or a horse than they were with a female. I can remember one funny occasion when the wife of one of the pastoralists was ill. She had a bad case of diarrhoea and her husband came on the radio and said to the doctor, 'The wife's crook.'

And there was a lady doctor up from Perth, filling in for the usual male doctor in Wyndham. Anyhow, it was obvious that the pastoralist felt very awkward talking to a woman about what his wife's problem was because he was humming and haring a lot and not quite getting to the point. But the female doctor kept probing him in an attempt to get a clear and proper understanding of just what he was on about. Anyway, in the end it all got a bit too much for the pastoralist and he blurted out to the female doctor, 'For heaven's sake woman, don't you understand? My wife, she's got the scours.'

Hans from Germany

You must know, it is ten years ago that Germany founded the fan club of the Flying Doctors from the Australian television series. It was translated into the German language and many Germans liked the actors of this series, and so they founded a fan club. I am a member of this fan club, too.

My name is Doctor Hans Henschel. In Australia they know me as 'Hans from Germany'. That is my name in Australia. I am a pacdiatrician in Germany; a doctor for babies and kids and youth to eighteen and I have a big practice. We are three paediatricians in this practice. I am the senior doctor. Two paediatricians must always be in the practice. This is our agreement so that the door of my practice is always open for the sick children. Parents can always find an open door. And, you know, I am a workaholic. I work Sunday, Saturday, seven days a week. I work, work, work, and then I think, I must come to Australia.

But I have always loved Australia. I don't know where that comes from—perhaps from the heart—but when I was much younger I was always very interested in Australia. In my life before I think I was an Australian, perhaps I could even have been an Aboriginal, I don't know. But it's a long time that I'm very interested in Australia.

I come here the first time in the year of 2001 and I see this country. Spectacular! I was infected. We say in Germany, we are infected with this country. I love, very much, the outback, the nature, the animals, the sunrises and sunsets; it's fantastic. To dream in the outback and to feel it, that is very great for me. And when I see the country the first time, I come to Alice Springs and I visit the Flying Doctor base there. This is my first real contact to the Flying Doctor. And then I realise, because of my profession as a doctor, there is much more in Australia than the country, the nature, the animals, the plants and all those things. There's also a very important health service. The Royal Flying Doctor Service, it exists, already, over more than seventy-eight years. John Flynn founded it and it is very important for the people who live and work in the outback, and for the people who are travelling there. And in the outback there are travelling much more Germans and if there becomes health problems the Flying Doctor helps, and it costs no money.

And this is why I founded, in Germany, the association to support the Royal Flying Doctor Service. I am President and I am the founder of this association and I guide this association, because I thought I should do much more to support the RFDS. And I knew many people in Germany who would give much more money if only they could use it as a tax deduction, and the fan club cannot do that. And so I founded this association. It's incorporated, so if they give a donation they can claim it on their tax return. We have a President—that's me—and we have an Assistant President, who is a doctor of law and he has done the statutes, and we have a cashier. You can find all about it at the website. But it is not so important for me to have much members

Doctor Hans Henschel has founded an association in Germany that raises over $50,000 annually for the RFDS—Jacob M van Splunter

because the most money we get in Germany, we get not from the members, we get from the people we speak to and tell them all about the organisation of the RFDS and what it is doing. Then, of course, many pharmacy factories and other factories also donate their money. But it's very important for me to get money to support the Flying Doctors.

So it is two years, nearly three years, since we have become an association. And now, I come to Australia two or three times every year, for four or five weeks each of those times, and I travel all over Australia and I visit as many of the Flying Doctor bases that I can to give them the money. This time we handed over more than $52,000, cash, to the Royal Flying Doctor Service bases, all over.

But, oh, I love Australia. So many, many Germans do. My fascination will be, Australia is a country where I can breathe. I like to be free in the outback, to feel the nature, to see the sky, to see the landscape, to see the sunsets and the sunrises. You cannot do these things in Germany. You can only do that in Australia. And if I will be in a town or a city for some days or weeks, I then must go back to the outback, to see the wideness again.

When I come back from my trips to Australia I see many people standing in the airport who are very sad to leave this nice country. If you go out of the aircraft at Frankfurt, a busy town, people don't look nice and much stress will be there in them. I'm sad to leave too, but it's just a little sad now because I know I will work very, very hard when I get back and then I can tell, 'Now, I must fly back to Australia.' So I am not so sad.

But after coming back from Australia, I will come back to my practice with much more inside power and I am happy once again to be in my practice. And all these emotions I bring with me from Australia, help me, and I can work ever much harder with that power. But after some weeks or some months, I know I must come back to Australia to refresh my motivation. So I'll be back here again after three or four months, and with some more money to give to the Flying Doctors.

Heroes out of Mere Mortals

When I was reading through the first book, *Great Flying Doctor Stories*, I came across one that was titled 'Peak Hour Traffic' and I thought, You know, hang on a tick, I've been writing history books about Tilpa for the past twenty-five years or so and I've never heard this story before.

So I rang the RFDS base at Broken Hill and I was speaking to the lady there and she told me I should go back to the source and see if I could clear up whether the old character named as 'Joe', who featured in the story, well, maybe he was someone else and things have been changed around so as not to incriminate the guilty, so to speak. Because, for the life of me, the name Joe just does not ring a bell, that is, of course, unless his real name's been changed, just in case, and it's actually old Clem who the story's about.

And also I was thinking about how it says in the story that this character Joe lived in the caravan park when there's never really been a caravan park in Tilpa. Oh yes, there's accommodation rooms at the hotel, and Carol and Bernie Williams, who own the Tilpa Trading Post—the store—they now have a couple of cabins and sites for caravans. But they didn't have them back then, when the story took place, and they're certainly not situated next to the pub. They're next to the building where the first Flying Doctor clinics were held. Actually, the funny thing about Tilpa is that, what now is the store was originally the hotel and what's now the pub used to be the store. So they've sort of swapped functions.

But my line of thinking is that, if that story about the old feller in the book was about Clem, well, I can understand that because Clem was a very private sort of a bloke, just like the Joe character. What's more, Clem would also be the sort of bloke that, if two cars drove past his caravan on the one day, yeah, he'd say that the traffic was getting too much for him.

So I reckon that it might be about old Clem and I know a fair bit about him because Clem was a bit of an institution around here. I say was because he's dead now. He was also a Tobruk Rat. Originally he came from, I think it was, out Tibooburra way or Broken Hill, maybe. From recollection, a couple of his sisters used to live in Broken Hill, where they taught piano.

But Clem was a fencing contractor in the Tilpa district for, I'd say, about forty years and, oh, wasn't he a perfectionist, especially when it came to fencing. The words 'It's just about right' weren't in his vocabulary. If the fence wasn't absolutely perfect, he'd go and pull it out again and put it back in at his own expense and in his own time. He was that sort of a bloke was Clem. Then when his working days were behind him he moved into a caravan over on the opposite side of the Darling River, across from the hotel, and it's quite possible that, as the story in the book said, when the Flying Doctor came up here to run their clinics they kept an eye on him.

I'll just tell you a little story about Clem that'll give you some idea as to what a sort of tough and independent character he was. On one occasion, he wasn't too well, he was crook, and he realised that he needed to visit a doctor. So rather than ringing up someone he knew at the hotel or anyone locally and asking them if they could give him a lift he literally walked over to the edge of the road and hitched a ride the 150 miles or so, all the way to Cobar to see a doctor.

And that's where he died. He died in Cobar. And he'd expressed a wish that, if he did die out this way, he wanted to be buried in the Tilpa cemetery. Then, well, one thing led to another and because the Tilpa cemetery was actually situated on private ground and the people who owned the property didn't want him buried there, Clem ended up having to be buried in Cobar, which is something we were all sorry about. So, basically, that was Clem.

Now, as for Flying Doctor stories, I could tell you a few of those because my family have been involved with the medical clinic here in Tilpa since it first came into being, back on 18 September 1969. My mother had been a Matron with the Red Cross in the Second World War so, being a trained nurse, she took on the role of, well, not quite District Nurse but at least Clinic Coordinator, when the RFDS clinic first came into existence in Tilpa.

And that, in itself, is another story; because how my mother got out here to Tilpa was that, well, she married a local of course, and that local was my father. But there's a funny little story about that, too, because my mother and my father first met in my mother's grandmother's house in Wilcannia. That was on the Wednesday before my mother's aunt was to marry Dad's uncle, the following Saturday. At that time Dad, whose name was Roy McInerney, was only sixteen years old—I think he acted as the best man for his uncle—and Mum was only nine years old. And to her dying day, Mum swore that the moment she saw this young, sixteen-year-old, Roy McInerney, she said, 'That's the man I'm going to marry. He's the one for me.'

But Dad was never one to do anything in a hurry because, you see, it was twenty-six or so years later, when he was forty-three, that they got married. So there'd been a whole lot of life going on and a whole lot of water under the bridge, between times. So that's how Mum got to Tilpa and when she got there she took on the Clinic Coordinator's role and she did that right up until I got married in 1973. After Mum finished, one of the other ladies in the district, Pat Luffman, she took on the role for a few years, until she and her husband retired to Cobar. Then, carrying on the family tradition, my wife, Jill, she took on the job as Clinic Coordinator and she's been doing it ever since. And on the few occasions we've been away over the last couple of years our daughter's taken it on. So you could say that it's been in the family for three generations.

But as to some stories about the Tilpa Clinic, I can remember one of the very, very early ones. This was after the days when they had a punt going over the Darling River, at Tilpa, and we used to hold the monthly RFDS Clinics in a couple of rooms in a house that had previously been the old Puntman's Cottage. One room was for the doctor and the other room was for the dentist, and the verandah acted as a waiting room, sort of thing. So everybody would line up on the verandah.

The Puntman's Cottage was owned by the local Postmaster, Fred Davidson. Fred lived and had his post office in a separate building in Tilpa and had, for some reason or other also acquired the old Puntman's Cottage, which then became known as Fred's Flats or The Villa Davo. And it was just lucky that he did because years later the building came in handy when the post office building burnt down and the 'office' was shifted to the 'Flats'.

But in those earlier days, with the dentist, all his drilling equipment was powered off a 12-volt battery and, as well as me being the official driver to get Mum into the clinic, it was also

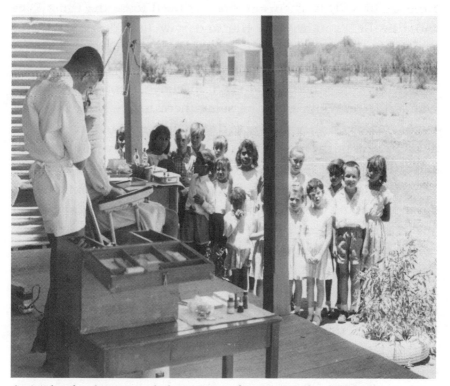

A visit by the dentist made heroes out of mere mortals—RFDS

my responsibility to make sure I brought along a fully charged 12-volt battery. The only trouble with that was, as the clinic wore on, the power in the battery tended to wear down. So if you happened to be the last one in the queue, it was a case of the drill going at a slow woo ... woo ... woo. And it's not very funny to start to get a filling with a very, very slow drill. In actual fact, there's been a couple of cases where they had to send out an SOS for someone to pull a battery out of a vehicle somewhere and use that before the old battery went flat and the drilling equipment stopped completely. So the trick was that, if you had to have any fillings, you tried to make sure you got there nice and early.

I can remember one clinic in particular when Ted Eslake was the dentist. Actually, I think that Ted first started with the Royal Flying Doctor Service in Broken Hill, as a dentist, and later on he became the Director for the south-eastern section of the RFDS. It's a bit like Clyde Thomson, how he used to be the Chief Pilot with the RFDS at Broken Hill and now he's the CEO there. Anyway, I can remember this particular RFDS clinic when Ted was the dentist. And you must remember that this was an afternoon clinic because they'd already been to Louth or Wanaaring or White Cliffs or somewhere before they flew into Tilpa. But when they got there Ted had twenty-one patients to deal with and the last three, would you believe it, were all extractions.

So, by the time Ted gets to them, the sun's slowly going down, down, down and the RFDS pilot's watching the sun get lower and lower and lower and, of course, he's getting very, very toey because we only had an outback dirt airstrip at Tilpa so there was no lighting or flares or anything back then. Anyhow, it's getting very late and the sun's setting and the pilot's getting extremely worried about all this so, in the end, to save time Ted lined these three blokes up—the ones that needed the extractions—and it was like working on a production line. It was a jab ... 'A needle for you.' And jab ... 'A needle for you.' And jab ... 'A needle for you.'

When he'd finished doing that he waited for the shortest possible time then he came back to the first feller and asked, 'Is it numb yet?'

'Yeah, I think so.'

'Good.' And so it was yank and out come the tooth. 'Here's a wad of cotton wool. Chew on it.'

Then he went to the next feller, 'Is it numb yet?'

'Yeah, I think so.' So out come that feller's tooth and, 'Here's a wad of cotton wool. Chew on it.'

Then the same thing to the third one. 'And here's some cotton wool. Chew on it.'

So there's the three fellers, still sitting there like stunned mullets, munching on these huge wads of cotton wool and Ted calls out to the pilot, 'Okay then, let's chuck all this stuff into the car and go out and get on the plane.'

And I've got a sneaking suspicion that they took off only about half a minute after last light. And so that would've been back in about 1970, because by November 1971 we had a new Community Centre in Tilpa, which had a separate room for the doctor. Unfortunately, though, the dentist was not so lucky because he had to work in a corner of the main room.

But that old area we had for the dentist, I tell you what, it made heroes out of mere mortals, because the only thing they had around the dental chair, to screen it off, was a bit of a curtain sort of thing. That's all there was between you and the audience. So everybody knew if you were whimping or not. Oh absolutely, if you screamed, everybody in the district of Tilpa knew all about it.

Naturally, things have changed over the years. We've now got a three-roomed demountable building for the RFDS doctor and whatever nurses arrive. And the dentist, she's now got her own room off the end of the hall. Mind you, she's still using the same old dentist's chair that Ted Eslake used away back then. So it's a pretty well-worn dentist's chair and a lot of us can still recall a life-changing event occurring while we sat in that chair, getting our teeth pulled or drilled or what-have-you. Of course, that's the few of us that remain living in the district and who can still remember back that far.

And what's more, the Flying Doctor people have tried a few times to get that old dentist's chair back and put it in their museum at Broken Hill, and every time they try, we've said, 'Not on yer life. That's part of Tilpa's history, that is.'

How the Hell

I'm afraid I don't talk about it too much because I still get a bit emotional about the whole thing. But it was 1966, about this time actually, February, bad dust storms. Terrible dust storms. You see, there was a big drought throughout central Australia at that time. I don't know how long it actually went on for but I was told that there were seven-year-old kids living out there that had never seen rain. Then when it broke, later in '66, I happened to be in Alice Springs and when the rains came, almost everyone in the whole town went down to the Todd River, just to look at the water going past.

I was only new to the Northern Territory. I was only a young feller out there with my best mate, Ken McEwen. We'd done everything together ever since we were little school kids. Anyhow, I'd never seen a dust storm in my life and I don't think Ken had either, and when we first arrived in the Territory it'd been so dry that there was hardly a scrap of vegetation anywhere and the little that there was looked like it just wanted to blow away. So on a regular basis we'd get these huge dust storms. I remember when I was in Alice—and I filmed it happening—it was as clear as anything, then, in the distance, you could see this mountain of dust and it rolled in like a massive cloud from the west and engulfed everybody and everything.

And when the dust started coming through town it got so dark that the street lights automatically came on and you could see all the street lights and the car lights turn blue. And that's true because, apparently, the silica in the sand turns the lights blue. Then sometimes the wind stops and it's deathly still but the dust is so fine that it just hangs up there in the air, like it's suspended. Oh, it's real eerie, I can tell you.

So anyway, we had quite a few terrible dust storms the particular year it happened. At the time I was working for a Canadian company called ODE [Oil Drilling Exploration]. ODE was doing a lot of contract well-drilling, out in central Australia, for oil and gas. They contracted for companies like X Oil and French Petroleum. I think they were also involved with Shell because Shell was also drilling madly all over the place in search of oil, even over in western Queensland.

How it all worked was that there was another company, Austral Geophysics, and they'd go ahead of us and do some preliminary drilling then get all the relevant information up on maps. Then Austral would go to X Oil or French Petroleum or whoever owned the leases, show them the maps, and the oil companies would decide where they wanted to drill and they'd come to ODE and say, 'Righto. Put down five holes for us over in this particular area.'

Then we'd charge them whatever-it-was per foot and we'd bring the rig in, put it up, drill the hole, have a look, finish the hole, knock it down, pull the drill rig down, put in what we called a 'Christmas tree' and then we'd move off to the next place to drill another hole. A Christmas tree was a structure that sealed off the drill hole for safety because of the gas. Oh, there were all these painted valves on it and illuminated safety signs bolted to the chain wire fence that surrounded it. They stood out like dog's balls in the desert, that's why they were called Christmas trees.

That was forty years ago and I was out there for most of that year, working all around the place. We drilled all around what they called the Mereenie Fields. The tourists now call it the Mereenie Loop Road. I remember one Easter, for a bit of a break, we went out to what was then known as Ayers Rock. And at Ayers Rock, back then, there was only the Caretaker's hut, a bit of a rough Caravan Park and an old motel that was built from fibrolite. And over that particular Easter there was only the four of us and three other tourists. That's all there was. Now, today, I believe there's well over a thousand people who actually live there, and that's just the people who are looking after the place. So there wasn't much there, back in 1966, believe me.

In those days they were drilling madly all over the place—RFDS

Anyhow, when we were drilling we worked seven days a week and as far as the structure of the team went, we had three shifts going and on each shift we'd have two Roughnecks, a Motorman, a Derrickman and a Driller. So in all, I'd say we'd probably have anywhere up to twenty blokes living out on the actual rig site, and you'd work your way up through the game. You'd go from a Roughneck to a Motorman—that's the feller who looks after all the engines you drill with—to a Derrickman, to the Driller and then you'd become Tool Pusher.

The actual accident happened to the bloke who was the Tool Pusher. He was like the boss of the oil rig, the head man while we were out there in the desert. I don't know why they called him a Tool Pusher because he certainly didn't push any tools. We were the ones that done all the big tool work. And this particular Tool Pusher, he was a nice bloke who, I must say, was very good to work for, yet he was also very strict.

Anyhow, as you might gather, living and working out in such remote places there wasn't much to do with any spare time we had. So, yeah, for a bit of play, when we had a bit of time off we'd just grab the old Land Rover and we'd go out shooting donkeys or camels, and sometimes the Tool Pusher would come along as well. The donkeys and camels weren't for eating, just for sport. Oh, they were everywhere. When we'd fly in and fly out you'd see herds of up to four hundred of them, all over the place.

But anyhow, on this particular day I was working a shift and some of the other blokes went out shooting and the Tool Pusher went with them. And while they were out there, driving about, they hit a sand dune and over they went. But when the Land Rover rolled over the Tool Pusher's head got jerked out the window and it got squashed in between the top part of the door and the sand. Really, he was lucky that it was sand or otherwise he'd have been killed instantly. Still, he was very badly injured. He was unconscious. He couldn't move or anything.

Anyway, one of the blokes walked back to camp and grabbed the old Bedford truck—an old pole truck. So they took that out and brought the Tool Pusher back and put him into one of the air conditioned dongas, which is a portable room, a bit like a little transportable. And they got him into a bed and, naturally, he was covered in blood and sand and everything.

In the meanwhile, a dust storm had been hanging around for a bit and it was starting to build.

We had another bloke out there who was second-in-charge of the rig, a Canadian bloke. He was a Driller. From memory, I think he had a bit of first-aid experience. So the Driller, he got one of the blokes to call into the Flying Doctor base at Alice Springs and the doctor there sort of instructed us how to dress the Tool Pusher's injuries and clean him up a bit by using what we had in our first-aid kit.

The Tool Pusher was still unconscious, at this stage. In fact, he really wasn't very good at all and he was getting worse, as was the dust storm. So things weren't looking real flash.

Then, with the Flying Doctor Service, I believe what happens in an emergency situation like that is that the doctor makes all the immediate medical decisions and the pilot has to decide if it's safe enough to fly. They work as a team. We had an airstrip there, of course, so the Driller spoke to them and he said, 'Look, this feller's not real good. We can't move him at all and, to be honest, he's not going to last a three- or four-hundred kilometre drive, over a dirt road, all the way into Alice Springs. He's just not going to make it.'

And while all this's going on, outside the dust storm's getting worse and worse. So the pilot asked what the conditions were like out our way—which, by then, were pretty horrible—and then he had a discussion with the doctor along the lines of, 'Well, do we fly through a dust storm like this and risk all our lives—the lives of the doctor, the pilot and a nurse—for the sake of, perhaps, saving just the one life.'

It was a tough call but, in the end, they decided that it was best to hold out until the next day when they'd check on the condition of both the Tool Pusher and the dust storm before making any final decision. But by the following day the condition of both the Tool Pusher and the dust storm had gotten worse. In fact, the Tool Pusher was fading.

In the meantime there was an Aboriginal settlement about 150 kilometres away from where we were, called Areyonga. It's one of the furtherest settlements on the western side of Alice Springs, right out towards Kings Canyon. And someone from over there, at Areyonga, made an emergency call into the Alice Springs RFDS to say that they had a lady out there who was going through a tough time having a baby and she was in need of urgent help. So the people from the RFDS got together and sort of said, 'Well, we've got an emergency at Areyonga and we've got another one over at the drilling site. But the dust storm's still very bad so, what do we do, do we head off or not?'

Anyway they made their decision to go, and they flew off and, first, they went over to Areyonga to pick up the lady who was having trouble with the baby, then they set off over our way. By this stage the Tool Pusher was slipping away.

It was day time, but because of this big dust storm it was terribly dark. You could hardly see your hand, right in front of your face. Of course, they didn't even have radar or anything like that in their aeroplanes back then so it was obvious that the pilot was going to have great difficulty just trying to find us, let alone attempting to land the thing. Also, our strip had no lighting. All it had was a bloody wind sock and there was no way he'd be able to see the wind sock through all this dust. The only way we could be of any help was to get all our vehicles and put them down on the end of the strip, with their lights on, so that when, and if, the pilot found us he'd be able to use the vehicle lights as some sort of guide when attempting to put the plane down.

We knew he was coming in from the west, from Areyonga, and I think our strip ran north and south. So we did that, we lined up all our vehicles, with their lights on and, like I mentioned about when the dust came through Alice Springs that time, the dust here was so heavy that all the lights on the vehicles turned blue because of the silica.

With the pilot not being able to see anything, the best he could do was to try and keep in two-way radio contact with our people on the ground. And so we were in our vehicles and some of us would flicker the lights on and off and we'd also grabbed a couple of spotlights, that we used for roo shooting, and we shone those up into this blanket of dust, in the vague hope that the pilot might see them and get some direction.

So we waited, with the Tool Pusher hanging on by a thread, as we flickered our vehicle lights and shone the roo spotlights up into the dust. And then we heard him. At first, you could hear this very dull sort of droning and, as the aeroplane got closer, the louder the droning got. And we were just sitting there saying, 'How the hell is he ever going to get down through this dust.'

But then, he appeared. Somehow he come out of the browny-black sky. And I tell you, if ever there was a mob of grown men— and tough ones at that—go to water, that was it. At the first sight of that Flying Doctor's aeroplane breaking through the dust storm the emotion got to us all and we were jumping up and down like little kids and we were cheering. Oh, there were tears—the lot—because, see, we knew straight away that our work mate was going to be saved, you know. Anyhow, down, down, down he come and he landed on that strip and he taxied up to us and there was a frantic rush to put the Tool Pusher in the plane, and away they went.

Now I'm not exactly too sure what happened with the Tool Pusher after that, but he did live, and that's the main thing. I never saw him again but I believe he eventually came good. And I also don't know what happened to the lady who was having a difficult time with the baby. But, I mean, they might well have saved two or even three lives on that one day, and through that terrible dust storm.

So yes, the old Flying Doctor, aye. As I said, it still gets to me. But anyway, perhaps that might give you a real insight into what the RFDS do and how they go about their work. And taking into consideration, of course, that forty years ago they didn't have the sophisticated planes and equipment that they have now. In fact, I think it was one of those old three-engine Drover aeroplanes he was flying that day. So the expertise of those pilots was unbelievable because, how the hell he came through that huge dust storm, I just would not have a clue.

In the Footsteps of Flynn

I suppose I could almost talk under water, but have you heard about 'In the Footsteps of Flynn', with Fred McKay. I think that's a beautiful story because it really depicts, you know, the greatness of Fred McKay and, in particular, the modesty of the man.

To start with, I'll just have to go back a bit in time. Fred McKay told me this yarn himself. Well, it's not really a yarn, it's a true story, and I remember the day that he told it to me, up in Queensland. Fred was born in Mackay, in northern Queensland and when he was a youngster he became very, very ill. I think he was probably around the age of nine or ten. Anyhow, when he told me this story he couldn't remember just what the exact illness was but apparently he was in and out of consciousness so, naturally, his family was desperately worried about him. But Fred clearly remembered, at one particular stage, opening his eyes and seeing his mother sitting on the end of his bed, looking desperately worried. Of course, she was unaware that her young son was observing her. And Fred said that he watched his mother as she looked to the heavens and in simple prayer she said, 'Lord, if you make my little boy well, I'll make him a Minister.'

And, you know, Fred went on to become one of the most celebrated ministers in the land, I suppose. And that's right, it's true, because when Fred told me that story he chuckled and he said, 'Stephen, my destiny was already carved out for me from such a very young age.'

Anyway, throughout Fred's ministerial training, John Flynn recognised the incredible qualities that Fred possessed and every time they'd meet, Flynn would always try and talk Fred into becoming one of his Outback Padres. Actually, it's my own thought now that, even at that early stage, John Flynn was looking down the track for a successor and he had Fred in mind.

Back then, John Flynn's title would've been the Very Reverend John Flynn because he was the Superintendent of the Australian Inland Mission, an organisation that was inextricably linked to the beginnings of the Flying Doctor Service by Flynn's unerring drive to create both a medical and spiritual Mantle of Safety for all remote and outback peoples, regardless of colour or creed.

But still, Fred didn't want anything to do with it. He wasn't going to be talked into anything by anyone. He was quite tunnel-visioned about the matter and he'd already planned that, after he became ordained here, in Australia, he was going to head off to Edinburgh, in Scotland, where he'd continue his theological studies. Still, John Flynn was determined never to give up, so he persisted, and every time they met he'd come up and try and convince Fred that his true calling was right here in Australia as an Outback Padre with the Australian Inland Mission.

Then Fred's first church was a Presbyterian Church at Southport, on the Gold Coast, in south-eastern Queensland. By then he'd met the love of his life, a nurse, named Meg. Because

And John Flynn simply said, 'Just go and listen to them and you'll get your calling from there'—RFDS

Fred was just ordained, I suppose his correct title would've been Reverend Fred McKay. But Fred loved the water and, on this particular day, after he'd finished his sermon he went home and put his togs on and went down for a swim, and it was while he was there that he looked to the far end of the beach and he saw quite an unusual figure coming towards him. I say unusual because it would've been quite a sight for Southport beach to see a tall, thin man wearing a three piece, pin-striped suit, with a hat on, walking along the sand. And as the figure got closer, Fred realised that it was John Flynn.

Naturally, Fred's first thoughts were, 'Here we go again. He's come to try and talk me into becoming an Outback Padre.' And that's exactly what John Flynn was about to do because he'd come back this one more time to try to convince Fred that he should join 'Flynn's Mob', as they were called. So they greeted one another and they sat down on the beach and John Flynn started his convincing.

Then, you know how, when you sit on a beach, you unconsciously play with the sand. You just pick it up in your hand and you let it run through your fingers. Well, there they were, sitting there on the beach and John Flynn realised that they were both running sand through their fingers. So Flynn stopped the conversation and he said to Fred, 'Fred,' he said, 'the sands of Birdsville are much finer than the sands of Southport.'

And that's what changed the life and the destiny of Fred McKay. That's what started his great career. Fred told me later, he said, 'Look, Stephen, I don't know whether it was divine intervention or what but, at that precise moment, I knew exactly where my destiny lay.'

So that's when Fred McKay agreed to join John Flynn's Australian Inland Mission. But then immediately after agreeing to become an Outback Padre, Fred had a sudden pang of anxiety and in his anxious state he said to Flynn, 'Look, what am I going to say to these people in the bush when I go out there?'

And John Flynn simply said, 'Nothing. Just go and listen to them and you'll get your calling from there.'

That satisfied Fred and so they stood and they shook hands on it and then they started walking off the beach. And when they walked off the beach, John Flynn was slightly ahead of Fred and Fred clearly remembered trying to step into the indentations left on the beach by John Flynn's footsteps—and what giant footsteps they were. So right up until just prior to Fred's death, which was a couple of weeks shy of his ninety-third birthday, Fred remained a very prolific public speaker who spoke about the tremendous work of both the Australian Inland Mission and the Flying Doctor Service. And that's the reason why Fred's talks were always titled 'In the Footsteps of Flynn.'

In with the Luggage

Just by the way of background, I'm the Director of Aviation and also the Chief Pilot of the Queensland Section of the RFDS, and I've been here for about seven years. This revolves around an event that happened some years ago. So let me just tell you the story as I'd tell it if we were sitting around having a beer.

It was some years ago, three or four, I can't remember exactly, and, as a Senior Manager, I don't fly all that often though I do try and fly occasionally, just to let the troops know that the 'old man'—that is me—can still do it.

Anyhow, I was flying a Super King Air aeroplane and it was the second job that we had for the night. The first job was a close one. I think it was Goondiwindi, in the south-east of Queensland. Then the second job was to pick up an old chap out at Cunnamulla, which is further out west.

When we left Brisbane it was a typical wet winter's night, very, very cold, and it was also a typically wet winter's night in south-

Super King Air—RFDS

western Queensland, and also very, very cold. Then to compound matters, while flying out there, at all levels there was a strong westerly. From the fuel-burn point of view for the Super King Air aeroplane, in the mid 20,000 feet levels, where I would've liked to have been, the wind was about 120 knots on the nose. Even down in the mid-teens, where I was flying, it was still about 70 or 80 knots on the nose.

So it took an awful long time to get out to Cunnamulla and the fuel flow was high because turbines are more thirsty at low level. Anyhow, we eventually got there—by we, I mean myself and the Flight Nurse—and I remember I had to make an instrument approach because there was rain and a fair bit of cross wind. But we landed safely. By this time it was about two o'clock in the morning and, as you might imagine on a night such as that, I wasn't at all too pleased with the world.

Then we always kept about half a dozen fuel drums in a shed at the airport at Cunnamulla and something about Cunnamulla is that you've always got to brave the brown snakes. The only saving grace to all this is the fact that the Shire out there is very, very supportive of the RFDS and their employees always gave you a bit of a hand to roll some fuel drums out, even if it was two o'clock on a cold, wet and windy winter's morning. So I wasn't bitten by a brown snake. I survived that and, after quite a deal of time, the ambulance came back with our Fight Nurse and, from memory, there was also a Nursing Sister—or perhaps it was a young doctor—from the Cunnamulla Hospital. They had with them this old chap who'd had what you and I would euphemistically call a cardiac event.

Now, quite often in the more remote parts of Queensland, particularly within that older generational group, you encounter people who have never been in an aeroplane before. It happens a lot, especially out in those places, and this old bloke was no exception because it was patently obvious that he'd never flown before. So the old chap's there, looking a bit anxious about the whole thing and he's on the stretcher and he's all hooked up with these things that are beeping and carrying on. At that stage my

Flight Nurse and the Nursing Sister, or whoever it was, from the Cunnamulla Hospital, were about 20 or 30 feet away doing the hand-over process.

I was preparing to load the old chap and I had the left-hand wing locker of the King Air open. Now the wing locker is the luggage compartment or an equipment compartment at the back of the left-hand engine. It's exactly like the boot in a motor car and it's where we keep our loading equipment and all sorts of things, like spare stretchers and that. Well, I had this wing locker, or luggage compartment, propped open with a stay, similar to the stay you use on the bonnet of your car.

So this old chap, he wasn't in real good shape so he was pretty short of breath. But as I was preparing to load him, he beckoned with his gnarled finger for me to lean down to where I could listen to him. It was fairly windy, and he was obviously quite concerned about something so I put my ear as close as I could to his face and he sort of pointed towards the luggage compartment and he whispered to me, 'You're not gonna put me in there are yer?'

And I was quick enough, even at two o'clock in the morning to see the humour in this. In fact, it was the only thing that had made me smile all night. So I called out to our Flight Nurse, 'Nurse, if Mister so-and-so is well behaved and he promises not to put his arms or his legs out the windows, do you reckon we could let him travel inside the aeroplane with us?'

Now, for a start, you can't put your arms or your legs out of the window of a pressurised aeroplane. But she was a smart girl, the Flight Nurse, and she also still had her wits about her, even at two o'clock in the morning, so she replied, 'Well, just as long as he behaves himself, I suppose we can make an exception, just this once, and put him inside with us.'

And this fellow, oh, he was so very, very grateful, even privileged, that we'd allowed him to fly inside the aircraft with us. And we didn't tell him any different so then we loaded him into the King Air and I closed the wing locker and off we went. Then other than that wonderful slice of humour, I suppose the only other good thing about that long, cold and wet winter's night was that by going very high and taking advantage of the 120 knots of tail wind we got the old chap into Brisbane in pretty much record time, where he'd get better care for his cardiac event.

So that was the silver lining to the otherwise dismal cloud. It's an interesting story, and a true story. I can't remember the names, and I suppose I could reconstruct the date if I went back through my log books. But it was just one of those events in life that I always have a wry smile about.

It's Alright Now

It was about ten years ago this August, I suppose. We were living south of Broken Hill, on a property only about 15 kilometres out of Menindee. Do you know where the Menindee Lakes are? Well, we were there. I was actually out in the paddock cutting wood with a chainsaw and my wife, Margaret, she said something to me so I put the chainsaw down and I came inside and left it for a while.

Now, I didn't have much fuel left in the can, hardly any at all. There was only fumes in it really, but I didn't put the lid on it properly and I had leather-soled boots. Then after we loaded some wood, I went to pick the can up and the static electricity went from my fingers to the top of the can. And you know, as static electricity does, it just went zap and it blew the fumes up.

Then of course, when it exploded, flames blew up the length of my cotton shirt. The only trouble was, I'd been wearing the shirt beforehand, when I'd done some cleaning with kerosene, and I think there must've been some kero still on it because, next, the shirt caught alight. Then it went from bad to worse because it was a fairly new shirt and it was one of those that only do up to half-way down the front. You know what I mean; it didn't have buttons right the way down. So then, when the shirt got on fire, there were flames everywhere and we—the wife, Margaret, and I—we just couldn't get it off, over my head, and my wife had leather gloves on and all.

I even tried rolling around on the ground but that didn't work either because the flames, they just seemed to be following me around. We got the shirt off in the finish but, you know, I'd been burnt pretty well by then. My chest was all burnt and my hands were burnt, and my face and under my face and my ears and my head, that sort of thing, down as far as my waist. Luckily I wasn't burnt any lower than the waist.

Getting ready to chainsaw—The Hansford Collection

Then once we got the shirt off, Margaret called on the UHF and somebody came on and she got them to ring the Flying Doctor Service. So then she got me back home and the ambulance came out and they took me to the Menindee Hospital. Then the Flying Doctors came out from Broken Hill and landed at Menindee and they took me down to Adelaide, and I ended up in the Royal Adelaide Hospital. And that's about the last I remembered about it for about fourteen days or something like that.

But I don't know what degree of burns they were. All I know is that some of the burns on my chest were pretty deep because, when I was in hospital, they kept on prodding around at me and I said, 'Well, that can't be burnt too bad because I can't feel it.'

'That's the problem,' the doctor said. 'It's burnt so deep that all the nerves are burnt, too.'

So they must've been pretty bad and then I got the infections and that didn't help much, either. I suppose I was there, in the Royal Adelaide, for about a couple of months before I come out again. So the burns were bad enough but then that infection wasn't too good either because the pain from the infections was worse than the burns.

But since then I've had about another fourteen operations; you know, patching parts up and more skin grafts and things like that. But no, it's alright now. I'm alive, that's one thing about it. The worst part is the hands, you know, because I've got to wear gloves all the time.

So that was one episode when the Flying Doctors took me down to Adelaide. The other one was with the motorbike accident and the lip. That was in October, not the same year though, more recent, it was. But this time I was out mustering sheep and I hit a stump in the grass and, when I did, the stump kind of catapult me into a tree. And although I always wear a helmet, I didn't have a full-face helmet on so when I hit the tree, my face come down and hit the handlebars and it just ripped the skin from, oh, from the right-hand corner of my mouth and it just took the skin back, top to bottom, right down under my chin and right back to the teeth and gums.

Anyway, I knew I was in a bit of a mess so I picked myself up and got back on the bike. But then I had the thought, Well, I've been out here nearly all day mustering these sheep so it'd be a waste of a lot of time and effort if I just let them go again.

So I went and put the sheep in the yard first. Then after I'd done that, I rode the 15 kilometres back home again. And when I come in the back door, before she even seen me I said to Margaret, the wife, 'Don't panic.' I said, 'I just took a bit of skin off.'

And Margaret turned around and just took one look at me and she was nearly sick. Oh, there was blood everywhere and there were flies all stuck to it and everything by then. So Margaret rang the RFDS and we drove to Broken Hill and the Flying Doctors flew me to Adelaide, and when I got into the Royal Adelaide Hospital they stitched all that up. I think I had about a hundred and forty something stitches in my face, and in the gum. I didn't lose any teeth or anything but they had to sew the bottom of the gum, on the inside of the lip, first. Actually, I think they did more inside sewing than anywhere else, really, and then they finally sewed up the outside. Anyway, when the surgeon come back in and seen me the next morning, he said, 'You certainly made a bloody mess of it, didn't you?'

But, you know, it didn't feel too good there for a while but it's alright now. It's a bit numb, but it's not too bad. It's going along alright. But that was only a little episode, that one.

Just Day-to-Day Stuff

Well, I don't know if I've got any sort of real 'feel good' Flying Doctor stories because most of it was just day-to-day stuff, really. Stuff that goes on all the time. I was a pilot with the service for about 27 or 30 years in South Australia. I was at Port Augusta for about fifteen years after the RFDS took over the air-ambulance side of things up there, then I came down to Adelaide and flew out of there.

Back then, Port Augusta was considered as a place where the, so called, traditional Royal Flying Doctor Service work happened; you know, stuff like going out on clinic runs and that. It was a fair time ago now, so, when I started, it was pretty basic, well, very basic, actually. The hot ship of the day was a Beechcraft Baron. Then they went on to the Chieftains and the Navajos, which served us well for many years. They were beautiful planes but they weren't pressurised. So then it was time to move on to pressurised planes, which improved the comfort levels for the crew and, of course, the patients who would arrive in a much better state. It's just progress so you simply go along with it. Nowadays, I don't think people wouldn't even get in a Beechcraft Baron.

With the flying side of things, I'd say that, mostly, it was more difficult back then than what it is now. Nowadays the aeroplanes have heaps better instrumentation and navigation equipment. So while we were still doing the same things, now you don't have to work at it too much. I mean, we didn't even have radars or altimeters and GPS [Global Positioning System] wasn't even thought of. So, basically, it was watch and compass stuff; just time and distance, really.

It's like a seeing eye dog, now. You just look at the GPS and you know exactly where you are. Yeah, we had a few nav [navigation]

There was little instrumentation in the early days, basically just watch and compass stuff—RFDS

aids around the place, to get some sort of cross-reference, but out in the backblocks there's nothing much there so you really had to work at it, especially during the night. So to find some of those more remote places we relied on a decent amount of good luck, a bit of good management and a hell of a lot of local knowledge. You know, sometimes you'd be flying out in the middle of a dark night and if you saw a light you'd say, 'Oh well, that must be it.'

From Port Augusta we'd regularly do clinic runs up to Oodnadatta and Marree. We used to do Tarcoola and Cook and all the other settlements out along the Transcontinental Railway Line, right out to the Western Australian border. Nowadays just about all of those little settlements are closed down. Then I think they still go out to Maralinga and Hope Valley Aboriginal Settlement and Yalata Community, of course. Coober Pedy was always there. Mintabie, they still go there, and the other opal fields like Andamooka.

But we also used to do a lot more station people back then too, as far as clinics went. We'd go to all the station homesteads up the Birdsville Track and those places. We'd even overnight at Birdsville, sometimes. They just had RAD phones—radio telephones—in those days. The RAD phones were the only real means of communication, actually. That's what they had the Medical Sessions and the famous 'Galah Sessions' on. All that came through Port Augusta. They had the main transceiver there, at Port Augusta, for all of South Australia. But now they've got telephones or satellite phones or whatever.

So that was the basic day-to-day stuff and then, of course, you'd occasionally get called out on emergency retrievals. They could happen any time of the day or night though, for some odd reason, most of the worst ones seemed to happen at night. The retrievals were always the urgent missions, like road accidents, and so we'd have the entire crew plus all the retrieval gear onboard.

But they were pretty full on and, as I said, a lot of it was road accidents. You'd see some tragic circumstances, say, where you'd have the father down the back of the aircraft on the stretcher and you're trying to fit the mum and the kids in as well and you'd try and screen them from what they might see as far as the father's condition went. We never used to like to do it but sometimes we'd have to put some of the family members up the front, in the cockpit. But we only did that when it was really necessary, like when one of the family members down the back had died and so you were trying to keep the others well away from view.

Over my time we had a couple of major accidents. I don't remember what year it was, but there was a big bus smash up north, between Coober Pedy and Mount Willoughby. That was a major smash where we actually landed on Mount Willoughby Station airstrip, which was right next door to the accident site. I don't know how many fatalities there were but it was like a war zone. The doctor at the time was a New Zealander and he just sort of lined everyone up and, basically, we crammed as many of the injured as we could into the aeroplane and flew them back to Coober Pedy. Then we spent the next few days ferrying people from Coober Pedy back to Port Augusta Hospital or down to the Royal Adelaide Hospital, depending on their severity.

Then in later years there was another big bus accident up near William Creek; same type of thing, you know, it was a roll over. School kids, I think they were, on an excursion from New South Wales, somewhere. The bus ended up upside down. The only people that were there before us were the ambulance officers from Coober Pedy. They'd driven straight out as soon as they got the news and they reckoned there were kids just thrown all over the ground.

I was in Adelaide at the time. We had King Airs then and it was one of the worst nights as far as the weather went. We were flying the retrieval teams up to Coober Pedy and there were thunderstorms all over the place. It was horrific. Just getting to Coober Pedy was terrible. I was up flying around the 29,000 feet mark, trying to dodge the thunderstorms all the way. For that one we also had planes coming in from Broken Hill to help out as well and they were experiencing the same weather problems.

Then, once we got to Coober Pedy—we used Coober Pedy as our base—once we landed there, we went up by road to the accident site to help pull out the most severely injured. Then it was just a mad scramble to get them back into Coober Pedy Hospital. And again, we spent the next few days ferrying kids from Coober Pedy back to Port Augusta Hospital or down to the Royal Adelaide Hospital, depending on how bad they were.

So yeah, that was a bit of a long night, too. But as I said, most of the time it was pretty much just day-to-day stuff.

Love is in the Air

This happened in 1965 or '66. My maiden name back then was Astbury. I was nineteen at the time and I was at Rottnest Island, holidaying with my friend, Jan, and I fell off a push bike. How the actual accident occurred was that we were out bike riding and, do you know Rottnest Island? Well, there's one hill on it and we were up the top of the hill and I said to Jan, 'Let's just freewheel down to the bottom.'

Famous last words because I came off my bike, didn't I, and oh, I was in a terrible mess. Amongst other things I smashed down on my face and cut right across my lip. Then I put my head down into my lap and when they got me to the Nursing Post on the island I was bleeding like mad and the Nursing Sister thought that, maybe, I was haemorrhaging and there were all sort of things the matter with me. But actually, it was mainly just my face and my shoulder and my knees. But it was scary. And being nineteen, that's the stage of your life when you think you're just so gorgeous.

This all happened towards the evening. So the Nursing Sister decided to call the Flying Doctor. Then there was a bit more drama because, with it becoming dark, they didn't have electric lights on the runway so they had to light flares along the side. From memory they were just like lighted sticks in 44 gallon drums or something like that, placed along the runway. I'm afraid my memory of all that isn't too clear because I was in shock and I was bleeding from my face and I was all mushed up. I just remembered these flares. Anyway, the Flying Doctor arrived in the dark and, when I eventually got on board, I said to the pilot, 'Look, do you mind if I take a friend.'

'Okay,' he said.

Well, Jan was my age. She was blonde, vivacious and quite gorgeous looking. So I'm lying in the back of the plane—there I am 'dying'—and in the front of the plane all I can hear is this chat, chat, chat, chat. Like, I didn't know just who Jan was talking with but it was certainly a male. I can't actually remember anyone else being up there other than a pilot and Jan. I can't even remember if there was anyone else in the back of the plane with me. All I could remember was that Jan was chatting to this chap all the way to Perth.

So it would've only taken about ten or fifteen minutes to fly from Rottnest Island to Perth. It's not very far. You can actually see Rottnest from Fremantle. So I arrived in Perth and they took me to Royal Perth Hospital in an ambulance and I was there for a week to ten days having operations on my face and all that. Oh, I had skin grafts and all sorts of things. I really mushed up my face, badly. I remember my aunty coming in to visit me and she took one look and she burst into tears. 'Oh Laurel,' she said, 'why couldn't you have broken your legs or something, instead of smashing up your face?'

But anyway, I healed and they sent me home to recuperate at my parents farm at Harrismith, which is south-east of Perth,

Rottnest from the air—Rottnest Island Authority

near Wickepin, in the wheat-belt. So there I was, recuperating at my parents' farm and, the next thing, well, Mum got this telephone call from a male person who said he was from the Royal Flying Doctor Service and he was ringing just to enquire how I was getting on. Mum said that he sounded very caring. You know, 'How's your daughter? She was in a bad way and we got her across to Perth and we got her to hospital ...' Bla, bla, bla.

Oh, I thought, that's pretty amazing. He's being so very nice, you know, ringing to see how I was after my accident.

So Mum explained to him that I had to have skin grafts and I had to have stitches here, there and everywhere.

'Oh, that's good,' he said. 'I'm glad she's recovering. And by the way,' he said, 'the lass that accompanied her over, she was very nice, too.'

Then he asked Mum if he could possibly have the name, address and/or phone number of 'the beautiful-looking girl who accompanied me over from the Rottnest Island'. So there was an another reason for him ringing. There was a bit of hocky-docky romance going on in the plane that he probably wanted to follow up on.

But Mum being the old fashioned lady she was said, 'Oh no, I don't think I could give you that. It just wouldn't be right.'

And as far as I know, nothing else happened. So that was 40 years ago. I've still got scars, but I healed fine. You know, it was just one of life's little accidents.

Matchmakers

HG Nelson: HG Nelson with you on 'Summer All Over'. We have Jacqui from Yandina on the line. Jacqui, how are you this morning? Now, you've got some connection with the Flying Doctor Service.

Yes, well, back years and years ago I used to live with my, then, husband, John, and my two baby boys, in the south-west of Queensland at a place called Yaraka, which is unheard of. Yaraka's at the end of the railway line that goes out from Rockhampton then down past Blackall. And once a month the Flying Doctor people used to fly out from Charleville to run medical clinics in each little area around the place and, when they came down our way, sometimes they'd stay overnight with us.

So I think this was probably in the late 60s, when I was in my mid-twenties, and we were all reading the Peanuts comic books. Do you remember those? Well, we kind of thought that the Snoopy character from the Peanuts comics would look good on the nose-cone of the Flying Doctor aeroplane. You know the drawing where Snoopy's doing his 'Red Baron' act and he's sitting in a plane with his flying goggles on and a scarf blowing out behind him.

Anyhow, we teed it up with the RFDS pilot and doctor that the next time they were going to come out to Yaraka on a clinic run we'd have the paint and brushes all ready. Of course, we didn't know if it'd be approved by Tim O'Leary, who was the Head of the Flying Doctor network back then, but we decided to do it anyway. And if Tim asked any questions when they got back to Charleville, then the pilot and the doctor would tell him that they didn't have a clue how the painting got there, nor who did it.

So on the day, as soon as we heard the plane buzzing overhead we whooped out to the airstrip and, while my two little boys were looking on, we painted Snoopy on the nose-cone. The actual plane was named the 'Allan Vickers'—Allan being one of the original doctors who worked with John Flynn. After he retired, I think he actually died while he was coming back from England on a boat and they buried him at the Cape of Good Hope.

Anyhow, so we did this paint job on the nose-cone of the aeroplane and when Tim O'Leary saw it he thought it looked great and so it stayed on, and everybody loved it. After that, each time the 'Allan Vickers' was serviced, the engineers painted an extra whisker on Snoopy. So I reckon he might've got a bit hairy before that particular RFDS plane was replaced. Then, when they finally did replace it with a new plane, they even got a sign writer to paint a new Snoopy on the nose-cone of that one as well. And they've had new planes since and I gather that Snoopy's still on

While my two little boys were looking on, we painted Snoopy on the nose cone of the RFDS plane—Jacqui Plowman

there. He's become, more or less, the mascot for the Charleville Flying Doctor Service.

> HG: So if you see a Flying Doctor plane with the Snoopy character from Peanuts drawn on the nose-cone, now you know the story of how it got there.

Then, of course, the Flying Doctor Service had an awful lot to do with my ex-husband and I getting engaged. Both Tim O'Leary and Allan Vickers were incorrigible romantics who seemed to want everybody in the same miserable state of marriage because both of them were always trying to match-make people.

> HG: Well, that's an aspect of the Flying Doctor Service I didn't know about. So it's not only a medical service?

No, they did all sorts of things. They'd find you a partner whether you wanted one or not. I remember with, John, my husband-to-be, though I didn't know it at the time ...

> HG: Tell me more.

Well, this was long before the Snoopy episode because I was working out at Dalby, which is west of Brisbane, and John had a property with his brother out at Yaraka. We'd met a couple of times, that's all, and we used to write to each other occasionally, but just as friends. I mean, it was a bit far to pop down to Yaraka from Dalby just for a dinner. Anyhow, one time, John wanted to survey a boundary track because he was thinking of taking a tank-sinking plant out to the edge of his property. Mind you, these were pretty big properties. So he set off and, as you do in the country, you always have a gun in the vehicle with you.

Anyway, John was on his way out when he met up with Jimmy Davies, a 100 miles from nowhere. Jimmy was an old 'dogger', meaning that he made a living out of the bounty money he earned from shooting wild dogs, dingos in particular. So they started having a chat, out in the middle of this nowhere, and Jimmy asked John, 'What're doing out here?'

So John explained how he was thinking of taking a tank-sinking plant out and he just wanted to survey the area.

'I may as well come along with yer, then,' said Jimmy.

So they both jumped into John's vehicle and while they were driving out they saw a dingo and John grabbed his rifle and took a pot shot at it. The only trouble was that he had some faulty ammo in his rifle and the gun blew up in his face, damaging his right eye. So then Jimmy had to drive John home and when they got there they called the RFDS. Anyhow, both Tim O'Leary and Allan Vickers came out in the plane and by the time they finished patching John up and got him settled, it was too dark to take off, so they decided to stay the night then fly John to hospital the next morning.

As I said, John and I had only met a couple of times before and while we did write the occasional letter, there was really nothing in it. Now the accident must've occurred on a Melbourne Cup day or close thereafter because I'd won some money in a sweep so, feeling a little flushed with money, I decided to ring John on impulse, that particular night. Then when I rang up to have this chat with John, the phone was answered by someone who had an Irish accent. It was Tim O'Leary and so he told me about the shooting accident and he mentioned that they were going to take John to Brisbane the next day. So a couple of days later I rang around and found the hospital where John was and I went down to visit him.

Then, when Allan Vickers found out that I'd been to visit John, he suggested to the doctor—the eye specialist—that the best thing for John to do, in his current situation, was to spend a weekend in the country to recuperate; perhaps even a short trip to some place like Dalby, even. It was all a set-up, of course, so John then caught a bus out to Dalby and he arrived on my doorstep. I didn't know he was coming or anything. In actual fact, I was doing the ironing and I heard this knock ... knock on the door and when I opened it, there was John.

'I'm here,' he said.

And ten days later we were engaged.

HG: Well, that's an insight into the Flying Doctor Service that I didn't know about. Not only can they analyse mystery photographs, as John in Ingleburn is about to inform us, or solve crossword clues as I suggested they might, but they also match-make as well as fix a myriad of ailments such as broken arms and bung eyes ... and all at the same time.

Mystery Photograph

HG Nelson: And now we have John from Ingleburn on the air. So what's your Flying Doctor story, John?

Thanks HG, I've got one that I thought was a bit interesting. I've flown over Australia quite a number of times and, I mean, it's brilliant, absolutely brilliant. I've taken shots of Lake McKenzie. I've taken shots from across the centre. Actually, one time I was coming back home and I spotted the Birdsville Track. I knew what it was straight away because I'd been out through there quite a few times, you know, and it's just fascinating to see the beauty of this land. You know, the colour, it's just brilliant.

But back in '98 I was flying over to Europe with Singapore Airlines and we were about 10,000 metres high. Anyway, I'd had a couple of scotches and, as we were passing over Alice Springs in the Northern Territory, I thought I'd take a photograph out of the plane window. Anyway, we weren't on the right angle for me to get a shot of the Alice and, naturally, I couldn't get the bloke— the pilot—to turn around so I took a shot out of the left-hand side of the plane.

Anyway, I didn't think much of it and when I got back home a few months later, I got the film developed and there was something there, on the ground, and I just couldn't work out what it was. It sort of resembled an airstrip, but I knew that there wasn't one there—well, there wasn't supposed to be one there. Anyhow, I was stumped so I had a bit of a think about it and my reckoning was that the Royal Flying Doctor Service were always in the air around the Territory and, if anyone knew what this thing was, they would. So just on the off-chance, I sent the photo to the Flying Doctor base in Alice Springs and in the letter I asked them if they could help me identify it. And anyway, an RFDS

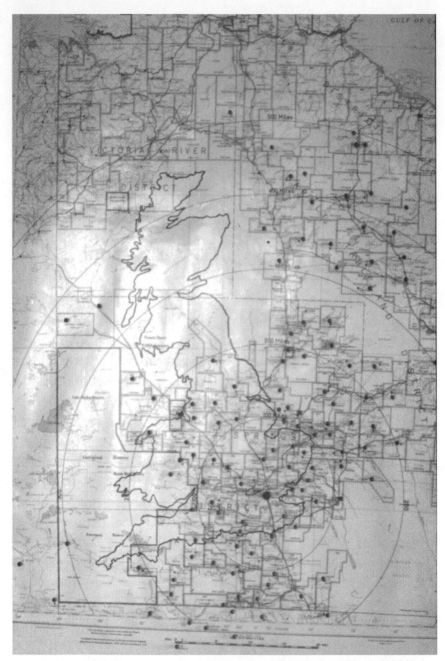

'I mean, the RFDS is in the air all the time up that way, so I reckoned that if anyone knew what this thing was, they might.' Note the outline of Great Britain embedded into the map, which gives some idea of the vast area the RFDS cover from its Alice Springs base—Neil McDougall pilot, I think it was, he wrote back and said, 'Yeah, as soon as I seen it, I knew what it was.' And it turned out to be the Jindalee BEA 'over the horizon radar transmitter', which is just north of Alice Springs.

HG: Isn't that interesting? So you're telling me that the Flying Doctor Service, in its spare time, answers questions from people flying across Australia. Absolutely fantastic.

So, yes, they're a great service, and that was an aspect of their work that I was completely unaware of. Well, I didn't know, I just thought, well, who else could help me identify this shot—this photograph—and then straight away I thought of the Flying Doctor Service. I mean, they're in the air all the time up that way, so I reckoned that if anyone knew, they might.

HG: Well, that's a terrific call there from John in Ingleburn and, obviously, about how the Flying Doctor Service solved the mystery of his photograph.

You know, they're better than the *Encyclopaedia Britannica.* Say if you got stumped on a crossword puzzle question. For example the clue is, 'Monkey'—three letters. You've already got the P and you can't work it out or you just completely can't think of anything, well, just ring the Flying Doctor Service and they'll solve all your crossword puzzle problems as well. Oh, they can do anything. I mean, I'd love to think that if people had barbecuing problems, you know, like how to clean barbecues, all they had to do was to contact the Flying Doctor Service. And they're also very good if you need to know how to get stains off carpet or off sheets, for that matter, or, let's face it, if you have any sheep crutching problems, well, all you have to do is get in touch with the Royal Flying Doctor Service and they'd be able to help you.

Next to Buckley's

This happened many years ago, when I was working up bush, at the Moomba gas and oil fields. Moomba's in the far north-east of South Australia so it's usually a desolate, dry country, as you might be able to imagine. But at this particular time there'd been a lot of rain and it'd caused flooding all through the north-east, and there was this guy who'd always dreamed of doing a walking trek from Innamincka, north-west through the Sturt Stony Desert and up to Birdsville, which is just over the border into Queensland. He was a very experienced bushman and he'd done all his research and all that sort of stuff, so he was well prepared. Then he decided to take a younger mate along with him, an English fellow, who was a very inexperienced bushman. So they decided to do this walk.

Now, it was the middle of winter and by then the weather was okay: bitterly cold at night, mind you, but the days were okay, and not too hot. As I said the experienced bushman had done his homework, right. They had a radio with them, plus all the maps and they had backpacks and a cart to carry their supplies. They'd even organised rendezvous points along the way, where they'd meet people and pick up fresh supplies.

So they set off from Innamincka and they'd been walking for a couple of days. But what happens up in those regions is that, when you get big rains, a lot of water comes down all the little creeks and what-have-you, and they overflow and then you get these huge floodplain areas—like surface water spreading out everywhere. Now all this surface water doesn't appear on a map because it's rarely there. So they were walking along and they came to this big lake, over a floodplain, which wasn't on the map. They then had to make a decision: what do we do? Do we take a couple of extra days to go around it or do we try and wade across?

As a trial, they walked out a couple of hundred yards and it was only, you know, a foot deep or something like that. 'Well, it can't be too deep,' they said, and they decided to walk across this lake.

But there must've been a washaway or a creek that they didn't know about or wasn't on the map, right? So they were wading along, carrying all their gear—the experienced fellow was strapped to the supply-cart—and suddenly they went from water that was about a foot deep to water that was right over their heads. They both went under and because they had lots of gear strapped onto them, they sunk like rocks.

Now, somehow the inexperienced Englishman managed to struggle to the surface. Then, when he got to safety he realised that his mate, the experienced bushman, wasn't there. So he went looking for him and some time later he found him, but unfortunately he'd drowned.

Anyhow, the Englishman's first thought was, I'd better get this guy back to the shore.

So he unstrapped all of the dead fellow's gear, and he left his own gear there and he started dragging his dead mate all the way back through this stretch of water. Eventually, he got the body to dry ground but then, when he went back to retrieve his gear, it was gone. Everything. He couldn't find it. So there he was, trapped out in the middle of nowhere, with nothing but the clothes he's wearing, which were, basically, just a pair of shorts and a tee shirt. That's all. He'd even taken his shoes off to swim. So now he's thinking, Well, what do I do now? How do I get myself out of this mess? I've never been in the outback before. I don't know how to navigate. I don't even know where I am. I don't have any maps. Nothing. I'm going to die.

Then he remembered that two days previously they'd crossed something that resembled a road, so he thought, If I can get back to the road I might be able to find someone or track someone down.

Obviously, he couldn't take his dead mate with him so he had to leave the body there and he starts backtracking. There's plenty of water because there's lots of waterholes, you know, but he hasn't got any food. Not a crumb. Nothing. So for two days he walks back the way they'd come and eventually he stumbles across this road, right. But, unbeknown to the Englishman, the road wasn't a real road it was what's known as a shot line, okay? Now, what a shot line is; with oil and gas mining they sort of bulldoze these tracks like grid lines so that when they fly over them, they can use them for survey lines, you see? Vehicles don't drive up and down them, they're basically put in and abandoned, right? But this guy thought it was a road. But it's not—it's a shot line.

So he thinks, Good, I've got to this road but now, what do I do? Do I sit here and wait for a car to come along or do I keep moving?

Well, he sat and waited for a while and there was no sight of a car so he decides it'd be better to keep moving. But then he was faced with another problem: Do I turn right and walk and see what I can find or do I turn left and walk and see what I find?

Now, what you've got to realise, this's out in the Sturt Stony Desert and the nearest town is Innamincka, and that's like 100 kilometres away. What's more, the guy's got no idea where he is; not even a clue. But he decides, for whatever reason, he doesn't really know: I'll turn left and walk down the road a bit and see how I go.

So he turns left and starts walking down this shot line, which really isn't a road. Then about 100 yards further on he walks over a rise and sitting there, in the middle of all this nowhere, is a wrecked telephone booth.

Now, what had happened was, about 15 years before the Englishman arrived on the spot, there'd been a little camp there that they'd used when they were grading the shot lines, and maybe drilling a couple of holes or something like that. So years ago there'd been a small camp there, you know, with five or ten guys, living in caravans for about four or five weeks before they moved on. And back then, what sometimes happened was that, with these little camps, they never used radios for communication. They only had one of those old wind-up telephones, right, and they'd just plonk it in the middle of a camp, stick a bit of a telephone box

He'd always dreamed of doing a walking trek from Innamincka, north-west through the Sturt Stony Desert and up to Birdsville—RFDS

around it and they'd run maybe 20 or 30 miles of telephone cable, above ground and, when they happened to come across another telephone cable, they'd just cut into that, alright. Then, when they abandoned the camp, they'd pick up the telephone box, wind the cable up and move on to the next site and set it all up again. But for some inexplicable reason, on this one and only occasion, they'd up and left and they'd abandoned this telephone and the wires.

So, you know, this guy sees this telephone box like it's an apparition. But it's been exposed to the elements for donkey's ages; the doors are hanging off, there's no windows, the old Bakelite receiver's all cracked, wires are hanging off it and, you know, there's a dirt floor. So the Englishman thinks, well, in for a penny, in for a pound. And he jumps into this telephone box, picks up the receiver, he winds the handle and, all of a sudden, out of the deadness comes this voice. 'Hello Santos, Moomba Coms can I help you?'

Now, for some strange reason this telephone box was not only still there but it'd never been disconnected, as well. And this guy just couldn't believe his luck, right? He's out in the middle of nowhere and finds a telephone box and an old wind-up receiver and he gets straight through to Santos Communications at Moomba. So the Englishman told his tale of woe to the communications guy. Then the Coms guy said, 'Look, okay, but do you have any idea where you are because we can't track you on this telephone line. We didn't even know it existed.'

'I've got no idea,' the Englishman said. But he tried giving him a basic outline, you know, like, 'We were walking between Innamincka and Birdsville and then two days later this accident happened and I backtracked for a couple of days and I came across this road and I turned left and I think I headed south, but I'm not quite sure.'

So the guy at Moomba said, 'Alright, well, tell you what, stay on the line, I've got a couple of old blokes who were out on the surveying camps years ago. They might remember the area so perhaps they can give us a rough idea of, maybe, where you might be.'

In actual fact the Coms guy didn't hold out much hope. But anyway, he rings up a couple of old blokes and they come in and get the story. They don't hold out too much hope either but they get out their old surveying maps—the ones they'd had stored away at the back of their wardrobes for the past 20 years or so—and they blow the dust off them and lay them out on the table. So there's these two old crusty miners, you know, looking at these maps and going like, 'Gawd, it could be this camp.' 'No it couldn't be that one but I remember this camp. That could be the one.' And between them they, sort of, figured out, 'Well, he might be somewhere in this region here but, you know, then he could be somewhere else. But if we were going to have a stab in the dark, here's as good a place as any to start looking.'

And that's when they got the Flying Doctor Service involved. As I said, I was working up there at the time. So they called me over and they said, 'Well, look, we've got a guy. He's out bush somewhere and he's found an old telephone and he's on the line and we're going to try and find him.'

So we got the helicopter pilot in for a briefing and these crusty old miners said, 'I reckon we should do a grid search, starting from here and just see how we go.'

'That's fine by me,' the chopper pilot said. 'We'll start at that point and just work our way back in a criss-cross pattern.'

And well, what you've got to realise is that the lost Englishman could've been at any one of about 150 possible old camp sites, okay? Anyway, off we all go in the chopper and this Englishman's still on the phone talking to Moomba Coms and he looks out of the broken down old telephone box and he sees this helicopter away in the distance, and we could see the phone box and we could see him waving and we're thinking, Oh God, this is unbelievable. It's a miracle. We've found him.

Now, from him making the telephone call to us finding him would've only taken, probably, an hour. Mind you, he'd already been wandering around out there for a couple of days without adequate clothing and, of course, no food. But as luck would have it, that was the first point in our search pattern. So we landed the chopper and the pilot, he switches the engine off and he walks over to this English guy, who's still standing there with the phone in his hand, wondering if what he's seeing is really real or not, and the pilot says to him, 'Excuse me, were you the guy who phoned for a taxi?'

And this guy couldn't believe it. Well, neither could we. All the cards had fallen his way. He told me later that he thought it was sort of a religious experience. Like, I know his mate died and all that sort of stuff but he said, 'I've never believed in God but gees, I do now because, you know, there I was out in the desert with next to Buckley's of getting found and all of a sudden an ancient telephone box appears that somehow gets me through to Moomba Coms and then a helicopter arrives out of nowhere to pick me up.'

Anyway, before we went back and retrieved his mate's body we flew the Englishman back to Moomba and, amazingly, he wasn't too badly exposed. His feet were really blistered and he had a bit of sunburn. But, you know, in the scheme of things, he wasn't too bad, though he did keep saying how hungry he was, which you could understand. So when we arrived back at Moomba, of course, all his clothes were shredded and, as we walked into the Health Centre I threw him a pair of overalls and said, 'Look mate, just put these on and we'll go and get you something to eat.'

And he went, 'Oh great because, like, I'm really hungry, you know.'

Well, he threw the overalls on and I took him over to the Moomba mess hall. Now, the Moomba mess hall is this great big, gigantic dining room, which can cater for about 400 workers, right, and the food's phenomenal. You can get just about anything. You know, this is around lunchtime and there's salads and sandwiches and four different sorts of hot meals and there's an ice-cream machine there, and desserts. It's like a huge buffet at a hotel. So we go into this mess room and this guy, well, here he is, an hour and a half earlier he thought he was going to die from starvation and now he walks into this food fest.

'Can I have anything I want?' he said.

I said, 'Go for it mate, you're the one that hasn't eaten for days.'

So he grabbed a plate and he piled it full of T-bone steaks, right. And I've never seen a guy go through three T-bone steaks so quick in my life. He just wolfed them down. And he'd just finished this enormous meal, right, and he turned to me and he said, 'Oh, cripes, I've just forgotten. I'm a vegetarian. I haven't eaten meat in ten years.' Then he added, 'But I tell you what, that was the best meal I've ever had in my life.'

Not a Happy Pilot

I suppose you could say that I actually started with the Flying Doctor Service back in 1987 when I was working with the Division of Child Health out at Charleville, in south-western Queensland. At that stage the nurses from Child Health were seconded across to the RFDS as Flight Nurses. From Charleville I moved back to Innisfail, in far northern Queensland, which is where I was born. And then in 1991 the structure changed within the Division of Child Health and we were employed by the RFDS. So since '91 I've been a Senior Flight Nurse, here in Cairns.

The area we cover is, well, we go right up to Torres Strait, then west out to Georgetown, and down south to just north-west of Townsville. So it's a fair area. And the daily structure, if there is a structure—and that's the beauty of the job because there isn't much of a structure—is that in the Cairns, Charleville and Mount Isa RFDS bases we help the doctor run the general clinics as well as on-call work. So we'll be on a four-week roster doing clinic work and also, because we've all got child health experience as well, we go out and set up a 'Well Baby Clinic'—that's like a Child Health Clinic. You know how, when you're in the city, you go and take your baby in to be weighed and to get advice and all that sort of stuff, well, that's what we do on the Well Baby Clinic.

The other thing is that, when you're on your four-week roster, you're on day call or night call so you have to stay in town and you, virtually, wait—just in case there's an emergency or whatever. Basically, it's a twelve-hour shift and so you know when you're going to work but, if there's an emergency, you don't quite know when you're going to come home from work. That's about the only catch, really.

But there's many, many happy stories. I suppose delivering a baby while you're in the air and then having to tell the pilot we've

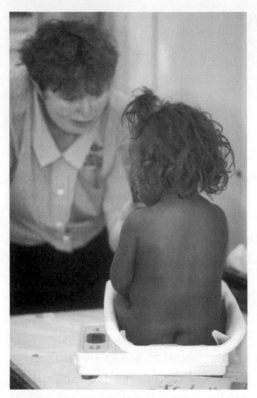

A Well Baby Clinic is set up for people in remote areas where they can have their babies weighed and get advice— RFDS

got an extra one on board still gives me a thrill. But that's nothing out of the ordinary, really. It just happens. But I was thinking about some other types of stories and I remembered once when I was working out of the Charleville base. This doesn't have anything to do with the delivering of babies. I guess it's really more just a comedy of errors, which, in turn, caused Bill McConnell not to be a happy pilot on this particular occasion.

Bill was an old and wise and very experienced pilot who'd been flying around out in the bush for years. Anyway, a seismic crew was out there in the outback somewhere looking for oil and they radioed through one night to say that one of them had been bitten by a snake and they thought he was going to die. So it was an emergency.

On this occasion there was Bill, a doctor and myself who headed out to this place to evacuate the bloke. Now, because we didn't normally go there—it was an airstrip that Bill didn't really know too well—he wanted everything prepared for our arrival. To that end, Bill gave them instructions about lighting flares along the strip to help guide him down and he also asked for a small fire to be lit so that, when he saw the white smoke, he could judge wind direction, which would help with his landing the aeroplane.

As I said, it was night, but when we got out to where Bill thought the strip was, there's nothing there. No flares. No fire. Nothing. So we're circling round and round, trying to figure out what's going on. What was even more baffling was that Bill had also prearranged a channel to talk to these seismic blokes on and now we'd lost complete contact with them on the radio. So we're flying round and round and round until finally another voice comes over our radio and says, 'Well, they had a bit of an accident on their way out to the airstrip. They run into a tree and their radio's out.'

Nobody had been hurt in the accident, thankfully, and we were told that they'd soon be out at the airstrip waiting for us.

'Okay, then,' we said. So we flew around for a while longer and then, 'Yes, there's the strip and they're there but the flares are pretty dull and I can't see any white smoke.'

Anyhow, being an emergency, Bill decided to go ahead and land anyway. Then on final approach we realised that, instead of lighting a small fire to produce a thin wisp of white smoke they'd basically built this huge bonfire and stacked it with old rubber tyres. So, instead of white smoke, there's this huge plume of black smoke blowing right across the strip, which, of course, made Bill's job of landing the aeroplane extremely difficult because he could hardly see the airstrip at all.

But as I said, it was an emergency so with Bill muttering curses at the seismic blokes' stupidity, he decided to continue with the landing. Down we came on final with me up the front, trying to help poor Bill negotiate his way through all this black smoke. Then just as we are about to put down, one of the seismic blokes decides that he'd better take a memento of the occasion. So we're only about 10 or 15 foot off the ground when—Flash!—

Bill's just about night-blinded by the flashlight of a camera. That was immediately followed by some very colourful and derogatory language coming from our pilot punctuated with, 'Just hang on!'

Considering all the circumstances of a strange strip, the darkness of both the night and the smoke, plus being blinded by flashlight, Bill did a great landing. Though, by now, he's not in a very cheery mood at all. So he gets out to have a bit of a go at these blokes and it was a Kiwi who'd been bitten. And I hate snakes. Anyhow, these blokes came over and they hand me a jar. 'Here it is,' they said.

'Here it is, what?' I replied.

'Here's the snake that bit him.'

And I just tossed the jar over to Bill, screamed with fright and ran back to hide in the aircraft. When Bill took a look at the snake he grunted, 'It's a child's python. That won't kill yer. It's non-venomous. It wouldn't kill a fly.' Then he walked off shaking his head at all the unnecessary trouble they'd put us through. I can tell you, he was not a happy pilot at all.

So, with me hiding in the aircraft and Bill having walked off, the doctor was left to manage the situation by himself. Anyhow, we ended up evacuating the bloke. I think, being a Kiwi and there not being any snakes in New Zealand he was a bit traumatised just by being bitten by one anyway.

Okay

I guess these two stories are about communication in its different forms. The first one is, perhaps, more rightly about miscommunication. It's about a young bloke who was a ringer cum jackeroo at Nappa Merrie Station. Nappa Merrie's out in the channel country, over on the south-western Queensland, north eastern South Australian border. The Cooper runs through the property. That's where the Burke and Wills monument is and The Dig Tree.

Anyway, history aside, this young fellow had been on a holiday to Brisbane where he'd befriended a young woman. He was obviously very serious about her because, after he came back to Nappa Merrie, he then made up his mind to return to Brisbane, with the express purpose of meeting the young girl's father and discussing future plans with regard to marriage or whatever. The only trouble was that, when they met, the young woman's father wasn't at all impressed with the young lad. What's more he told him so in no uncertain terms that of the only way the romance had any chance to continue was, as he said, 'Over my dead body.'

The young ringer had then returned to Nappa Merrie in quite a distraught state. Then, one night, when he was feeling particularly lonely he gave the girl a ring. But, as luck would have it, the young girl's father answered the telephone and was rather blunt with the ringer. In fact, he told the young lad, something along the lines of: Go away and slash his wrist. Which, of course, the young ringer did. He did exactly that.

It was at that stage I received the call to say the young ringer had cut his wrists and I advised them what to do to try and arrest the haemorrhage, until I got down there. We flew out from Charleville and, when I got down there to Nappa Merrie and went to the small room where the young ringer was, it looked like he'd done a pretty good job of it. There was blood all over the place.

To begin with, I resuscitated him. Next up, I had to examine the wound to see what sort of damage he'd done to himself. And it was while I was doing the examination that I felt a strange sensation running up my legs, and when I looked down I discovered that the floor was covered with meat ants. Now, I don't know what attracted them, whether it was the smell of the blood, or what, but these meat ants had decided to crawl up my legs, which was not very comfortable, I can tell you. Anyway, I then had to get rid of them before I could fix the fellow up.

Well, the young ringer survived, though I don't know what happened to him after that, though I don't presume his romance with the young woman from Brisbane went any further.

The second story, and perhaps a more humorous one, also deals with communication; though, more rightly, this time you could describe it as non-communication.

I was called to a motorbike accident about a couple of hundred kilometres west of Thargomindah, again in south-western Queensland. This fellow, he was a middle-aged Japanese bloke and he was riding a big motorbike. I can't remember what sort of bike it was, nor what size, but it was a big bike.

All is not okay—RFDS

Anyhow, he'd had this accident and, of course, he couldn't speak any English, and me, in my ignorance, couldn't speak any Japanese. What's more we didn't have access to telephone or radio, to get an interpreter or anything like that. Not out there. But I soon found out that we did seem to have one word in common, and that was the word 'okay'. We both knew the meaning of 'okay'. Well, I presumed he understood the term 'okay' because as I was diagnosing him, I'd do something and ask him, 'Okay?'

To which he'd reply with an, 'Okay.'

Anyway, this Japanese bloke had suffered, amongst other things, a fractured pelvis. In fact, his pelvis was in quite bad shape. So having diagnosed him and resuscitated him there were then certain procedures I had to perform before he was considered fit enough to be loaded on the Pilatus PC XII and be flown back to the hospital. And these were quite invasive sorts of procedures. In fact, they were not the sort you'd expect to have to do, out in the middle of the bush, including, amongst other things, the insertion of a tube into his bladder plus a physical rectal examination.

Of course, everything was done with an 'okay.' And everything was going 'okay' until we came to the rectal examination. Then as I began my examination I looked at him and asked, 'Okay?'

To which he sort of winced a little, but still replied, 'Okay'. Though, this time I noted that his 'okay' was not spoken in a very convincing manner.

Anyway, he got the appropriate treatment whether he liked it or not. Then we got him into the plane and we took him to Toowoomba, where he began his pathway to recovery, before being sent home to Japan.

But now, thinking back, I'm not sure just how much he actually understood about the procedures I did on him, nor why I had to do them. So I have the feeling that, by the time he'd returned to Japan, he was convinced that these rough Australian doctors were anything but okay.

One Arm Point

At the time of this story, my wife, Gail, and I we were teachers up at One Arm Point. Mind you, we're still with the Eduction Department. I'm now a District Director in Geraldton and a lot of the area that I'm responsible for goes into the outback from Geraldton. So I have a large spread of responsibility. Gail is now a school principal. So we've moved on in 30 years, but we still have a strong link with the north-west of Western Australia.

Now, One Arm Point is an Aboriginal Community about 200 to 240 kilometres north of Broome, on the Dampier Peninsula. The Aboriginals there—the Bardi people—had once lived on Sunday Island, which is probably about 10 to 15 kilometres off the mainland. But then, for a number of reasons, their community on Sunday Island folded so they moved into Derby.

But the tribe really suffered in Derby from drink and unemployment and eventually, after quite a number of years, some of the Elders decided that they'd like to return to their land. Now, setting up a community back on Sunday Island was impractical. That was out of the question, so they got a lease on the mainland as close as possible to Sunday Island, which is where One Arm Point is now. On a map, it's at the tip of the point that goes north-eastish from Broome, as well as north-westish from Derby. Cape Leveque is just near by. That's where there's a lighthouse.

So in 1975 Gail and I were asked by the Superintendent for the Kimberley to go to One Arm Point and open the school, which we did. By that stage, the Aboriginal Community had only been going for a year or two and we were the first teachers to go there. We were young. I'd been teaching for seven years and Gail had been teaching for six. So we were pretty inexperienced really, and we were certainly inexperienced as far as Aboriginal

When we arrived at One Arm Point we had no house and there was no school to teach in. We taught under a tree and we lived in a caravan—Rod and Gail Baker

Communities and Aboriginal people were concerned. But we said, 'Yes.' And we bought ourselves a Nissan four-wheel drive and headed off.

When we arrived we had no house and there was no school to teach in. We taught under a tree and we lived in a caravan. I must say that it was quite a cultural shock really, but for all that it was to prove to be a wonderful experience.

Anyway, we'd only been at One Arm Point for two or three weeks when a cyclone came through. And that was another experience, I can tell you. Oh, there was a lot of rain and a lot of wind, that sort of thing. It knocked down a lot of trees and it really put the road in terrible condition. We had the only four-wheel drive vehicle at the community and were the only ones who could get through when the road was that bad. Then, at about two or three o'clock one morning, there came this bang ... bang ... bang on the side of our caravan and, when we opened the door, a white guy, Brian Carter—he's married to an Aboriginal person there—said, 'Would you mind taking one of the young women to Lombadina, she's in labour.'

Now, because One Arm Point was so new, it had no medical facilities. Oh, there was a very short airstrip there, but it couldn't take the Flying Doctor aircraft, certainly not at night time. So basically, there was nothing at One Arm Point while Lombadina— the Catholic Mission about 30 to 40 kilometres south—had a serviceable airstrip, plus it had lay missionaries, and that included a nurse.

So Gail and I got ourselves dressed and we jumped into the Nissan and headed off around to the camp where this young woman was in labour. We pulled up there and her mother and her mother-in-law and a couple of other people carried her out on a mattress and put her in the back of our vehicle. She didn't look too well, at all. Then the mother and mother-in-law got in the back with her and we headed off to Lombadina. It was still dark. Thankfully, the high winds had passed by then, but there was still a fair bit of rain around and the road was, as I said, in a terrible condition.

Anyway, we'd been driving for, I don't know, about fifteen minutes or so, when we heard a lot of cries from the young lady in the back. And all of a sudden, one of the older women lent over and said, 'The baby's come. The baby's come. Will you stop. Can you get me a razor blade?'

Well, you know, we didn't have a razor blade lying around in the vehicle, but Gail hunted around and she did find a pair of scissors in the glove box. So they used this pair of scissors to cut the baby's umbilical cord then they said, 'Oh, can you give us some string?'

Well, we didn't have any string either, nor fishing line. I mean, we just weren't prepared for an event like this. But anyway, we did have some old carpet in the back of the Nissan so we pulled a thread out of the carpet and they used that to tie the baby's cord. So then we continued on to Lombadina, with the newly born baby, the mum and the two new grandmothers, all in the back.

We eventually arrived in Lombadina Mission at about sun-up and we got the lay missionary out of bed. She was lovely girl. She came out and took the mother and baby inside, into their clinic there, and tended to her. At the same time she got on the radio and called the Flying Doctor who gave us an estimated time of the plane's arrival at about seven o'clock in the morning. We then headed out to the Lombadina airstrip, again using our vehicle as the ambulance, and the RFDS plane landed and they took the baby and the mum. After the plane had taken off, the grandparents returned to One Arm Point with us.

But the baby was tiny. I think it only weighed about two pounds. It was quite premature. Now unfortunately, I can't provide you with a happy ending because, I don't know if it had anything to do with the baby being so premature or whether the cyclone had anything to do with it or not but, we found out that the baby died about a week later. So yes, it didn't make it. But that was the story.

One Lucky Feller

I'm a doctor at the RFDS base here in Kalgoorlie and I have two experiences that you may want to hear about. The first one: I can't remember the exact details, but the guy was a Driller's Assistant for an exploration outfit. He was with a small team of men who, I think, were drilling for gold. Anyhow, they were doing some drilling just over 200 kilometres south-west of Kalgoorlie. If you can imagine, they were in line roughly between Norseman and a place called Lake Johnston. So they were west of Norseman, and it was about four hours' drive, on an unborn track, from where they were working to the nearest airstrip at Lake Johnston.

Now, from what I remember, the phone call came into the Kalgoorlie RFDS base at around three o'clock of an afternoon, in November 2004. The first-aider from the drilling company rang to say that they'd just heard about an accident that'd happened about four hours out bush from where the company was. It was all a bit scratchy and second-hand but, from what I could gather, apparently these guys were out drilling and the drill rig struck a tree and a tree branch fell down on this 26-year-old guy and pinned him under it. The first-aider said that they had a lot of gear out there so they were quite confident they could get the tree off the guy but, due to the injuries he'd sustained, they didn't know if they could get him out to the nearest airstrip at Lake Johnston.

Eventually we got in communication with the accident site and when I spoke to them it sounded like the guy had some pretty serious injuries. He had a very nasty open-fractured leg, abdominal injuries and probably some chest injuries, as well as possible spinal injuries.

The next set of problems we faced were, first, how we could get to him and, second, if we got there, how to get him out. One option was to get the exploration company people to drive an ambulance out to the guy, pick him up, do their best and bring him down to Lake Johnston where we could fly in to meet them. But, as the first-aider had said, they weren't sure that, with his injuries, he'd survive the four-hour, four-wheel drive, trek from the accident site to Lake Johnston, over some pretty rough ground.

The only other option was for us to fly down to Lake Johnston, hop into a four-wheel drive and go out to meet him, assess his injuries and then, somehow, take it from there. That was all guesswork and, of course, that again meant he'd still eventually have to be transported the four hours over some pretty rugged ground to Lake Johnston.

Anyway, we eventually decided to fly out to Lake Johnston while the mines people headed off in an ambulance to try and get to the accident site.

Now, yet another problem was the available light. Naturally it's far better for a rescue operation like that to happen in the daylight, but we were rapidly running out of daylight. And the guys from the exploration company reckoned it'd taken them at least six hours to get out to the accident site, pick the guy up, then drive him over to Lake Johnston in the dark. They'd then, of course, have to put out kerosene flares or set up car headlights for us to land.

So we were in an extremely difficult situation, with this guy's life in the balance and daylight running out. But then, just as we were in the process of packing our aircraft we heard a flight of navy helicopters coming into Kalgoorlie. As it turned out they were on their way from Perth, back to Nowra, in New South Wales, and were stopping overnight to refuel. So after they landed, I went over and had a talk to one of their commanding officers and within about twenty minutes they'd received permission to help us out. So we loaded up a navy Seahawk helicopter and they flew myself and the Flight Nurse straight out to the accident.

It probably took us just under an hour to fly down there and we landed in a clearing right next to where the accident had happened. The ambulance had just arrived by then and they already had the guy on a stretcher and had given him a little bit of pain relief. So we took over and stabilised him, loaded him onto the helicopter and flew him back to Kalgoorlie in the Navy helicopter. Then from Kalgoorlie we put him into a RFDS fixed-wing aircraft, the Pilatus PC XII, and took him through to one of the trauma centres in Perth.

And he survived. Mind you, he ended up with quite a lot of injuries, including spine injuries and he spent quite a time in hospital but he survived and now he's okay. So he was one very lucky feller.

The other incident happened quite recently, and he was a lucky feller, too. We do clinic flights out of Kalgoorlie to the remote stations and roadhouses, and one of these stations is Madura Plains Station, which is just north of the Eyre Highway. I'd actually been there the day before to run a clinic and we were on our way back along the Transcontinental Railway Line. I think we were at Cocklebiddy, which is a roadhouse along the way, and

So we loaded up the navy Seahawk helicopter and they flew myself and the Flight Nurse straight out to the accident—RFDS

we got a call from the Manager at Madura Plains Station to say that they'd been mustering and a jackeroo had failed to call in on the radio. So they went looking for him in the mustering plane and they eventually spotted him, lying on the ground next to his motorbike and it looked like he was unconscious.

Then about a quarter of an hour later some of the other musterers were directed to him by the mustering plane and they rang to confirm that, 'Yeah, this guy's come off his motorbike. He's hit his head and appears to be unconscious and it looks like he's been fitting.'

Luckily we were only about half an hour away in the Clinic Plane so, yeah, they wanted us to come and get him. Now, when we do clinics, we only use a small charter plane. We can't carry patients with us. We just carry all the basic medical gear for the more minor medical first-aid treatments and pain relief and things like that. But the Flying Doctor plane, the Pilatus PC XII, you know, it's fitted out like an ambulance, with all the proper aero-medical outfit. So the RFDS in Kalgoorlie decided to send that out as well.

Anyway, the pilot and I, we landed at Madura Plains Station in the Clinic Plane and we jumped in a four-wheel drive and then it was probably a pretty good 50-minute drive out to the scene of the accident. When we arrived there we stabilised the injured jackeroo and we packed him up, put him in the back of the ute, and by the time we got him back to the airstrip at Madura Plains Station—which took about two-and-a-half-hours in total—the PC XII had arrived with a doctor and nurse on board and they took over and flew him to Kalgoorlie Hospital. So he was one lucky feller, too.

Over the Moon

My story goes back to January 1959, when I was a nineteen-year-older, fresh out of teachers' college in Perth and I took up my first appointment in the little school at Coonana. For those that don't know, and I guess there'd be many, Connana's a small railway siding township out along the Transcontinental Railway Line, approximately a couple of hundred miles east of Kalgoorlie, in Western Australia.

Up until that stage in Coonana, if you had a medical emergency and needed to get to Kalgoorlie, the only thing you could do was to catch the Fast Goods train. The passenger train wouldn't stop, only the Fast Goods train would stop. There were a number of drawbacks with that, the main one being that the Fast Goods only came through occasionally and even then it took four hours to get into Kalgoorlie; so, for a critically injured person, that could well be too late.

Anyhow I was just getting settled there and I was fossicking around trying to sort out what was what, when I uncovered a metal box. I guess it would've been about 2 feet by 2 feet and when you opened it up it created more compartments. I soon found out that it was an old Royal Flying Doctor Service medical chest, and that there were all sorts of medicines in it, which were all out of date. Then also, just sitting there was this unusable old wireless.

So, I got in contact with the RFDS people and they came out and they set the wireless up so that we could now use it and they replaced the medicine chest with a complete batch of new medicines. I got the job of being their contact so if someone was crook I'd ring the Flying Doctor base in Kalgoorlie and explain what was wrong with the sick person and they'd tell me the number of the medicine to take out of the box and I'd dispense it.

Now, when I first arrived at Coonana, most of the people who were out there were refugees from countries like Germany, Italy, Yugoslavia and whatever European countries. In fact, no one spoke much English, apart from me, which made things a little bit difficult at times, especially with teaching. But I got the idea that now we had an operational wireless I could use it as a teaching aid for the 20 or so children who hadn't heard much spoken English. So in the mornings, when the chat sessions were on, I'd get the kids involved. Our call sign was '8 BAKER TARE' and the kids used to get on the radio and they'd call through and chat and we also sent telegrams and received messages from people out along the trans-line. And that worked very well indeed.

Then one day a Commonwealth Railways bulldozer—or grader—came through Coonana. The driver was out there cleaning up the edges of the track and so, when I was talking to him, I said, 'Hey, what'd be the chances of you putting an airstrip in here.'

And typical, he didn't consult anybody, all he said was, 'Yeah, okay, I'll give it a go.'

So he got stuck into it and he graded an airstrip out the back of the school. Then after he'd finished I got all the kids together and in an emu fashion we walked up and back the thing, at least twenty times, to pick up any sticks, glass, tin or anything else that could cause a problem with respect to the aeroplane's landing. So now we were in the situation that, if there was an emergency, the RFDS plane could be in and out from Kalgoorlie well within an hour and a half, which was a far cry from an irregular four-hour train trip.

When I told the Flying Doctor people that we now had an operational airstrip they put us on their monthly clinic run. And you can just imagine the huge excitement of the twenty or so kids when the first plane landed. Because, even though they didn't grade the strip, they felt that they were virtually responsible for establishing it. Oh, they were over the moon.

The RFDS held their clinics in my office where the mothers or whoever came in to see the Flying Doctor. The other thing was

The kids welcome the first Flying Doctor plane to arrive on our new airstrip—Graham Cowell

that, with the clinic, the pregnant women out there could now have the opportunity to be checked by a doctor.

Also, another thing, once we'd established the airstrip, other planes, like crop dusters and people like that started to use Coonana as a stepping stone to other places out along the transline; say, from Kalgoorlie to Coonana, then Coonana to Rawlinna and so forth. And of course, that was absolutely wonderful for the kids because even though some of them had seen aeroplanes in Europe, they could now get close to them and see inside of them, and they just loved that.

I was also entrusted by the RFDS people to collect the ten shillings per year levy off all the people out there. Now, I don't know if you've got it over in South Australia, but in Western Australia, if you pay 'x' amount per year to St John's Ambulance then you get free use of the ambulance, if you ever need it. But if you don't pay that then, if you need to use an ambulance, you have to pay the full price per kilometreage. Well that was the same with the Royal Flying Doctor Service. If you paid the ten shillings per year you could be carted to wherever for free. So if you had to be flown from Coonana to Kalgoorlie then from Kalgoorlie on to Perth, it was all free, apart from the ten shillings per annum, of course.

And that caused some hardship because, it's got to be remembered that the people out there at Coonana, in those days, did not see much money because, even though there were a couple of Australian families living there by then, the vast majority were still the refugees coming out from Europe. And those refugees were heavily in debt to the Commonwealth Railways because, when they first arrived they had nothing but the job.

So the Commonwealth Railways supplied them with furniture, clothing, bedding, their food, and when they got their pay, not only did the Taxation Department take their bit out but the Commonwealth Railways took their slug as well. So they'd get their pay envelope and it'd state that they now only owed the Commonwealth Railways another £540, or whatever it was. For many, the only cash they got was Child Endowment and that's what they used when it came to paying their levy to cover themselves for the Flying Doctor.

So yes, they were very difficult times for many of those people, and I remember one family saying, 'No, we just can't afford it and, anyway, we don't use the Flying Doctor Service.'

But Murphy's law; guess which family had to use the Flying Doctor. It was them.

Anyway, that was the establishment of the RFDS in Coonana. As I said, it started with the discovery of an outdated medical chest and a disused wireless, sitting idle in the school house. And of course, when they were sorted out it opened up communications for the children. Then the opportunity came along with the arrival of the grader and the kids helping prepare the airstrip so they had a great feeling of ownership and pride in being involved, as well. Add to that John Flynn's ideology of placing a Mantle of Safety over the people in the bush, plus the huge contribution by the Royal Flying Doctor Service, and that's what happened in that small community. And to those people at Coonana, it was absolutely unreal.

Porcupine

I was born on 3 October 1950 and I got into strife on the Christmas morning of 1951, so I was too young to remember what actually happened. But I've heard all about it, of course, and I've still got the scars on my lungs. We were at Canopus Station, which is between Renmark and Burra, in South Australia. Later on, Dad sold Canopus to a bloke called Bill Snell, then Bill sold it to the South Australian Government and it was absorbed into a massive national park, the Danggali Conservation Park.

But right from the time I was born, I had an incredible bond with my father. Incredible! Oh, as a kid, I used to go everywhere with him. I was like his shadow. Anyhow, that Christmas morning, when I was about thirteen or fourteen months old, my dad was cleaning out the bath with power kerosene. Power kero was what we used to get rid of the greasy marks and stuff that had built up from the old dam water we washed in. And the kerosene was in this container—a tin—but he left it on the floor when he went off to do something else. Then I crawled along and, next thing, Mum heard the sound of an empty tin hit the ground and, when I started coughing and going on, she realised that her little boy had helped himself to the kerosene.

I don't know how much I drank but it was enough to be absorbed into my lungs, which started the coughing. Then, after that I became unconscious fairly quickly. But my father thought it was all his fault and he got really upset and he started to panic and he wanted to put me in the car and head straight off for Renmark. I think Renmark was something like 56 miles from Canopus, but it was just a dirt and sand track in those days, with fifty gates or something that had to be opened and shut along the way. So you know what a trip like that would've been like for a very sick little boy.

Anyhow, Mum said we weren't going anywhere. She reckoned I'd die if I was moved. So then they settled me down the best they could and they waited for the Flying Doctor to come on air. See, at a certain time of the morning the Flying Doctor Service kept the channel clear and if anybody had any issues they'd be able to get on the communications radio and talk to the doctor. But, because it was Christmas Day, it just happened to be the only time of the year that the Flying Doctor base wasn't open for their usual morning doctor's session.

I think the Canopus call sign in those days was something like ABS 6-CANOPUS and you'd get on the radio and say, 'ABS 6-CANOPUS calling Broken Hill, calling Flying Doctor.'

So that's what they did, and they just kept calling and calling but they couldn't raise anyone at the Flying Doctor base in Broken Hill. To make things even more difficult we didn't have any 240-volt electricity coming into the house. All we had was 32-volt power and the radio for the Flying Doctor, it run on a 12-volt battery. And of course, with all this continual calling and calling our transceiver used a lot of power which, in turn, kept old Butch Batty busy, running batteries backwards and forwards from the outside generator room and swapping them over.

Just to give a bit of background; Butch was a real identity of the district. He was a former clown who was working with Dad in those days. He used to call Dad 'The Engineer'. But poor old Butch was an alcoholic and every now and again when we'd have to take him into town to see the doctor or get his glasses fixed or something he'd get on the grog, then he'd come back out home and dry out.

Mum said that, on one particular occasion, they went to get Butch from the pub and when they got him outside there was a little feller—a young kid—selling newspapers and Butch just put his hand in his pocket, dug out what was left of his money and gave it all to the kid.

And Mum said, 'Oh Butch,' she said, 'what'd you do that for? That's all the money you've got left.'

'Misses,' he said, 'the poor little feller was battlin'.'

See, old Butch reckoned that he didn't need the money back in the bush so he just gave it all to the boy. Anyway, that's just a bit about Butch, and when I was unconscious after drinking the kero, he spent all his time swapping the batteries over so that we could stay on the transceiver calling Broken Hill. Actually, it was my mum who was on the radio, doing all the calling because, apparently, my father was nursing me. So things were pretty desperate.

Now, I'm not too sure how it works, though I think whenever you made an emergency call into the Flying Doctor's base it used to light up an instrument panel. But it wasn't until after the doctor had had his Christmas lunch and come back out to the base that he saw the emergency light was on. So he jumped straight on the radio and said, 'Where's the station calling the Flying Doctor?'

And Mum was back in a flash, saying it was her and, as I said, there was my dear old dad, the man I had this incredible bond with, at his wit's end, cradling me in his arms. *This is interesting. As I just mentioned that, the emotion's all just rushed up in me. Sorry about that.* So, yeah, well, and, well, then Mum hooked into the doctor and the doctor told her what to do. I don't know exactly what the instructions were but he told her what particular medications to give to me from out of our Flying Doctor's medical chest. And he also confirmed that, you know, my mother had done the right thing by me and to just continue to nurse me through it gently and, along with the medication, I'd be okay; I'd survive, which I did. And to this day I've still got scars on my left lung and whenever I have an X-ray I've always got to explain to the people that I got a scarred lung from that particular experience with the kero.

So I mean, they didn't have to fly me out or anything but there were plenty of times when the Flying Doctor did fly out to Canopus. In those days, when I was growing up, the doctor was Dr Huxtable and Vic Cover was the pilot. I've got photos of the family and all of us standing by the Flying Doctor's plane because Mum and Dad used to put on so many different fundraisers, especially after my stuff happened. I've even got cuttings from the newspaper in at Renmark where, you know, they wrote that Canopus Station raised something like £2500 for the Royal Flying Doctor Service.

For the fundraisers, Dad and Mum ran a woolshed dance every year plus a cricket match. I remember when we'd get up early and Dad would drive us into Renmark to get the ice and lots of ice-cream for the kids, which was in those big old canvas bags. And he'd bring home a heap of kegs of beer for the adults and they'd set up the kegs under a shady thing they called a bow shed. Basically, a bow shed was just a few sticks with some green mallee laid over the top of it, and that was the pub. And for the cricket match, Dad actually poured a concrete wicket out in the middle of the airstrip and, to this very day, I reckon I could just about walk you out to it, blindfolded.

Also, I remember how Mum used to get cardboard tea packets and she'd cut them straight through the middle with a sharp knife and pour the tea out into another container. All year long she'd save these empty tea packet halves. Then before we had a fundraiser she'd cover them all with leftover Christmas paper or whatever coloured paper she could get—or we'd both do it, me and her—and she'd make little handles and attach them to the boxes, then she'd fill them with homemade lollies, coconut rough and all that stuff, and all the kids that came along would get a couple of packets of lollies. Everything was free. I didn't see any money changing hands so they must've paid through the gate or something to raise the amounts of money they did.

Now, I've just remembered another story I was told. It was when Mum was pregnant with me. The airstrip was just off the side of the house and, anyhow, on one occasion the Flying Doctor flew out to Canopus Station to give my elders, Andy, Wally and Marion, smallpox injections or something like that. So they landed and then the crew came over to the house and the nurse said, 'Okay, who's gonna be first?'

And my brother, Wally, who was always the cheeky one, he raced forward, looking real tough, and he said, 'Oh, me, me, me, I'll be first.'

'Okay,' the nurse said, 'pull down your pants.'

Then the nurse got the needle out and started to get it ready for the injection. But when Wally saw the size of the needle, oh,

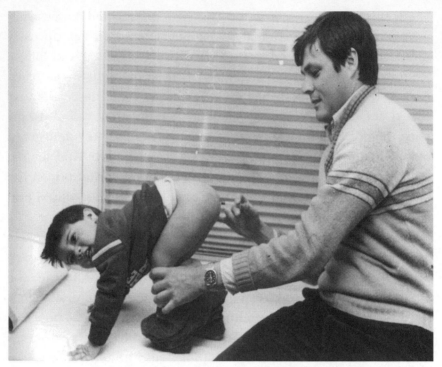

When Wally saw the size of the needle he was off like a shot—RFDS

he was off like a shot and he bolted through the scrub and they chased him everywhere, trying to catch him. But he was too quick and they all got tired, so then they decided that they'd get him later on, when he turned up back home again.

Anyhow, Andy was the eldest bloke so he got his needle, then Marion got her's. But young Wally was a pretty wise young feller and he hid out in the bush until he saw the Flying Doctor plane take off before he decided to come back home again. I must add at this juncture that Wally could also make up a pretty good story when the need arose because, when he eventually turned up later in the afternoon, he snuck in home, pretending he had a sore bottom and he announced, 'I've already had my needle so I don't need another one.'

'How's that?' everyone asked.

And Wally replied, 'I went and sat on a porcupine!'

Rabbit Flat

In 1975 and '76 I worked for a charter company who contracted to the Royal Flying Doctor Service in Alice Springs. We had a Beechcraft Baron. Anyway, I was wondering if you've heard the story about Rabbit Flat? It was in all the newspapers and magazines, as well as being on television and radio.

Of course, you know where Rabbit Flat is, don't you? Well, it's in the Northern Territory, out on the Tanami Track, on the way to Halls Creek, roughly 600 kilometres north-west from Alice Springs and about 150 kilometres from the Western Australian border. If you can imagine, it's typical Tanami desert, flattish country, just spinifex. So there's not a lot out there apart from this roadhouse on the Tanami Track at a place called Rabbit Flat. It's actually privately owned by a couple called Bruce and Jackie Farrands and, at the time this occurred, Jackie was pregnant and was about six weeks away from giving birth. Actually, I can give you the precise date; it was 6 August 1975.

Anyhow, the night before—on the fifth—I got a phone call from my boss asking me to take off in the Beechcraft Baron early the following morning to arrive over Rabbit Flat just on first light. Apparently, the Flying Doctor Service base had received a radio message via either Perth or Darwin or somewhere and it looked like Jackie had gone into labour. Bruce couldn't get in direct contact with the RFDS at Alice Springs, himself, because of the poor atmospheric conditions. Then just after the message had arrived the conditions turned so bad that radio contact was cut completely and they couldn't get anymore information about Jackie.

So we took off before sunrise and we flew out to Rabbit Flat. There was just myself and a nursing sister, Maureen Eason. I can't remember exactly but it took us something like an hour and

The population of Rabbit Flat doubled last night—RFDS

a half, flying out to the north-west, and we arrived just after first light at Rabbit Flat. We circled over the roadhouse to let Bruce know we'd arrived then, when we landed, he came out in his vehicle to pick us up.

The first thing Maureen said to Bruce was something along the lines of, 'Has anything happened yet? Is Jackie okay?'

'Oh sure,' said Bruce. 'She's already given birth.'

Maureen was quite surprised at that news so she said, 'Oh, so how's Jackie and how's the baby?'

'Well,' Bruce replied, 'the first baby's fine.' Then he said, 'And so is the second one.'

So there were two of the little buggers. Twins; both boys.

And no one knew. Not even Jackie's doctor knew that she was expecting twins. Anyway, the babies were fine. Bruce had them wrapped up in cotton wool, in a washing basket. So Bruce and I, we sat down and had a cuppa tea while Maureen attended to Jackie and got her ready to be transported back into Alice Springs. We'd taken a humidicrib with us so Maureen put the baby boys in the humidicrib and we put Jackie on the stretcher, in the

Beechcraft. Then just before we hopped into the aircraft, Bruce said to me, 'Oh, this'll be good publicity for Rabbit Flat, eh.'

'Oh yeah, okay,' I said, and I took off.

Well, it was a bit strange for Bruce to say something like that, you know, about wanting publicity for Rabbit Flat, because he was such a quiet sort of bloke; a bit of a loner, really. Well, you'd have to be to even contemplate going out there to live in a place like Rabbit Flat, in the first place, would you?

But anyway, on the way back into the Alice Springs I began thinking that he really must be keen on seeking some sort of publicity. So after I landed and my services were no longer required, I raced over and there was a phone in the corner of our hanger, and I rang the local ABC Radio in Alice Springs. A male voice answered the phone—I don't know who it was—and I said, 'Do you want a good story?'

He said, 'Yeah.'

'Well,' I said, 'the population of Rabbit Flat doubled last night.'

Now, the last thing I expected was to be quoted verbatim. But the next thing I know, it actually started hitting the headlines as a human interest story. I'm pretty sure it was on the front page of *The Australian*. If you go back and look at 7 August 1975 you'd probably find it in the paper, there somewhere. It even made the *Women's Weekly*, and I think it probably went into *Pix* or *Post* and most of those popular magazines at the time.

So it was a big story and it even went international because people in England even started ringing up Bruce. It was also actually written up in some publication or other over in England. Oh, Bruce had phone calls from everywhere, all over the world. So then it became a bit of a stampede out to Rabbit Flat, there for a while. But it got a bit too much for Bruce because he was left out there to deal with it all by himself until Jackie and the babies, Daniel and Glen, were ready to go back home.

Then, I think it was *A Big Country*, well, they went out there and did a television program on Bruce and Jackie and their lives in Rabbit Flat. In fact, just recently, *A Big Country* approached Bruce again because they were re-running some of their old stories and I think they wanted to do something along the lines of *A Big Country: Twenty Years On.* So they rang Bruce about doing a follow-up program. But Bruce's a bit shy of publicity these days. In fact, he's not real keen on it at all. He reckons he had enough back in '75 to last him a lifetime.

Rissoles

I reckon I might've been about one of the first recipients of the Flying Doctor Service. This was in 1929, back in the depression era when no one had two pennies to rub together. Things were pretty tough and Dad was out in the bush with the railways, so my Mum took work anywhere she could to get some money. Anyhow, she got this job, working as a domestic on a cattle station called Davenport Downs. Davenport Downs is on the Diamantina River, in the channel country, in south-western Queensland.

I was only about two or something so I can't remember exactly what happened but, apparently, there was a black gin—an Aboriginal woman—who was working in the kitchen as one of my mother's helpers. Anyhow, this gin was doing some mincing; mincing up leftovers to make rissoles. And so, yeah, she sat me up on the table where she was doing this mincing and she must've turned away or something because I stuck my hand in the top of the mincing machine and it took me finger off, right down to the first joint. It was the first finger—the index finger—of the right hand. Yep, right down to the knuckle. So she must've still been turning the mincer and she didn't see me stick my hand in the thing. I mean, I was only two or something so I lost the top of my finger in the mincer.

Now, there would've only been the old peddle-type radio back then and, I presume, that's how they got in contact with the Flying Doctor. So they came out to pick me up in what would've been, back in those days, an old canvas plane; an old biplane, an Avian or something like that. I think the Avians were about the first ones the Flying Doctor Service used. There's one up at the Museum in Longreach. I'm going to Longreach sometime this year because I want to find out for sure what exactly happened,

An early Flying Doctor's bi-winged aeroplane—RFDS

you know, whether my name or my mother's name is on their records out there.

Anyhow, the Flying Doctor came out and they flew me and my mother from Davenport Downs back in to Boulia Hospital. And, as they did in those days, they just took what was left of the minced up joint-bone out, pulled the skin back over it and then they sewed the fingernail back on. So I've got a nail on my knuckle, yeah, but I don't know where they got that from. Perhaps they fished it out of the rissole mince.

Then when we got back, the black gin had taken off somewhere. I don't think she'd ever seen an aeroplane before so when she saw the Flying Doctor plane come and take me away she probably thought she'd killed me and I was being taken off into the spirit world by this strange thing that flew in the sky.

Anyway, that's my story. As I said, I was only about two at the time and I've still got the fingernail growing out of the knuckle of the index finger on my right hand and, no, I don't know what happened with the rissoles.

Slim Dusty

I suppose you've heard of Slim Dusty the singer? He's dead now but, back in 1985 I published a book called *Slim Dusty Around Australia.* Basically, it was a collection of photographs, with only about two pages of writing, and it was about his concert days and all that sort of thing.

I'm not really into music, but I was just a fan, that's all. And how it all come about was that I was working in the Public Service and in my spare time I'd travel around with Slim and take lots of photographs. Like, I'd go behind the scenes. And I'd go into towns where he'd been and go to the local newspapers and, you know, I'd go to some of his record store appearances on the day he was to sign autographs and I'd attend some of the awards that he got, even the ones he received outside the music industry.

Anyhow, over time the collection gradually built up. So, in the end, I sorted them all out and put it together and I included about 250 photos in the book, which was about 100 pages long, and then I had a thousand copies printed and, really, the rest is history. They've all gone now, but that was my little mark on history.

Then in the 1980s, after I left the Public Service, I did some volunteer mission work up in the Kimberley region, up in the far north of Western Australia. I did a year in Derby, about four years at Lombadina Aboriginal Mission, another year up in the Kalumburu Aboriginal Mission, then another year in, what was originally known as Port Keats, which is now the Wadeye Aboriginal Community.

When I was in Derby I ran the School Hostel, on the outskirts of town, there. See, the church had a boarding hostel for the little Aboriginal school kids who lived up that Gibb River Road. And they'd come into Derby for the school terms and they'd board at

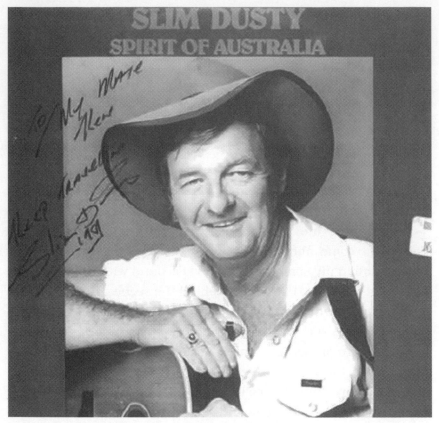

Slim Dusty was a great supporter of the Flying Doctor Service—The Hansford Collection

the School Hostel and go down to either Derby Primary School or to the Catholic Primary School. Our job was to look after them and feed them and clothe them and provide recreational activities for them and things like that and then, on their school holidays, they'd take off and go back to their communities.

Then one Sunday night, when I was in Derby, I was listening to the local ABC radio's 'Country Music' program and they were having an appeal to raise money for the Royal Flying Doctor Service. And I knew that Slim was a great supporter of the Flying Doctor Service. I think he even sung a song about it and I'm certain that he did a couple of concerts over in Charleville, where he donated part of the proceeds to the RFDS.

Anyhow, I still had a copy of the book with me so I rang up the radio station and asked if they wanted to auction a book. And when I explained what the book was about, well, the ABC got really wrapped in it, you know, because everybody up there loved Slim Dusty and they played him all the time. Anyhow they agreed to auction it over the radio, amongst all the listeners, and, I mean, I was only selling it for about $10 a copy and I think they ended up auctioning it for somewhere between $250 and $300.

So that was my small contribution to the RFDS.

Slingshot

Did you ever run into people by the name of Clarrie and Emily Pankhurst? Clarrie only passed away eighteen months or so ago, but he was the last of the Boss Drovers. I mean, this fellow could be on the road for anything from six to eight months with 1500 head of cattle from Wave Hill, which is in the west of the Northern Territory, over to Camooweal, just inside the Queensland–NT border, then all the way down south of Mount Isa, to be trucked from Dajarra. Camooweal was where they used to keep all their horses and that. So it was an amazing life some of these fellows had, wasn't it?

Actually, a book's been written for Clarrie and his wife, Emily. It's called *The Boss Drover*, and it's a great read. To tell you the truth, I know a lot about it because we lived across from the Pankhursts at Mount Isa, and me and my brother, we both went out with Clarrie, you know. So we know the guy first hand. None of it's fiction so if you give any credit to anybody for this story, I'd rather it be credited to Clarrie and his wife, Emily, formally of Mount Isa, because that's where they used to live when they weren't droving.

Now, I want to get this as close as possible; so this was in 1956. Clarrie and his ringers were yarding up some cattle out on a station property, well out into the Northern Territory, near Newcastle Waters, and this young fellow come off his horse and broke his leg. It didn't happen near the homestead because they were out a way. The young fellow, he had a few rib injuries as well, but mainly the leg was badly broken and, well, they had to call the Flying Doctor to come in from Alice Springs. But all around the particular area where they were at the time, where the accident occurred, there was a lot of scrub so there wasn't much room for a plane to land.

Anyhow, the pilot got the plane down alright, but because the airstrip was so short and because of all this scrub, plus they now

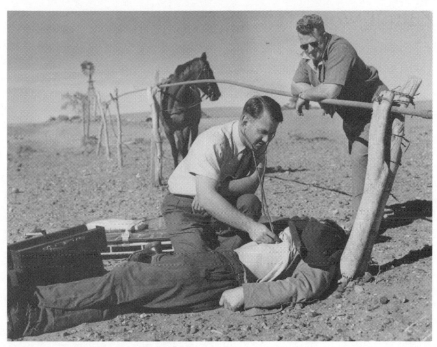

He wasn't looking too good—RFDS

had this young injured fellow on board, the pilot needed a much longer run up to get the aeroplane back in the air. So what they did was, they got three ringers to hang on to each of the wings and two ringers to hang onto the tail—that's eight of them—and these ringers just dug in their heels while the pilot built up the revs on the plane. And they held on for as long as they could and then the pilot gave them a signal out the side of the plane and he just took off like a slingshot. Vroom, off he went and he just made it over the scrub. He wouldn't have made it without them doing that, and they got the fellow to hospital alright.

But, Clarrie and Emily, they were both wonderful people. And, you know, these sorts of things come because people are ingenious in times of trouble. It's sort of like thinking outside the square. But as tough a life that those people had, and yes, Clarrie was a hard man at times, but he was always fair and honest. You know, once you got to know him well, he was a real friend and so was his wife, Emily.

Small World, Large Bruise

In the late 1970s I transferred out to Mootwingee Historic Site as a Ranger and, basically, we—myself and the Senior Ranger—looked after the Historic Site and around the National Park district. Mootwingee's in the far west of New South Wales about a hundred and something kilometres north-east of Broken Hill, as the crow flies.

Mootwingee's known as a Historic Site because that was one of the classifications the National Parks used at the time. It was only a relatively small area and like the Kurnell area at Botany Bay was called Captain Cook's Landing Place Historic Site, it was, in fact, part of the Sydney Metropolitan District, which included Sydney Harbour National Park, which was later called Botany Bay National Park or something similar. So, it's just one of the classifications they had; you know, you had National Park, Nature Reserve, and Historic Site, and each was established under the National Parks and Wildlife Act.

But the Mootwingee Historic Site was very popular with visitors, especially in the cooler months. And during those cooler months one of the local tour operators used to bus visitors—tourists—out from Broken Hill on a day trip to the Historic Site. So, upon their arrival, first, they'd come into the Visitors' Centre and have a look around at the displays and then they'd get back into the bus again and go down to a picnic area, where they'd have something to eat and they could go on a couple of designated walks and what-have-you.

Anyhow, on this particular day the bus arrived and the bus driver brought the tourists in and they spent their normal twenty minutes or so looking around the Visitors' Centre, which basically had displays of Aboriginal relics and fauna and flora of the area. Of course, we also used to sell a book on the Historic

Site plus other New South Wales National Parks publications. Then after they'd gone through the Visitors' Centre their bus took them down to the picnic area. The walk they were doing that day was the walk up and around the dam and past Snake Cave.

Snake Cave was one of the most significant parts of the Historic Site. It was a very large overhang, with a huge painting of a snake on it. I'd say that it'd be a good 20 or 30 feet long. I'm not up with what's happening now but, at one stage, I recall that they actually stopped people from going to Snake Cave unless it was by prearranged guided tours. So it's a fairly significant site.

Now, basically, the bus driver used to leave the tourists free to go around the walks and he'd stay at the picnic area and have a rest or sort out lunch or whatever. But then, on this particular day, about half an hour after they'd left the Visitors'

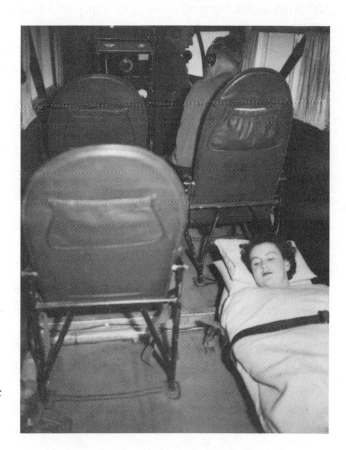

Being flown back to Broken Hill—RFDS

Centre, the bus driver returned to the office and said that one of the elderly ladies had fallen over and she appeared to have broken her leg.

That's when he added, 'And she's a very large lady.'

Anyway, my house was behind the Visitors' Centre and there was a fairly large garage there also. So I went and got the Stokes Litter from the garage. I'm sure you're familiar with what a Stokes Litter is: it's a light aluminium-framed stretcher, where the patient actually lies into it, as opposed to a conventional stretcher where the patient lies on top of it. Basically, it's designed for search and rescue. The idea is that, when you're taking someone over rugged terrain or winching them up a cliff, they don't fall off the thing.

At that time I had a Volvo station wagon, so I decided to drive that down to the picnic area because the alternative was to take the Toyota four-wheel drive tray top and I didn't think that'd be really appropriate for transporting an elderly lady around the place in. The Senior Ranger was also there, so he and the bus driver and I headed back down to the picnic area in the Volvo and we set off on foot with the Stokes Litter.

As it turned out, the bus driver had given us a very adequate description because, when we arrived at the scene of the accident, I could see a very large lady lying on the ground. She must've been 18 stone. Her arms were probably as big as my legs and she was obviously in a great deal of pain and had a very swollen ankle.

So we enlisted the help of a few of the male tourists to lift this lady into the Stokes Litter and we started the slow trip back to the picnic area. I can't remember exactly how long it took but, once we got back to the picnic area, I put the rear seat of the Volvo down and we slid her into the back, ambulance style. Then we drove the injured woman straight down to my house where I thought she'd be more comfortable.

There was a Flying Doctor radio in my house, as well as in the office, so we placed her on the lounge-room floor, as I'd intended, and got onto the radio. Now, on the Flying Doctor radio there's a little emergency button and when you press that, it emits a high-pitched sound which alerts the nearest RFDS base that somebody needs a doctor urgently.

So literally, within thirty seconds, there's a doctor on the other end. And what happens is, you press a button and a doctor comes on and says, 'Broken Hill Flying Doctor Service' to the caller who's on the emergency button. Then you identify yourself. So I identified Mootwingee and the doctor then asked what the problem was and I explained that we had an elderly lady with what appeared to be a broken ankle.

Then we went through the consultation process where the doctor asked a series of questions and established that the woman was in quite a great deal of pain. In such circumstances it was usual for them to prescribe a pethidine injection. If you know the system with the Flying Doctor kits, they're a large metal chest with a whole lot of numbered medicines and bandages in there, plus syringes and whatever. So on instruction from the doctor I removed one of the syringes and an ampoule of pethidine. I then proceeded to prepare the syringe by putting the appropriate amount of pethidine in it, then pressing lightly on it to ensure that there was no air in the syringe.

So there we were, with the lady on the floor and the Senior Ranger and I with this syringe. Now, I'd never given an injection before and, as it turned out, the Senior Ranger hadn't either. But because he was the more senior officer, well, he got the job, didn't he? In this case, with the patient being a rather large lady, we were instructed by the Flying Doctor that we were to give the injection into the arm.

Anyway, he went ahead and administered the pethidine which, after a short while, took effect as it obviously made the patient more comfortable. Because it was best not to move the injured woman, we kept her on the Stokes Litter all the time. Mind you, she filled it pretty well. But she seemed reasonably comfortable in it and we didn't want to disturb her, especially after the pethidine kicked in.

In the meantime, the doctor had informed us that he was sending out a plane to pick her up. Now, because the airstrip was only about, at most, 800 metres from the house, we waited until we heard the plane buzzing around. Then, when it was circling, ready to land, we picked up the Stokes Litter and we bundled the lady back into the Volvo and I drove her down to the airstrip. The RFDS were using a Nomad aircraft at that stage. They had a doctor, a nurse and the pilot and, basically, they took charge as soon as they arrived. The woman was taken out of the Stokes Litter, put onto the plane's stretcher, then into the plane where they secured her, and off they went to Broken Hill.

Then a few days later my wife, Robina, and I went to Broken Hill to do our shopping and, while we were there, we decided to call in and see how the patient was faring. We went into the hospital and found her in one of the wards. She had plaster on what, she informed us, was a triple fracture of her ankle.

And that's when I asked her, 'So, how's the ankle?'

'It's not the worst bit,' she joked.

Then she showed me her arm and, oh god, I could not believe that such a small needle could give such a large bruise. This bruise was a good 4 inches by 3 inches. It was huge. I mean, with someone who's overweight, yes, they do tend to bruise easily, I know, but this one was the biggest, blackest bruise I've ever seen. I just couldn't believe it.

But she was fine about it. She was in good spirits and was quite happy and she thanked us for all we'd done and we had a chat for a while. And though I didn't find out until some time later, it turned out that the lady was related to a counterpart of mine, one of the rangers in the Blue Mountains. Small world, isn't it?

Someone, Somewhere

I'm constantly reminded of the diverse types of people that we, in the Royal Flying Doctor Service, serve. And in doing so, it's important that we respect and embrace those differing cultures. Of course, with so many of the Aboriginal people being 'out there', obviously, they are a large percentage of our clientele both in their traditional areas, where they're more nomadic, as well as in communities or towns where they're less so.

I remember when I went to Port Augusta for a Consumer Network Group meeting. That's when we get together with our constituents to sort out how the RFDS can better serve their needs. And the majority of the people who attend those meetings are the station people, mostly white. Anyhow, it was the night before the meeting, so the few of us who were already in town were having a meal and there was music coming from the next room, a larger dining area that'd been partitioned off. So I opened the door and there was this Aboriginal group. Up front were a couple of people playing guitars and singing and another bloke was on the drums. As it turned out they were taking part in an Aboriginal workshop about Native Land Titles.

Anyway I introduced myself. 'G'day,' I said, 'I'm John Lynch, CEO of the South Australian Division of the Royal Flying Doctor Service.' Then I told them just how much I was enjoying their music.

'Do you sing?' they asked.

'Oh yeah,' I said, 'I sing, alright.'

Well, I can't sing, but I reckon I can. So anyway we did a couple of John Williamson and Kenny Rogers numbers together, then we sat down and we swapped a few yarns. And gees we had a good time. Then the next day they invited us into their morning tea, which was outstanding.

Actually, I've got to pinch myself sometimes in the knowledge that I'm privileged enough to work within the RFDS—RFDS

And that's what we need to do. We need to share the cultures. That was John Flynn's ideology; for each and every one of us within this greater organisation to serve the people who live out in the harshness, no matter what their colour or creed, in as much as nobody should be without access to health services, which was born out of the Jimmy Darcy story.

Now, are you aware of the Jimmy Darcy story? Well, it was big news back during the First World War when a young stockman by the name of Jimmy Darcy was working on a station property, up the Kimberley area of Western Australia and he fell from his horse and was severely injured.

In those days there was no medical help available up in the Kimberleys. There wasn't even a doctor. No radio. Nothing! So their best bet was to try and get Jimmy to Halls Creek, which was about 80 kilometres away, where they knew that the local postmaster, a feller by the name of Tuckett, had at least done a first aid course. So they loaded Jimmy into a buggy and took him along a rough bush track to Halls Creek. When they got there,

Jimmy was in such a bad state all that Tuckett could do was to give him a shot of morphine to try and relieve the severe pain.

Tuckett then decided to morse code over 3650 kilometres of telegraph wire to Perth to get help. Then, from the post office in Perth the doctor diagnosed Jimmy's injuries and concluded that it was a life or death situation and he needed immediate surgery. And, what's more, because poor old Tuckett had completed a basic first aid course, he was the unfortunate soul to be given the job.

So then, for the next seven hours the doctor's instructions were relayed by morse code all the way from Perth to Halls Creek while Tuckett operated on Jimmy with the use of just a penknife and razor blades. The only antiseptic that was available was Condi's Crystals. The only form of anaesthetic was morphine, and that just relieved some of the pain. Anyhow, the operation proved to be a success but, unfortunately, complications set in so then the doctor decided to come up from Perth.

Now, it took six days by a cattle boat for the doctor to reach Derby. Then it was a day and a half by car out to Fitzroy Crossing, followed by a further thirty-six hours—including breakdowns—in a smaller car to get within 50 kilometres of Halls Creek. They then had to travel the rest of the way by horse and sulky, only to find that Jimmy Darcy had died just the day before the doctor arrived.

That tragedy made newspaper headlines all over Australia and it really brought it home to John Flynn that, if there'd been medical services in the bush, Jimmy may well have survived. And I'm getting right off the track here, but also, at that time, when aeroplanes were first being used in the First World War, a feller named Clifford Peel pointed out to Flynn that, with the use of aircraft it was now possible for patients to be transported by aeroplane. Then, of course, add to that the communications expertise of Alf Traeger and so this wonderful organisation was born.

Since then, of course, we've developed and become more advanced, and more sophisticated. We've even expanded to include Capital City inter-hospital transfer and organ harvesting. But we should always acknowledge the traditional owners of this land as well. We should acknowledge the courage and commitment of the people that've been prepared to go out and explore and develop the harshness of our outback, and who provide us with the wealth. And that's something we must never lose sight of.

Then at the same time we should also acknowledge our own people, those who work within the RFDS. I see it as a privilege that's been bestowed upon us to be able to carry the mantle of serving what we've created. Because it doesn't matter what time of the day or night it is, or what the weather's like—unless, of course, it's absolutely foul and it's impossible to get out there— there's a courage and commitment from our staff to deliver services, above and beyond the call of duty.

And it's not only the lifesaving adventures that should be noted. It's also the day-to-day occurrences: the simple things. We had a Community Health Nurse who's now working in either Canada or Alaska where she drives sled dogs to do medical clinics. When she was with us at our Port Augusta base, every morning she'd go to the bakery and buy fresh bread to take to whatever Clinic outpost she was heading to that day. She'd also take some daily newspapers so that the people out there could read up-to-date news, which was a real rarity, and sometimes she'd even take out icy poles or some such for the kids. And you know, that had nothing to do with her nurse's training. None of that was in her brief. She just cared enough.

So I reckon we're lucky to be part of this great organisation. To tell you the truth, I've got to pinch myself sometimes in the knowledge that I've been chosen, or that I'm privileged enough to work within the RFDS. Because I reckon that, every one of us— all our staff—when we wake up we know that, at the very least, during the course of that particular day somebody within our organisation will make a difference to someone, somewhere. That's our lot, and I love it.

Statistics and Brief History

Queensland The first base of the Flying Doctor Service was established in Cloncurry, in north-western Queensland, in 1928.

Victoria The Victorian Section was formed on 9 November 1934 and was the first of the Sections of the Australian Inland Aerial Medical Service. Because there was no need for Flying Doctor services in Victoria this section went outside its state borders and took over the responsibility of providing medical services in the vast and remote north-west of Western Australia, in the East and West Kimberley. The section's first base at Wyndham became operational in 1935.

New South Wales The New South Wales Section was formed in 1936. Its Broken Hill base, in the far west of the state, was initially jointly operated by the South Australian and New South Wales Sections and became operational in 1937. It later became known as the South Eastern Section.

Central Formerly known as the South Australian and Northern Territory Sections, this section was formed in 1936 and has since been changed to Central Operations and is administered from South Australia. Initially it operated (from 1937) out of Broken Hill, jointly with the New South Wales Section. This arrangement continued until the Central Section opened its own Flying Doctor base at Alice Springs in 1939.

Eastern Goldfields Although the Eastern Goldfields Section was officially established in 1937, in the Kalgoorlie area, the 'Goldfields Flying Doctor Service' provided a medical service for people in the outback as far back as the early 1930s.

Western Australia The Western Australian Section was officially registered on 14 June 1936. However, a provisional Section Committee had already purchased a de Havilland Fox Moth Aircraft in 1935. The section's first base at Port Hedland became operative on 10 October 1935, and the first medical flight was made on the opening day.

Tasmania Although emergency medical flights were operated in Tasmania going back as far as the 1930s, the Tasmanian Section of the Flying Doctor Service was the last section to be formed in 1960.

RFDS GROWTH STATISTICS

	1928	1948	1968	1988	2005
Number of Aircraft *	1		19	34	50
Number of Doctors	1			27	115
Number of Nurses				41	117
Patients Attended	225		43,562	102,554	234,783
Health Care Clinics			332	3,734	11,239
Aerial Evacuations			3,072	11,259	33,339
Number of Landings	50		2,959	24,379	57,857
Telehealth			21,163	24,748	73,694
Kilometres flown per year		320,461	1,863,611	7,392,128	19,524,359
Bases	1	8	14	16	20
Staff (F/T + P/T)				261	639

* In 1928 The aircraft was leased from Qantas. Up until the late 1950s/early 1960s many of the aircraft used by the RFDS were chartered rather than purchased

Sticks in the Mind

Well, all up, I was flying for forty-five years, and the last eighteen of those were with the Royal Flying Doctor Service. It was a marvellous time really, as well as a great way to finish one's flying career and, I must say, the RFDS were a great crowd to work for. They were just wonderful people. And it goes without saying that the people in the outback were marvellous as well; a hardy variety of Homo sapiens. Then, of course, we also had great aeroplanes to fly, particularly the turbo prop ones. And what tremendous machines, they were.

As far as stories go ... let me think: well, there's one that I've quoted before. Actually, it might've even appeared in a Flying Doctor publication at some stage of the game, but it's one that really sticks in the mind. It happened before we received our first King Air, so it was back while we were still flying the Queen Airs, which probably made it about 1983.

Anyway, we got an emergency call one night to go to a place called Cape Flattery. Cape Flattery's in far north Queensland, about 120 nautical miles up the coast from Cairns. It's where they have a big silica sand mine. In those days they used to bring the larger vessels in as close as they could to the little bay area behind the hill, then they'd take the silica sand out on smaller barges, called lighters, and load it up onto the larger ships with cranes and so forth.

But one vessel that came in on this particular day had a lot of Korean seamen on board and one of the unhappy fellows managed to get his hand and arm caught in a winch, which, I must add, is not something to be recommended. Actually, it might be more accurately described as exquisitely painful. So they called on us to go up there to get him. 'This feller, he's in a real bad way,' they said. 'His arm's shockingly damaged and he's bleeding badly.'

If we wouldn't have been able to take him out when we did, at the absolute minimum, he would've lost an arm, or else he probably would've been dead by the morning—RFDS

Of course, the weather had to be bad, didn't it? You know, it's Murphy's Law. You could put your money on it every time. I went with a Nursing Sister, Stone was her surname. So we took off in the Queen Air from Cairns, with this not-very-promising forecast, and as we got closer to Cape Flattery nothing improved. In fact, it got worse. When we arrived, the place was nothing but cloud and rain.

Now, Cape Flattery was just a sandy surface airstrip that ran sort of north-west/south-east, with a bunch of kerosene flares along each side to provide the light. There were no navigation aids there and, by now it was about eight o'clock at night and, being night-time, of course, that made it even worse. So I was faced with the immediate decision of: What do I do?

Anyhow, we went down to what they call 'the lowest safe altitude'. That's as low as you can go in cloud and still have a nice clear buffer from any of the surrounding high terrain. And, oh dear, it wasn't looking too good at all.

We had the radar on, which I had in weather mode just in case there were any storms amongst all this stuff, which, luckily, there weren't. It was mostly rain from stratiform cloud. So I turned the radar into mapping mode and picked up the coastline and the area around Cape Flattery and very quickly devised a circuit and an approach to the airfield, using the radar on the aeroplane. This particular action was not approved, of course, not at all. But under the circumstances, considering the condition of the bloke, I figured that the risk was worth taking. It was a calculated risk, put it that way.

Of course, I had escape clauses all the way along. There was absolutely no point in compounding the tragedy by ending up with a crashed aeroplane and two dead crew members: myself and Nursing Sister Stone. In a case like that, the final analysis, of course, doesn't help the patient at all.

So anyway, I worked out this circuit diagram and, by using the radar, I was able to track myself down to a downwind leg and a base leg and line myself up into where the radar indicated the runway should've been. So I started letting some flap down, and the gear extended, and in I came on a fairly low powered setting. So what you're doing is that you're bringing the speed back to— I forget what it was in the Queen Air—but it'd probably be approaching about 100 to 110 knots.

We didn't have a radar altimeter on board so we were just using the pressure altimeter. I'd already made the decision that, when we got to the 300 feet indicated then, if I didn't have visual siting it'd have to be, 'Well, sorry mate we've done our best. We'll just have to put on the power, pull the gear up, pull the flap up and go home.'

But would you believe, I was just about to say, 'Well that's it.' when lo and behold these dim runway lights appeared from these kerosene flares. So I plonked the Queen Air down, and I must say that it wasn't the most gentlemanly of arrivals. But that didn't matter. It was still pouring with rain and we sloshed our way down the strip. Then we turned around and taxied back up again and, I can tell you, there was a tremendously grateful group of people there, waiting for us, with this very, very sick Korean feller.

So we took him back to Cairns and they saved his arm, which was tremendous because, I mean, I'm no doctor but I'm guessing that if we hadn't been able to fly him out when we did, at an absolute minimum, he would've most certainly lost his arm, or else he probably would've been dead by the morning.

Stories about the Flying Doctor

Howdie,

I did my best to get some stories on the Flying Doctor. I have this letter from Etheen Burnett who was round in the Gulf Country but being well into her eighties and has had bad health for the last six months. Even so she has typed out these two stories in the hopes that you may be able to use them in your book if it be at all possible.

I have had no experience re: the Flying Doctor Service but I saw plenty of planes flying over me when I was droving out of the Gulf Country straight after the war, but never had to call them.

With the good roads and most of the places having their own planes now and of course with big four-wheel drive vehicles, I think all that may relieve the pressure on the Flying Doctor Service. But, I know that the Flying Doctor will always be there, picking up the pieces if called upon.

Regards

Jack

* * *

Etheen's letter

I remember one day my niece and I returning from the stock camp were told the Flying Doctor was due to land to see a patient from a neighbouring station. We quickly drove out to the air strip about three miles away to make sure there were no cattle on it. As we drove along it we noticed the plane landing on one end so we quickly drove off into thick grass on the side. My niece was standing on the running board and I had one arm on the door above the glass window.

No one noticed an ant hill in the long grass which we duly hit. What a jolt! My niece fell off the running board skinning her shin badly. My arm was cut by the glass and both of us were bleeding profusely when the Doctor got out of the plane. The patient whom he had come to see with a broken arm was there and on alighting the Doctor looked at us and asked which one is the patient? Of course we thought we would be okay but after three days my niece developed blood poisoning and had to be taken away by the Flying Doctor. She and I still have the scars of that accident.

* * *

When Dr Tim O'Leary was Flying Doctor in Mt Isa he was very particular about treating patients with dysentery especially children. He insisted only fluids and no solids whatsoever. One child he was treating did not seem to be improving so he flew out to see him. While examining him the child vomited and brought up fruit cake. Can you image what our Irish Doctor said!

The Crook Cocky

HG Nelson: HG Nelson with you on 'Summer All Over'. Now, you have some Flying Doctor info, Clinton.

Yeah, just a little story here, HG. Back in 1984 I was doing a bit of an outback adventure and I ended up in a little whistlestop town called Kajabbi, which is out near Mount Isa, sort of in the Cloncurry arca, in north-western Queensland. And I stayed there for a few days in the local pub. Now, when I say a township, basically, there was just a pub. That's all. There was nothing much else there, at Kajabbi, though I believe that, at one time, it was a rather large place but, over the years, it'd declined to the state of it being, more or less, just the hotel.

But the story is; I was in the bar at about eleven o'clock one mid-week morning. There were about four people in the bar and all the talk was around the doctor coming to town. And I was quite amazed. I thought, 'Well, what would a doctor be doing out here?' In my mind, of course, I was conjuring up ideas of a buckboard arriving and a doctor jumping out with an old medical bag—that type of thing.

Anyway, about twenty minutes later I heard the sound of an aircraft. It circled around overhead a few times and, along with everybody else, I went outside and, with drinks in hand, we all watched the aeroplane land on an airstrip, which was just in behind the hotel. When I say 'everybody else' I mean the whole four people that were in the bar.

Then about five or six minutes later a doctor came in and, by that time, a few more people had drifted into the pub. Now I believe that there was just the doctor, on his own, because I didn't see a pilot. So I assume he was piloting the aircraft himself. But anyway, by now I'd pieced it together that this was the Flying

Doctor who'd come to visit and that the pub was a regular stop for him; meaning that he came, like, once a fortnight or whatever, stopped off and all the people who wanted to see him would drop in at the pub for a medical consultation.

Anyway, the doctor disappeared out to a back room, followed by one guy and when the guy returned I noticed that he had a new dressing on his hand. After him, a couple of other people went out to the backroom for a while before returning to the bar. Then about ten minutes later the doctor, himself, came out into the bar and I saw a fellow go over and talk to him. And this fellow looked like he was of, some sort of, Indian extraction.

Now, I couldn't actually hear what the conversation was about but it seemed quite intense because this Indian fellow was nodding to the doctor in a very concerned fashion. Then, after a while, the Indian guy turned and he nodded to his wife and she went outside and, when she came back into the bar, she was carrying a cockatoo in a cage. It was a golden-crested, well, a silver- or sulphur-crested cockatoo. To explain, the lady, herself, I think she might've been of South Sea Islander extraction, with blonde hair. As I said, the husband looked like he was Indian. I found out later that he was Fijian Indian and, apparently, he and his wife had lived there, in Kajabbi, for many years.

So I'm sort of taking this all in and by now I'm thinking: surely the doctor's not going to look at the cockatoo, you know?

But anyway, the cockatoo came out of its cage and it got on this Islander lady's shoulder and I watched as the doctor went over and lifted its wings. Then after he'd taken a good look underneath each of the wings he lifted its comb up and took a check around its head area. Now, I was absolutely amazed that this aircraft had flown into this little country town and here was the Flying Doctor actually diagnosing a cockatoo.

HG: Oh, they can do anything, the Flying Doctor Service.

But I was just spellbound, H.G. I just couldn't believe it was happening. The whole scenario was just absolutely crazy. But

I was absolutely amazed that here was the Flying Doctor actually diagnosing a cockatoo—The Hansford Collection

anyway, after he'd checked over the cockatoo, the doctor spoke to the South Sea Islander woman for about four or five minutes then she thanked him very much for his expert advice. Then she popped the bird back into the cage and placed the cage on the bar.

The next thing I see is the hotel owner talking with the woman who had the cockatoo and out came a plastic bag and they put some crushed ice in the plastic bag and then they fattened it out, sealed the end off, put a few pegs on it, and sat the cockatoo's cage on top of this bag of ice. So I assume that the Flying Doctor had diagnosed that the cockatoo was suffering from heat stress and, believe me, it was very hot.

Then the doctor, well, he grabbed his gear and he disappeared out the back door. And I was amazed that everyone sort of automatically got up and, with drinks in hand, they wandered outside, to the back of the pub, and they watched as the Flying Doctor gunned the aeroplane up and down the airstrip and away he went out into the wide blue yonder.

But that always stuck in my mind. To think, well, you know, here in the middle of nowhere, which it was because Kajabbi is a long way outback, was the Flying Doctor arriving, not only to look after the local people—you know, to put a dressing on a guy who'd obviously hurt himself plus, probably, talk to a few other people—but also he gave service to this lady's, obviously, much-loved cockatoo, which, I may add, thanks to the Flying Doctor, is most possibly still alive and well at Kajabbi today.

The Easter Bunny

In total I worked with the Royal Flying Doctor Service for nine years. That was at both their Broken Hill and Dubbo bases. For much of that time I was employed as an Emergency Flight Nurse and well, in the end, I more or less left because I got married and we moved over here to Walgett, in the central north of New South Wales. That's the only reason why I finished up. But I really loved my time with the RFDS, and I actually kept a diary through the years I was working for them so I've looked up a few stories, if you're interested. I guess they're both about determination of spirit, but in very different ways. What's more, both incidents happened up at Tibooburra, in the far north-western corner of New South Wales.

Well first; one time we got a phone call from a very distressed husband up at Tibooburra. He told us that he'd delivered their last nine babies, all by himself, and there'd been no problems. That's right, nine! And he'd delivered every one of them. But now he said that he was having a bit of trouble delivering their tenth baby. His wife had been in labour for quite a while and, to make matters worse, she didn't want any medical help. In actual fact, she was adamant that there be no medical intervention. No doctors. Nothing. She wanted all home births—just natural—and that was that. No argument. So there he was, this distraught husband, hiding in the next room, out of earshot from his wife, whispering to us over the phone, 'The baby just won't come. What to do?'

From what he was telling us, we surmised it was probably a breech birth because it wasn't coming down well at all. Anyhow, we had a clinic plane in the area so we sent that out and, you know, they arrive and they went in to see how the wife was going and she gets very upset, particularly with her husband, because

199

he'd gone against her wishes and he's asked us to come in to help her. In fact, she's downright angry with him. She was still in labour at that stage and had been for a good twenty-four hours or so, which was very unusual for a tenth child. They should come, probably, within about an hour.

So they tried to settle her down and talk her into coming back down to Broken Hill with them to have the baby in the hospital there. Anyhow, much against her wishes, they eventually managed to coax her on the aircraft and I was in radio contact, waiting at the other end for them in Broken Hill.

There was little change during the flight but then, just as the clinic plane was coming into Broken Hill, they told me over the radio that they thought the baby was coming. So I was telling them what to do and where to find the delivery packs on the aircraft. Still and all, she hadn't had the baby by the time they landed so I got straight onto the aircraft and helped the woman out into the waiting ambulance. Even at that stage she was still complaining about our intervention.

Then, just as we were going over the bridge on our way to the Broken Hill Hospital, we delivered a breech baby in the back of the ambulance. So, we ended up with a hell of a mess and I virtually finished cleaning up the baby and the woman in the ambulance bay of the Broken Hill Hospital.

Now, once the placenta is delivered the mother, more or less, stops bleeding and she can stay fairly comfortable. Anyhow, after I'd cleaned everything up, I turned around to the woman and I said, 'Look, how about we just take you into the hospital and get you checked out?'

But the attitude of the woman hadn't changed one little bit. 'No, no,' she said, 'it's alright.' And she packed the placenta up and she wrapped the baby up and she wandered off to get a taxi downtown so that she could catch the next bus straight back to Tibooburra.

I tell you, it's amazing some of the mums you come across. She was a tough one, alright. And this was her tenth child. But I did feel for her poor husband. I imagine he would've been in the bad books for quite a while, after she got home.

So that was one incident, and the second one was ... well, actually, you do have to laugh at times, don't you? As I said, it's another one about the strength of spirit but, in a very different and funny sort of way.

This happened around Easter time and we got a call from the bemused nurses up at Tibooburra saying that they'd just been out in the ambulance and picked up a man who'd been wandering down the Barrier Highway in quite a distressed state. Now, it was extremely hot at the time and, as it turned out, this man was schizophrenic and he'd either broken out, or got out, of a Psychiatric Hospital near Morisset, which is just south of Newcastle, on the central coast of New South Wales. How on earth he found his way out to Tibooburra, I couldn't tell you. I wouldn't have a clue.

Anyhow, he'd told the nurses at Tibooburra that the reason why he was in the area was that he was off to pick pears. Now, mind you, we are talking about the far north-western corner of New South Wales and, as you might imagine, the nearest pear orchard could've been anywhere up to a thousand or so kilometres away. So I think he was in the wrong place.

But, that's not all. What really got the nurses going was that this poor man was not only off to pick pears but he'd also somehow got it in his head that he was the Easter Bunny. So when they found him, he was walking down the road stark naked,

He'd somehow got it into his head that he was the
Easter Bunny—The Hansford Collection

apart from wearing his underpants on his head and, for added effect, he'd stuck a carrot up where he shouldn't have—up his rectum. But the nurses said that he wasn't violent or anything because, apparently, when they went out to get him, they simply stopped and asked him if he'd like to hop in the back of the ambulance and in he hopped, no problem at all.

Anyhow, first of all, we found out where this man's father was and contacted him because we thought he might be worried about his missing son. But when we got onto his father and explained the circumstances all he said was, 'Yes, he does that kind of thing, quite a bit. You should've seen what he did last Christmas.'

So then, we flew out to get him and we took him back to Sydney and, again, he got in the plane, no problems at all. But, oh, he was totally off the planet. He had no idea where he was or who he was, other than believing he'd come out to Tibooburra to pick pears and that he was the Easter Bunny. And, what's more, there was no way he was going to let us take his underpants off his head or take the carrot out of his rectum. In his mind, he was the Easter Bunny and that was it. So he stayed that way the whole trip back to Sydney. But you'd think it'd be uncomfortable, wouldn't you, particularly with the carrot.

The Flying Padre's Story

You may well ask, What connection does an American have with the Australian Royal Flying Doctor Service? Well, to begin with my wife, Becky, is one of several Americans who have worked for the RFDS. She's currently the Tourist Facility Supervisor at the Broken Hill base. The Museum there also identifies Reverend Doctor John Flynn's ethos of a Mantle of Safety to serve the people of the outback. That not only includes pilots, doctors and nurses, but also ministers on patrol. Over the years these padres have travelled by everything from camel, bicycle, motorbike, and automobile—as Flynn's successor, Reverend Fred McKay did in an old International truck. Then there have been a few more fortunate ones, like myself, who fly an aeroplane. I'm known as a Flying Padre. I can reach a destination in hours where, in earlier days, it could've taken days or even weeks.

I'm the seventh Flying Padre, with the Uniting Church's Far-West Ministry—currently in its fortieth year. I am currently flying our third aircraft, a 1974 high-wing, single-engine Cessna 182, which is a great aeroplane for remote airstrips and extreme conditions.

But before I tell my story, just a bit of background. I'm originally from Cedar Rapids, Iowa, USA, which is where you'll find industries such as Quaker Oatmeal and Collins Radio. My first love was aviation but, at the age of eighteen, when I took my physical for the 'draft' I was told, 'Sorry, you measure 203 centimetres. We can't take you for the Air Force or any of the services because you're just too tall.'

Then, when I got on the bus to return back home, I remember very clearly asking myself, so what else do you want to do with your life? And an internal voice—and I suppose it had greater dimensions—replied, Well, I've always liked church. I'll go into church work. It wasn't an angry voice but more of an okay, God, you win, take me kind of thing. So that was the way I decided to go.

Then Becky and I met at university, after she'd returned from a Brazilian high school exchange. She saw me singing in a musical group for their orientation week. Then in the second week I met her at a church coffee house. It was love at first sight. That night, I walked her home, and I've been walking her home ever since. We married in 1969.

Becky was also aware of my passion for aviation. My first posting, following seminary, was to a small village up near the Canadian border. There was a little airport and flight instructor in Milan, New Hampshire. So when Becky got a job as a State Social Worker, it was just a case of, 'Hey, we've got a little money. Go get your flying lessons.' Six hours of lessons later I flew my solo and I finished my licence in quick time.

But we soon learned that hot summers were short, usually only a week or two, and the long, dark nights of winter could last for months. It could reach forty degrees below zero [Fahrenheit!] and it seemed like shovelling snow was everyone's hobby. I could tell you about the time I tried to keep the Volkswagen's engine oil warm overnight. I was advised to plug in a light bulb by the engine, then put a blanket over it. Not only was the oil warmed but, a couple of hours later, the blanket and the car caught fire. The good news is that, conveniently, there was snow everywhere and we saved the car by throwing snow on the engine compartment. I could also tell you about the nails in that house becoming so cold in the dead of winter that they'd contract and pop like pistols being fired at close range. Ministry can be so exciting!

So, it was a difficult two years for us. The highlight was my learning to fly and organising a successful 1974 air show. Four groups benefited: our own Methodist parish, an orphanage in South Carolina, the Catholic Church down the road, and Father Tony Gendusa, a flying priest in Rabaul, PNG [Papua New Guinea].

However, before another New Hampshire winter came Becky and I would move to Melbourne, Australia, where we thawed, retrained and tested ourselves in many ways. I had accepted a hospital chaplaincy internship at the Austin Hospital, Heidelberg. After eighteen months, I happily moved on to teach at St Leonard's College, in East Brighton. Becky worked at Trans-Australia Airlines.

After two and a half years living in Australia we moved back to the States, to Atlanta, Georgia, where our son, Matt, was born. Then when my residency in pastoral counselling was finished, I became the Director of the Atlanta District Counselling Service. It gave me eight years of building skills, which would come in very handy later. We left 'Hotlanta' for central New Hampshire for seven more years of good pastoral town and rural country work before I ended up serving as a Church Pastor near Boston, Massachusetts.

Boston was a tough placement especially when you see churches losing their vision and wearing down their memberships. You could liken it to when someone you love loses their way. So, for a break, we came over to Australia for holidays. We were at Narromine, in central New South Wales, visiting the parents of an Australian friend who was studying in Boston, and I remember as we drove past the local airport, on the way to the Dubbo Zoo, our friend's father asked, 'What's your hobby?' And I told him that I truly loved flying and church work.

'Well,' he replied, 'you know, we've got a Flying Padre position open in Broken Hill.'

And I asked three questions: 'What's a Flying Padre?', 'Who broke Broken Hill?' and 'Where do I apply?' Then it took eight months or so but everything got resolved and we started work in Broken Hill on 1 May 2002. And though tragedies do happen, the job's a delight; the people have been absolutely wonderful. Here in the outback, I don't have to shovel snow, and I haven't set fire to my automobile ... not yet, anyway.

Now, to my story: I was minding my business one cold and blustery Sunday in, gosh, I think it was back in September 2003, when the news first reported that Mrs Luscombe had gone missing. She was a Broken Hill resident who suffered from dementia. She lived alone, on the south side, near the Broken Hill Airport, where a carer, a neighbour and some relatives kept an eye on her.

Becky and me beside The Flying Padre's Cessna—Reverend John Blair

Every day she'd walk part of the perimeter of the airport with her dog, Dazzie, a blue heeler cross, and occasionally a neighbour's dog would join them. But when Mrs Luscombe hadn't shown up by dark a neighbour became concerned, even more so when the neighbour's dog returned home alone. Basically, all Mrs Luscombe was wearing for weather protection that day was a light jacket. So the police were called, the relatives were notified and a full-blown ground search was organised that Sunday evening.

Becky's office, at the RFDS base, was just a stone's throw from the search headquarters at the airport. So, with still no sign of Mrs Luscombe by Monday morning, after dropping Becky off at work, I stopped in and—as a New South Wales Regional Police Chaplain—I offered to fly my Cessna in an aerial search. I was well aware that people had previously gone missing into the vast surrounding desert, never to be seen again. It was an urgent situation.

Because of Mrs Luscombe's condition, she wore a signal-emitting necklace that sent out a beep, beep, beep to a tuned receiver. One of the relatives said that they had put fresh batteries in the necklace. We only hoped that she was still wearing it. So I got into my Cessna with a couple of SES people who had a radio and an antenna receiver system to track the necklace. We took off and spiralled south and north from the airport, thinking that Mrs Luscombe and Dazzie, the dog, were more likely to head toward town rather than going out in the bush. But, after two-and-a-half-hours without a response from our receiver I thought, well, surely they'll find her in their wide-cast ground search.

But, you know, the ground search continued on Tuesday then on the Wednesday and still without any sign of her. By Friday morning the weather had warmed up and I got a Police Search Director's call saying, 'Look, we're going to have to shut down the search but, for the sake of the family, would you mind taking just one more aerial run?'

I was happy to do that. They double-checked the radio equipment to make sure everything was working properly. It was another very windy day and I wanted to go slowly to do a visual search as well. I started my increasing spirals and then laps on the southern side at about 700 feet above the ground. Then we were about 10 or 12 miles south of Broken Hill when Josh, the chap who had the signal meter said, 'Turn left!' So I did and he called out, 'Mark it.'

Then, Leslie, the SES volunteer in the back of the Cessna, marked the latitude and longitude from her hand-held GPS. We did this four times, from different directions, measuring the numbers each time. Below us were two water-filled dams and a couple of power lines. Being windy I wanted to avoid getting fried on the wires, but I got down as low as possible and when I saw something of colour in the water, my first thought was, Gee, I hope that's not her.

At this stage, because we were just tracking a piece of jewellery that might've popped off as she'd walked along, we couldn't positively confirm if we'd found Mrs Luscombe or not. When we landed back at the search base we marked out the spot on a map and handed copies to the ground searchers. Then I waited on the ground for another 10 minutes before I overflew the motorbike searchers and others and I circled the exact spot to give them direction. And that's where they located Mrs Luscombe, lying near the dam.

By the time I landed back at the airport I still hadn't heard the actual outcome. But as I was tying the Cessna down, one of the ground staff, who was nicked-named 'Flies', came over and his voice broke as he said, 'They found her ... and she's alive!'

I was then informed that Mrs Luscombe had been found lying in a roughly dug hole, dehydrated, sunburned and semi-conscious, though still communicative. But because of the rough terrain, the SES people had to get a four-wheel drive vehicle in there to retrieve her. From there she was driven with as much care as possible to a waiting ambulance, before going on to hospital. So we all felt pretty good and when I returned to the search headquarters, the extremely anxious family was now shedding tears of relief and happiness.

So that's how Mrs Luscombe was found. I believe she's now living in Adelaide with family, and has had extra years of life, care and love. And with the Uniting Church Flying Patrol celebrating its fortieth year, what a memory that particular event is for me. And to think that it's the same satisfaction felt, almost daily, by the Flying Doctors' staff. I just wish everyone could be a part of such an experience.

But, of course, Dazzie, the dog, was the real hero. Apparently, it was he who'd led Mrs Luscombe to water. Then, when a hole was dug, that faithful dog had laid on top of her to keep her warm enough to avoid freezing.

Now, don't quote me on this. But I heard a story sometime later that one of the family came to visit Mrs Luscombe and because she was a victim of dementia, naturally, they didn't want to scold her for what had happened. But quite understandably, the family member said to her, 'You know, you really gave us a fright.'

And in a moment of clarity, I understand Mrs Luscombe's response was, 'Well, you know, I didn't have such a good week either.'

The Souvenir

In 1958 I was working up on the west coast of the Cape York Peninsula at a place called Rutland Plains Station, which is about 180 mile north of Normanton. The property, itself, was about 15 or 16 hundred square mile, and it bordered on an Aboriginal settlement, up on the Mitchell River, called Kowanyama.

Now, I did two long droving trips that year, of about five weeks each, taking bullocks from Kowanyama, down the Mungana stock route to the railhead at Mungana. Anyhow, just before the last trip we were mustering up some 800 bullocks and the Head Stockman from Rutland, well, he came to me on the quiet and he said, 'Now, Goldie, I could use a feller like you, so there's a job here after yer've delivered this mob, if you'd like it.'

Good. That was fine by me but then, during the droving trip, one of my molars—I forget now if it was a pre-molar or a back

I did two long droving trips that year—Stockmans Hall of Fame

molar, but, anyway—it started aching. And I tell you what, if you've got a toothache while you're out droving and you just can't go to sleep, you generally end up doing a night watch for someone else, you know. But anyway, after we had the bullocks trucked at Mungana, I came back to Rutland to work there and, at that stage, the molar wasn't quite as bad.

But then, after about another three months, this toothache came back and it began getting worse and worse until, eventually, an abscess grew on it and I had a huge swollen jaw. And, you know, with all the pain, you try everything from putting tobacco in the thing or if you drink enough brandy or whisky that deadens it sometimes, and cloves, they're good, too.

At that time we were at a mustering camp on Rutland Plains Station named One Mile, which was about 15 mile from the homestead. It was called the One Mile because it was one mile from the Kowanyama boundary. So the Station Manager from Rutland said that my best chance would be for me to catch up with the Flying Doctor at the Kowanyama Aboriginal settlement, on his next monthly clinic visit.

'Okay,' I mumbled. 'Good.' Then he told me to ride into Rutland Homestead on such and such day and he'd drive me the 20-odd miles over to the settlement to meet the Flying Doctor.

Well, the day finally arrived and I rode into the homestead and the manager drove me over. It was dark when we got to Kowanyama and the doctor, Tim O'Leary, his name was, well, he had all these Murries—that's what they called the local Aborigines—he had them all lined up, giving them injections, checking them over and so forth, doing a clinic. Now, Tim was a great character and a very well-known and liked doctor with the Royal Flying Doctor Service, and after he'd finished treating all the Murries, I remember the manager saying to him, 'Tim, I've got a white stockman here, Jack Goldsmith, aged twenty-four and he's got a jaw like a lumpy jaw bullock.' Lumpy jaw's a disease that bullocks get.

'So you're Jack Goldsmith?' Tim O'Leary said.

And I said, 'Hello, so what have you heard?'

Then he gave a sort of grin. 'Oh, only rumours,' he said, 'just rumours.' Then, he said, 'Okay, let's have a look at this tooth.' And after he had a bit of a poke around he said, 'I shouldn't even attempt to pull that molar. It's got an abscess on it and a bad one at that.'

'Well,' I said, 'I'm not leaving here until it's out.' And I tell you, I wasn't going to budge an inch until that molar was gone.

Anyhow, he says, 'Okay then, I'll give it a go. Sit on that box.' And there was this box alongside a post in the building; just a wooden box, you know, about 70 pound or 50 pound, in weight. It's what they used to put butter into.

'Take your belt off,' Tim said.

Now, I didn't know what he was on about but I took me belt off, anyway, and I gave it to him. Then he got the belt and he tied my head to the post, by the forehead, so I couldn't move. So he strapped my head to the post, and then he started to work on the tooth, with just a huge pair of pliers, under the light of a dull globe, hanging down from the ceiling. And he pushed and he pulled and he yanked it this way and that way. I doubt if he even used anaesthetic and, if he did, it didn't do nothing to ease the pain. By this stage I was starting to feel pretty faint with it all, I can tell you. But the molar wouldn't budge.

Now, there was some Murries still there and they were watching all these goings on, and all with a bit of a smirk on their dials. But I had to put on a brave face, see, because I had a big rep up in that country because I used to mill a lot; you know, scrap around and brawl and fight and all that. So all these Murries reckoned I was real tough, except I wasn't, especially when Tim really started getting stuck into me with the pliers. Oh, he was huffing and puffing and pulling this way and that until I could feel the crunching sound of my molar and jaw. Now, I don't know if you can go numb with pain, but I reckon that I did. And then I started sweating all over and going from pale to paler and all this while these Murries were looking at me like they were enjoying every moment of it.

Anyhow, Tim eventually got it out. And I tell you what, I can still remember it. There he was, Doctor Tim O'Leary, standing there with this huge, bloodied tooth in his pliers, holding it up to the dull light and saying, 'No wonder it was so difficult to get out. Look,' he said, 'the roots are crossed.'

And apparently, when the roots are crossed, half of your jaw comes out with the molar. So there Tim was, looking very proud of himself, and he turned to me and he said, 'And what's more, that's only the second tooth I've ever pulled.'

'Well then, keep it fer a souvenir,' I replied, half jokingly.

So that was one of my experiences with the RFDS, and that was with Doctor Tim O'Leary, back in 1958. And for the life of me, I don't know where that molar ended up. I never saw it again after that, so I reckon he might've taken my word and kept it as a souvenir, aye.

The Spirit of the Bush

My name is Esther and I am the first female pilot of the Royal Flying Doctor Service within the Central Division. That is only the Central Division because, as you might be aware, the RFDS already, I believe, has had a female pilot over in Western Australia, somewhere, and also there has been another female pilot up in Queensland. I was just reading the book again the other day and the Queensland pilot, her name was Beth Garrett. Her husband initially worked for the RFDS in Queensland and he died, and years later, I think it must've been in the late 1960s, she started flying there. So she was one of the real pioneering women doing it.

But for me; how did I get to become a pilot for the RFDS. Well, it is a long story. I was three months old, initially, when I first came to Australia from Holland with my parents, and we lived here till I was the age of four. Then we lived for two years back in Holland and then we went to the United Arab Emirates for a few years and to Nigeria, to Holland a bit again then back to Australia. And the last time when we just landed here in Australia, in 1989, in July, I literally come off the plane and we drove from the airport to where Dad had a home in Sydney and I just looked around and I thought, I'm home. This is it. Australia is my home.

But my parents, they left again after another four-year stint in this country and, of course, I stayed and it took me in total six years to get my permanent residency, and I got stuck here, and I have no regrets at all. I love it.

Then in 1996, after I got my pilot's licence in Bankstown, Sydney, I went looking for the 'famous first flying job'. I had planned to look as far as Sydney to Dubbo but I ended up in Darwin, and the further I got into the outback the more I loved it. So yeah, that was it. I was hooked with the outback.

But to get a job with the RFDS, it was just through a lot of experience in different areas of flying and general aviation. I've worked in the Northern Territory in places like Arnhem Land, Darwin, Kununurra. I've done night freight from the big cities like Sydney to Brisbane and Melbourne and I was also based in Queensland doing what they call bank runs. That's where all the documentation from the bank is needed to be back to their state office, or their head office, at the end of each day. So from the smaller towns, all over Australia, you've got all these aeroplanes that leave at six in the morning and they deliver, not just bank documents but also overnight freight. Then at four in the afternoon they backtrack their steps before they return to the main city again. And that happens all over Australia.

Over that time, already, I'd applied to all the Flying Doctor bases, Australia-wide, and one day the Chief Pilot from the Central Division in Adelaide was nice enough to call me up and say, 'You have an interview.'

By the time I got there, Norm just came up to the door straight away and said, 'How fantastic.' He said, 'You are the first female pilot I am meeting.'—RFDS

So here I am at the Royal Flying Doctor base, at Port Augusta, at the top of Spencer Gulf, in South Australia. I've been here now for about eight months and the Central Division covers anywhere from Adelaide to Tennant Creek, in central Northern Territory, and from over near the West Australian border which, I think, Cook is the nearest place, then over to about Mildura, which is into north-western Victoria. I think, off the top of my head, it is something like 840,000 square kilometres. But of course, we have a Flying Doctor's base in Alice Springs and another base in Adelaide, so we only do the area south-east of the Riverland if Adelaide is busy doing other stuff and we only go up to Alice Springs sometimes, because they always cover their own area.

The plane I fly is a Pilatus PC XII. They are our newer aeroplanes. It has a single-engine turbo prop so they're a cheaper plane to operate than our previous plane, the King Air, which has a twin turbo prop. The PC XIIs have a shorter land and take-off than our King Air's do, so they have become a great success. And I think that the South Australian section of the RFDS has got the highest flight time of PC XIIs anywhere in the world. But they're very expensive, up around five or six million dollars, all fitted out. That's why we were doing some fundraising at a rodeo last night. Every little bit helps.

But I was very accepted as a female pilot. It has been great. In the first few weeks I was working in Port Augusta one of my first night shifts I was on, I was sent to Peterborough, which is about 150 kilometres south-east of Port Augusta. As we do at Peterborough, the lights need to be put on by an Airport Manager. The Airport Manager at this time was Norm. So the Coms [communications] people here in Port Augusta contacted Norm saying when we are expected to be in to Peterborough and he would go out and turn on the lights. And apparently the Coms people, when they were talking to Norm, they were saying about 'she' and 'her' in regards to the pilot. So by the time I got there, Norm just came up to the door straight away and said, 'How fantastic.' He said, 'You are the first female pilot I am meeting.'

That was so nice and a few weeks later there was an article in the *Peterborough Times* about, you know, the first female pilot working here, and Norm was such a gentleman that he actually made a copy of it and sent it to the base here in Port Augusta. So that was just a really lovely reception and a good thing to remember. But it was very funny that, often in the beginning, people would come up to me and start talking about the patient as if I am supposed to be the flight nurse. Of course, by now, I think most people are used to me being the pilot.

But the outback people are the most wonderful, and their support for the Royal Flying Doctor Service is just absolutely fantastic. I was saying that I was at a rodeo just last night and the RFDS had a little tent there and they were being supported by the people. Wherever you are, it's just amazing. You know, it makes me almost always so proud to be part of it because I can be just going on a four-wheel drive trip on my own and you meet some people and they say, 'Oh, where do you live and what do you do?'

And I say, 'I live in Port Augusta and I am a pilot with the RFDS.'

Well, the people just look at you and they go, 'Oh, that must be such a fantastic job, working for the RFDS.'

And anybody, whether they are German or Japanese or Australian people they all have heard about it. It's like there's some sort of invisible communication out there, in the outback, and that was what John Flynn was fascinated about too. Even though, of course, nowadays, you do have different means of communication, the attitude in the bush is still just amazing.

I remember when I came from Broken Hill to Port Augusta for the first-time interview and I came through the mountains from Wilmington, and the mountains were nice and green and as soon as we got over the mountains everything was that yellow dead colour. Then five kilometres further on you see the power station and then there's Port Augusta, and I loved it just so much that I said, 'If things would change, or anything like that, I might just buy a little farm here, up in the hills near Wilmington.'

And I was just talking to the organiser last night, at the rodeo, about it and she asked me, 'Why would you like a little farm?'

'It's always been my dream,' I said, 'to have a little farm with a few horses, you know.'

And she said, 'Oh well, if you get any horses, you don't need to buy a farm. I've got 2000 acres. You can just put them up there.'

You know, where else in the world would someone just offer land like that to another person? It's as if it was, 'Oh, don't worry about it. Take some of mine.'

So I said, 'You must be joking. I could not do this.'

She said, 'No, I mean it.' She said, 'If you have a horse and you want to put it somewhere, give me a call and you can put it up on my land.'

It was like the most normal thing ever, you know. And where would you come across anything like that? I think only in Australia, in the bush. It's the spirit of the bush. It was just so simple an offer, but so very nice.

The Tangle with the Motorbike

I'd actually moved from Adelaide to Western Australia. Then my ex-boyfriend had a friend who was a real estate agent in Katherine and, this real estate agent, she needed someone to look after a station property that she was selling in Arnhem Land. So yeah, we decided to do that and so we flew up there, out to Mountain Valley Station, up in the Top End of the Northern Territory.

But at Mountain Valley I was doing little bits of everything and I didn't like that too much. I even ended up being the cook and I didn't really enjoy cooking. I wanted to find some place where I could get involved with the mustering and everything, so I ended up going down to Mittiebah Station to work there. Mittiebah's in the Barkly Tablelands area of the Northern Territory. It's about 1.8 million acres, so I got to do some mustering and stuff like that, and no cooking.

Out at Mittiebah they had composite cattle; it's like Brahman and Shorthorn Cross and then they second cross with something else. It's basically just a whole lot of different types of cattle that are bred to get what they want as far as beef quality and temperament and stuff goes. And, also, we were trialling a different sort of technique where we don't try and stress the cattle out too much. It's like low-stress cattle-handling. Because if you get them all agitated they'll get stressed out and start to lose condition, and that's the last thing you want. So we weren't allowed to use dogs or stockwhips or any poles or anything like that and we weren't even supposed to make too much noise in the yards or anything.

Actually, I haven't learnt all that much about it yet, because of my accident. But we're doing a course this year where you learn to use pressure release and make the cattle work off you. Pressure release is when, say, the cattle are all in a mob, in the corner, and you want them to go through the gate. Well, you've just got to walk in on them and once they start moving, you back off and they'll go through the gate. Of course, if you educate the cattle they're a lot easier to handle and they sort of know what to do and so they work off you. We still use horses and motorbikes and stuff, but the horses are easy on them and, though the motorbikes make a bit of noise, I don't think they stress them out too much, either.

But about the accident—the tangle with the motorbike—that happened on 12 December 2005. I was riding a Honda XR 250 at the time and I was mustering some cattle with my Overseer, Mike. Anyway, Mike and I, we'd sort of done one back bit of the paddock and we were pushing the cattle—the bulls—up along the fence line. They'd settled pretty well, so Mike decided to leave me with that lot and go and get the next mob of cattle from the other side of the paddock. Then, yeah, we were going to meet at a fenced-in bit called 'the cooler', where we could hold them on water. Probably they call it the cooler because that's where the water is and the cattle can cool down there. It's certainly not a meat cooler.

So, I was pushing these bulls along, then I left the fence line and I took the bike out around the mob a bit and, while I was doing that, I hit a hole. But because I was only going very slow I decided to give the bike a few revs to jump it out of the hole but, when I did, the bike stalled. So then I put my leg down to try and hold the motorbike upright but, because I was in the hole, the bike rolled back and I lost balance and it fell on me. At first I didn't realise what had happened because my initial thought was, 'Oh, I've gotta get the bike off me.'

But then, when I tried lifting the bike, I noticed that my jeans were ripped up around the area of my inner-left thigh. So I had a look and, yeah, there was the clutch lever stuck right into my leg.

Anyhow, I still had to try and lift the bike up and pull the clutch leaver out of my thigh. And I was really worried about doing that because I thought that, when I pulled it out there might be a great spurt of blood or something because, maybe, I'd cut the main artery that's there. So that was the first thing I thought of, the blood spurting out, and I sort of freaked out a bit about that.

But anyway, yeah, I eventually pulled the clutch leaver out of my thigh and no blood spurted out. That was good because it meant that the main artery wasn't broken. Perhaps it was only just sort of punctured or something. The cut, or the gash, in my thigh was about seven centimetres by four centimetres. That's what the doctor told me later, anyway. And yeah, there wasn't much blood at all, so I was really lucky with that.

But, just to be safe, I ripped the sleeve off my shirt and I tied it around my leg to act like a tourniquet. I was thinking that that was what I was supposed to do, though I found out later it's what you're not supposed to do at all. But I didn't know that at the time, so I tied the ripped shirt sleeve around my leg and then my idea was to get back on the motorbike and ride home, back to the station. The only trouble was that, when I tried to stand up, I couldn't put any weight on my leg, so then I was stuck out there.

As I said, I was still off the fence line, but I did manage to get over there and put my helmet on the fence, like on a picket, because I thought that was the only way they'd find me, by seeing the helmet on the fence. And then I just went back and crawled under a native berry bush because I knew that when Mark reached the cooler with his cattle and saw that I hadn't arrived yet, he'd realise there was something wrong.

So, I just waited there in the shade of the berry bush and, naturally, Mark came back along the fence line looking for me and when he found the cattle but not me, he really got a bit worried. So he kept on coming along the fence line and, it was just as well that I'd put the helmet on the fence because, when Mark got there, he didn't see me, but he saw the helmet. So he stopped there and had a bit of a look around and, yeah, that's when he found me.

But when he asked me what was wrong, I didn't want to freak him out too much, so I just said, 'Oh, I've just cut myself and I can't stand the bike up.'

'That's okay,' he said, 'I'll stand the bike up.'

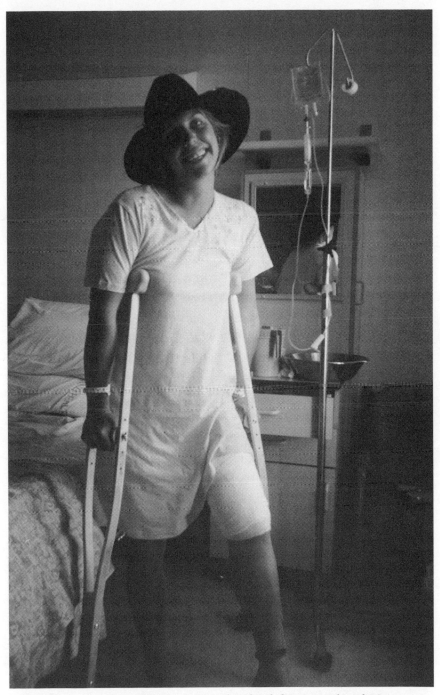

So I had a look and, yeah, there was the clutch lever, stuck right into my thigh—'Myf' Spencer-Smith

Then I said, 'Oh, and when we get back, I might have to go to town, though.'

'Why?' he said.

And I pulled my jeans over a bit so he could have a look and he goes, 'Oh fuck, Myf.' And he nearly vomited. He said, like, 'Don't worry about the bike, you stay there and I'll go and get help.'

Then he rode back to the station and he got the Bore Runner, which is the dude that checks all the bores on the station and the Bore Runner came to get me in one of his bore utes, and he also brought along a big bottle of water, thank goodness. Then, because the bore ute's got a big 900 litre diesel tank on the back and there's not much room, the Bore Runner, he got me in the front of his ute. It's got like a bench seat and so I sort of lent against him and stuck my leg out the window for the trip back.

Yeah, so then the Bore Runner, he took me back to the station and he put me on the table in the kitchen and everyone started coming in to have a good look, while they were having a cup of tea. But the cook there, Kay, she had some sort of nursing training so she took over then. The first thing she decided to do was to cut my jeans off and I was a bit freaked out about that because I don't wear undies when I work. It's more comfortable, that way. And so I was freaking out, like, because there's a couple of guys in the kitchen and I'm, like, whispering, 'Hey, Kay, I don't wear undies.'

So Kay got everyone to leave the kitchen and then she cut my jeans off to see just what damage had been done. While she was doing that the others had been on the phone, calling the Flying Doctor and all that sort of thing to find out what they needed to do. Apparently the doctor told them that I was meant to have morphine, which I didn't have. I didn't want it anyway, because I wasn't in that much pain. Well, I didn't really have that much time to think about the pain and so, maybe, that's why it didn't hurt just then. So yeah, Kay just tried to dress the wound as best she could and they said that the RFDS were going to send a plane out to get me.

But then there was some sort of complication about flying out to pick me up—and I can't quite remember what it was—but our airstrip was just a graded strip and, maybe, there was something wrong with it, like it'd rained the day before and it was too wet to land an aeroplane on it or something. So they decided to drive me over to the station next door, to Alexandria Station, where they had a really big, all-purpose airstrip. The same company owned both Mittiebah and Alexandria Stations. So we jumped in the car and it was about an hour's drive over there, I think.

Anyway, the RFDS arrived at Alexandria Station and they picked me up and then, while they were flying me over to Mount Isa, they had a close look at the leg and, yeah, there was still heaps of dirt and stuff in the hole in my thigh so they just sort of redressed it and then put a drip in me, just for liquid.

Oh, and they also asked me if I wanted some morphine, but I said, 'No, I'm okay,' because I didn't really have any pain until I was nearly at Mount Isa, and that's when it really hit. Still, I wasn't really keen on that sort of thing. But anyway they said, 'Well, it's better to get the morphine into you now, before the pain gets worse, otherwise it takes too much morphine to get it back down again.'

So they gave me one millilitre of morphine then and, when that didn't do anything, they gave me another two millilitres.

Yeah, so then I arrived at Mount Isa and they took me by ambulance from the airport to the hospital. I think the accident happened at about one o'clock in the afternoon and I left Alexandria Station just after four o'clock, maybe, and we got into Mount Isa at about six at night. I can't really be sure about that because I didn't have a watch or anything, but that's what I told the hospital people, anyway.

Then the next day, they cleaned out the wound in surgery. I don't know too much about what happened there because they knocked me out, thank goodness. But apparently they had to, like, really open the wound up to get into it, to scrub all the dirt and rubbish out of the hole in my thigh. And after they'd done all that, they packed the hole back up with seaweed. I really don't know what the significance of the seaweed was but I think it was to help with the healing somehow. Then five days later I went back into surgery and they took out the seaweed and stitched it all up. But then the terrible heat up there, in Mount Isa, got to it, which made it worse there for a while.

Yeah, so I had twelve stitches along the top there, inside my left thigh. And the accident happened on 12 December 2005, only about a week before I was supposed to leave Mittiebah Station, which was a bit unfortunate. But, yeah, that's about it. So there you go. Cool!

Too Late

When you go out to live in a place like Wittenoom, up in the north of Western Australia, you soon realise that you're a long way from anywhere. Like, it's not the sort of place where you can just get up and wander down the street to go and visit the doctor; though, I think at one time, they used to have a doctor come over from Tom Price once every so often and—in the hope that he'd keep up the service—everyone in town would front up and pretend that they had something wrong with them. But when that ended, then the Royal Flying Doctor Service virtually took over the medical side of things.

The first dealings that I had with the RFDS was through my brother. He was running tours of the gorges, out from Wittenoom, and everyday the Flying Doctor base at Port Hedland would call, just to check that everything was okay. My brother had two vehicles so, if he was out on tour, at a certain given time the Flying Doctor base would call me and I'd just answer, 'Whisky ... go ... go' or whatever. I just can't remember what my call signal was now. But that was my first experience.

Flying out of Port Hedland—The Hansford Collection

Then I became a member of the Wittenoom St John's Ambulance. We had a pretty old ambulance and there were just a few locals and we'd get called out if there was an accident or whatever. Like, at one time, a man was riding a motorbike up the gorge, with his girlfriend as a pillion. They were from the caravan park. He was sixty-six and she was sixty-four, I think. Anyway, a kangaroo jumped out and hit him. Bang, over they went and he broke his tibia and fibula.

Luckily, both the girlfriend and the motorbike weren't too badly damaged so the girlfriend rode into town, in the moonlight. She wasn't a small lady either, and she went to the power house, where the generators were, and the guy there called us. So out we went in the old ambulance to find this bikie. Anyhow, we patched him up the best we could and got him back to town then we called the Flying Doctor to fly out and pick him up. So that was one occasion.

But even I had to use the Flying Doctor. See, we'd had a lot of rain and the creeks were flooded right near the town so I drove out for a swim with the dog. Anyway, when I got out of the car, I felt this sting on my leg. At first I didn't take much notice, but went I hopped in the water, all my hands and feet started burning. I knew something was wrong then, so I hopped back in the car and drove straight back to town. By the time I got back home I was in a real mess. As it turned out, I'd been bitten by a marsh fly. I think that's what they're called ... or maybe it's a march fly. They're like big blow flies that come around after the rain and, as I found out, I'm extremely allergic to their bite.

So I raced inside and called the Flying Doctor. We had a RFDS medical chest in town; you know, one of those huge boxes that contain all the various medications and so forth, which, mind you, you were supposed to check regularly, just to make sure nothing was out of date. Anyhow, the doctor said to get some Phenergan: that's an antihistamine. So the girl that had the medical chest, I called her and she brought some Phenergan over and gave it to me.

'There you go, that should fix it,' she said.

But it didn't because the itch—the irritation—didn't go away, at all. Then she took a look at the Phenergan and said, 'Oh, this's only a child's dosage and, what's more, it's out of date.'

So then I had to call the doctor back again and he was very upset. 'Well,' he said, 'is there anyone there that can give you an adrenalin injection?'

Now, I had a small amount of medical knowledge, enough to give myself an injection, but my partner at the time, he said that he'd give it a go, which is typical of males … trying to be the hero. So I sorted out the injection for him and handed it over.

'What do I do now?' he asked.

Typical. And so I just held my leg up and said, 'Put it in there.'

So he gave me an adrenalin injection and that settled everything down. Then the next day—and you won't believe this—I'm sitting in my lounge room and another marsh fly landed on my arm and it bit me. And, oh, the side my mouth, my tongue, everything was swelling up and I had to call the Flying Doctor straight away, again. So I had another adrenalin injection then and I had to have another one the next day because the reaction to that bite was far worse the second time around.

And that's what I mean; you know, if I was in, virtually, any other town I'd just go down to the local pharmacy and tell them that I needed adrenalin and ask them to keep it in stock at all times—and there'd be no problems. So it's in situations like that when you realise that you're a long way from anywhere.

Then, another time, we had a man. I won't mention his name, but he was a local, in his sixties, and he'd previously had an operation for throat cancer. He'd had his voice box removed so that when he spoke he had to hold a cloth over this hole in his throat. Anyway, we didn't know it then but they'd apparently given him all the treatment they could and they'd said, 'Well, sorry, but that's the best we can do for you.'

So it was January and, you know, up there in the north, you get stinking hot temperatures. We had visitors from Austria, as well as my daughter from Sydney, all staying at my place at that time. We'd all had a few drinks when I got a call from the partner of the bloke who had throat cancer, to say that he'd collapsed and there was blood everywhere.

It was in the middle of the night by that stage and when we went down to their place we found out that the woman had been sleeping at one end of the house and her partner was sleeping up the other. Apparently, he'd woken up when he knew that something terrible had gone wrong and he was stumbling about, trying to find his way out to the woman and he'd collapsed in the kitchen, near the fridge. What'd happened was that, the veins had burst in his throat where the cancer was, so there was blood all over the walls where he was trying to find the light switches. It was dreadful. So we called the Flying Doctor straight away.

In those days the RFDS was still flying into Wittenoom and we had lights and everything at the airstrip. So some people went out there in the old ambulance and turned the lights on and waited for the plane to arrive and bring the doctor back in. The bloke had stopped bleeding by then so we got him back into bed.

Anyhow, when they brought the doctor back from the airstrip, the first thing he said was, 'Why didn't you clean him up?'

'Well,' I replied, 'we weren't game to touch him because there's just blood everywhere.'

And so we loaded him into the ambulance and we all went back out to the airstrip and we helped to get him on the plane. I can tell you, I breathed a real sigh of relief when I saw that Flying Doctor's aircraft begin to taxi down the airstrip to get ready for take-off. I had the man's partner beside me. I was trying to comfort her. But then, all of a sudden, the plane stopped and it turned around and it came back to where we were.

Apparently, as they were getting ready to take-off, the woman's partner had started bleeding again. The doctor said that that's the way people with throat cancer go in the end. The blood vessels in their throat burst and you can't do anything about it, so the doctor had said, 'No, this isn't going to work. We're too late.'

So they came back and they got her this time and they took her off with them to the hospital at Port Hedland. Then I thought that, with all the heat, you can't just leave it so I went back to their house and I tried to clean up all the blood. That was about two or three o'clock in the morning, and he died in Port Hedland. So the doctor knew that he wouldn't last the night. Then someone drove up there, to Hedland, the next day and they brought the woman home. But at least she was with him when he died.

Touched My Heart

Talking from the viewpoint of an ex-RFDS pilot, I guess you always remember the times that touched your heart or touched you emotionally or whatever. One very poignant story in that vein was a call we got in at our Port Hedland base to go to Geraldton, which is on the coast, about 300 or 400 kilometres north of Perth. And understand that in Western Australia we've got RFDS bases in Jandakot, which is in Perth, then there's Kalgoorlie, Port Hedland, Meekatharra and Derby. And I think there might've even still been a base at Carnarvon back when this happened because then they closed Carnarvon down in the early to mid-90s.

But yes, we were called in to pick up this young sixteen-year-old girl who'd been riding her pushbike in a storm and she turned in front of a car and got hit. She was declared brain dead but they had her on life support just to keep her body alive, and our job was to pick her up in Geraldton then take her down to Perth where they were going to harvest her organs.

But the thing was that the girl's parents came down in the aeroplane with us. And I could only imagine just how difficult it must've been for those parents, to have this happen to their gorgeous daughter and, you know, she didn't look marked at all. She was just beautiful and, of course, being only sixteen it had been the parents' call to allow her body to be made available for the harvesting of organs.

The thing is, I've got daughters as well and I just couldn't help thinking if I would've been able to make that same decision. You know, whether or not to donate their organs, especially at a time like that. Because, how on earth, as a parent, could you work your way through a logical process to reach such a clear decision when it's all compounded with the trauma of the accident and everything else.

Then, what's more, once that decision had been made, they chose to come along with us and sit in the aeroplane beside their daughter; who, as I said, was on life support. Oh, they were just so brave, strong and wonderful. I just so admired them. My heart went out to them, having to sit in that aeroplane for the hour or so's flight time, looking at their beautiful, unmarked, young daughter and knowing that it'll be the last time they'll ever see her.

So, that's one that really touched my heart and, I guess, another one I'll remember forever is when I was with the Check and Training Captain. That's when you go out on a normal call and the Check and Training Captain comes along to have a look at what you're doing and how well you're doing it. Then after the flight's over, you sit down together and you're given a précis of your performance. You know, if there's anything that could've been done better or worse or whether it was all fantastic.

Anyway, I was working at Port Hedland at that time and we actually got called out to Geraldton to pick someone up. Along with the Check and Training Captain, we had a doctor and a nurse with

I'm sure that every pilot and every doctor and every nurse has got a similar story or two to tell—Neil McDougall

us. You understand that not all flights normally have a doctor on board, but we happened to have one on that particular day.

Now, I can't remember what that particular Geraldton retrieval was for, but, while we were there, we got an emergency call to say that there was a lady at Carnarvon who was bleeding internally. Apparently she'd been in hospital there for a while and they hadn't had any success stemming the bleeding. And so they'd used up their supply of blood and it was imperative that someone get her down to Perth quickly, where there were more blood supplies.

So we shot up to Carnarvon straightaway. When we landed at Carnarvon, the doctor and the nurse went into the hospital to try and stabilise the patient enough to bring her out to the airstrip. Anyway, they did that and they brought her out to the Carnarvon Airport. The story was that she'd given birth to a baby two weeks beforehand and she had post-partum bleeding. See, when the afterbirth comes away, the patient normally stops bleeding. But this woman didn't stop bleeding. She was thirty-four years old and this was her ninth child.

We'd already been in contact with the medical authorities in Perth to make them fully aware of the urgency of the situation. To that end, they were going to meet us, with the blood supplies and a full medical team as soon as we landed at Jandakot Airport.

Now, when they put the woman in the aeroplane and I sat in the pilot's seat, the stretcher was sort of close behind me, to my right. And as we were about to take off, this poor woman reached her arm back and grabbed my hand and she said to me, 'I'm scared.'

And like you'd naturally do, I replied, 'It'll be okay. Everything'll be alright. We're on our way. We'll have help for you in less than an hour.'

Anyway, we wasted no time in getting going and on our way down to Jandakot we got all sorts of special flight clearances through military controlled airspace and so on. So we went the most direct and quickest route possible and, what's more, I had the throttle to the wall, so to speak. Also, as we got nearer, they even cleared the air traffic in the Jandakot zone.

Then, just one or two minutes from Jandakot, the doctor said, 'She's died.'

Still, we went straight in and landed and I taxied very quickly to where the medical team was waiting. I pulled up and before the engines had even stopped, people were in the aeroplane trying to revive her. And they tried to get her going again for about forty minutes. But they just weren't successful. She was dead. They just weren't successful.

And I'll remember that for as long as I live. That was a real toughie. It was just so sad. But, you know, I'm sure that every pilot and every doctor and every nurse has got a similar story or two to tell. So, I guess, the thing you've got to keep reminding yourself is that our success rate is a hell of a lot higher than our failure rate.

Tragedies

It must be stressed that tragedies do happen, and over my twenty or so years of flying for the RFDS there are two that immediately come to mind. Perhaps the saddest event in which I ever had to be involved was an accident that occurred at King Junction Station, which is west of Cairns, on the Mitchell River. It was January, in the middle of the wet season. And for some strange reason, even though the wet season's the time when people aren't as busy on their property as they normally might be, it always seems that, if anything wrong is going to happen, it always happens in the 'wet'.

Anyway, Ray Piggott had a high-winged, single-engine, Cessna 182 in which he'd been out inspecting the property. Two of his children, a boy and a girl, heard his plane returning home and so they decided to go down on their little motorbike to greet him. The boy was on the front of the bike, the girl on the back.

It was just on sunset and Ray was landing into the east, which meant that the sun was directly behind him. He was on final approach when the children arrived at the airstrip. But because they were looking into the sun's rays, of course, they were blinded to the approaching aeroplane. Then, just as Ray was about to touch down, the children rode across the airstrip about 100 metres in front of him. By the time Ray saw his children, it was too late.

There was nothing he could do. It was a one in a million chance and he collided with the bike. Though they missed the prop and the wing, the tail of the plane knocked the children from their motorbike. As it turned out, the young son, who was on the front was only slightly injured but the daughter was badly knocked about.

The RFDS was called and I flew out at once in the Queen Air with a doctor and a flight nurse. It was dark when we arrived at

King Junction. I'm not sure if it was raining, but I remember it was still very wet. Anyhow, they'd organised for some cars to light the airstrip and all went well with the night landing. The doctor attended the patients and reported that the daughter was in a dangerous condition; critical, in fact.

So we loaded both of the children onto the plane, ready for the trip back to Cairns. All looked well for a quick evacuation but then, on taxiing for take-off, we struck a spring, which had caused a soft patch to form on the airstrip. Of course, in the dark it's impossible to see such a thing. Anyway, we got bogged.

Fortunately the Flying Padre, Reverend Tony Hall-Matthews, had flown in that afternoon after he'd heard about the accident. And so, when they saw we were bogged, Tony drove up to our aircraft. We told him that we were well and truly stuck. One main wheel and part of the nose wheel were bogged so it was going to be some time before we dug ourselves out.

With the young girl being in such a critical condition, it was imperative that she reach specialist medical help as soon as humanly possible, so I asked Tony, 'Would you be able to fly the girl back into Cairns?'

Tony had never done anything like this before but his immediate reply was, 'Yes' and he was only too happy to declare it a mercy flight in the hopes of saving the daughter's life. So then we were able to transfer Ray's daughter and her mother on to Tony's aircraft, and I think the Nursing Sister as well, and they flew off to Cairns.

It then took us a couple of hours to dig the much heavier Queen Air out of the bog. Well, we ended up virtually lifting and pulling it out with a tractor, then Ray drove the tractor down the strip so that I could follow him and not get bogged again. Remember, of course, all this was going on in the dark. But then once all that was done we flew the young boy to Cairns.

Unfortunately, the next day we were advised that the daughter had died of her injuries in Cairns Base Hospital. But during an emergency situation like that, of course, you're always so busy that there's little time to stop and think. However, afterwards, I spent quite some time contemplating the terrible impact the accident had on that family, especially for Ray, being the father and pilot of the aircraft that hit the children, and also, of course, the poor mother who had lost a child in such tragic circumstances.

Another event that had a profound effect on me was the death of the Cape York grazier, Fred Shepherd. I knew both Fred and his wife, Ruth, very well. They were good people and had been great mates all their lives. They worked hard together and they worked well together. Then late one afternoon we had a call to go to Marina Plains Station, north of Cairns, near Princess Charlotte Bay.

Again, it was the wet season. Fred and Ruth had been out contract mustering for the manager of the property, Louis Komsich. Fred was thrown from the horse and the horse had rolled on him. Things didn't look too good at all and we got there as quickly as we could. From memory, I think it was about an hour and a half flying time from Cairns to Marina Plains, maybe not even quite that.

Anyway, it was after sunset when we arrived for the evacuation. There were no hills and I knew the area very well. I also knew the airstrip well so I felt that, with it being such a delicate emotional situation for those on the ground, I could land safely enough without giving them the extra burden of having to put out flares to light the airstrip.

Bogged aeroplane—RFDS

We landed safely and the only people present were Fred's wife, Ruth, and Louis Komsich was also there. Louis was very upset at what had happened and Ruth, though she exhibited a practical side, was extremely distraught. With darkness closing in, the doctor immediately attended to Fred and suggested that, even though there was little hope of Fred surviving, we should get him away from there as soon as possible.

At that point I felt it hardly appropriate of me to ask a woman—especially someone's wife, who'd just witnessed such a terrible accident—to go and put out flares so that I could take off. It'd only be more upsetting for both Ruth and Louis, plus it'd waste precious time. So knowing the area as well as I did, I decided I'd take off by using just my landing lights.

Having made that decision, we next had to solve the issue of a mob of cattle and some horses roaming on the airstrip, and I did ask Louis to drive a car down to clear the area. When that was done my landing lights proved sufficient light to guide me down the strip and I took off without any problems, leaving Ruth and Louis behind. Unfortunately, on our way to Cairns the doctor confirmed that Fred had died of his horrific injuries. This was extremely upsetting to me because, as I said, I knew the Shepherds very well. But at least I knew I'd done everything in my power to give them the best possible help.

Then about a week or so later the DCA [Department of Civil Aviation] called me in. Apparently, the doctor who was on board with me—and I won't mention names—had written a report to them saying that he was frightened about my taking off without the extra guidance of flares. This was deemed to be a dangerous manoeuvre by the DCA and I hadn't met department requirements.

I strongly disagreed because I never did anything that I didn't know I was capable of doing. I didn't take any risks. It might've seemed that way in a written report to someone like the DCA, but because of my extensive experience in charter work and many years of flying in the bush, what I'd done was a perfectly safe manoeuvre for someone like me. In the worst case, if I'd had an engine failure or anything like that after take-off, it wouldn't have been any problem in turning around on one engine and get on to final approach again and land with the landing lights. So basically, it didn't worry me one scrap.

Anyhow, I was called to Brisbane. I walked into the room. There were two people there from the DCA and they started to question my 'irresponsible behaviour'. So I explained that the reason I hadn't asked for flares to be put out was that for me to have had those people to go running around and organising flares would've been even more upsetting in the situation, especially for Ruth. Plus, of course, it would've been wasting more precious time. Then to finish off I simply stated to them, 'Well,' I said, 'taking all that into consideration, what decisions would you have made under those same circumstances? You've got an extremely upset man. Plus, you've got a distraught wife with a dying husband. So what do you expect me to do; just sit there and do nothing?'

Well, they didn't have an answer to that. They were silent for some time then they sort of, almost, congratulated me and said, 'Well, Mister Darby, we won't be going any further with this so you won't hear from us again.'

And I think from then on they had a much deeper understanding and a much more tolerant attitude towards that which was reported to them as having been 'irresponsible behaviour.'

Two in One

Now, I've had a couple of story ideas about my time as a pilot with the RFDS and one incident occurred with my Flight Nurse, Penny, who was by then my wife—still is, of course.

We were living up at Derby, in the north-east of Western Australia, and, well, we started our clinic circuit at 6.30 on the morning of 31 December, when we took off in the Queen Air aeroplane from the Derby RFDS base and went to Fitzroy Crossing. That's about a fifty-minute flight. We did a few hours clinic work there at Fitzroy, then we went on to do the clinic at Halls Creek.

It was late afternoon by the time we'd finished at Halls Creek. Then on our way back home to Derby we were asked to divert back to Fitzroy Crossing to pick up a patient. So we did that, we returned to Fitzroy, picked up the patient and then flew back home to Derby. This was now New Year's Eve.

Anyhow, we were invited over to our next-door neighbour's place for a champagne and chicken dinner, to celebrate the coming New Year. It'd been a bit of a day for Penny and I and so we were both really looking forward to that. So we got home, had a shower and we were just about to get dressed when the phone rang. It was the Derby base and they said, 'Look, Jan, sorry, but the patient you picked up from Fitzroy Crossing has deteriorated and we really need to get them to Perth.'

So it was goodbye to the chicken and champagne. Instead, we threw on some gear, rushed back out to the airport, loaded the patient, strapped ourselves in the Queen Air again and we took off at about 8.30 that night. Things were going pretty well until around Mount Newman, where we hit line after line of thunderstorms. At the time I remember using the descriptive expression that the lightning was 'hitting the ground like a picket fence.'

But the outside action was almost overshadowed by the turmoil going on in the back of the aeroplane. Being subjected to such severe turbulence the rear end of the plane was virtually fish-tailing as we were flying along. Of course, that didn't help things much at all because before long the doctor who we had on board with us soon became all but unconscious through airsickness, which left Penny as the only person still 'standing'. So there she was, being tossed around, desperately trying to keep the patient's neck immobilised by placing sandbags around the head to support the foam neck brace.

It was just after midnight when we landed in Meekatharra en route to Perth and it already felt like we'd been to hell and back, so to speak. But much to our relief, the Flying Doctor crew at the Meekatharra base very kindly came out to greet us with a cup of coffee and best wishes for the New Year. No, it wasn't chicken and champagne, but still it was greatly appreciated. In fact, that particular cup of coffee was absolutely bloody marvellous.

We then refuelled at Meekatharra before we took off and we headed on and arrived in Perth, to deliver our patient, just before dawn on New Year's Day. But by the time we landed, I estimated that Penny and I had been on duty for something like nineteen continuous hours, which is something that you'd never be allowed to do these days of far more strict regulations. And to the best of my knowledge, the patient survived and—you could say for effect that—the doctor who'd been so airsick on the journey took a little longer to get over the experience.

And that story—and it's a true one at that—could well be called, something along the lines of, 'Talk about tour of duty' or 'Happy New Year.'

So that was one story. Now, the other one you could possibly title, something like, 'Did you feel the pain?'

That came about after we'd been out to Balgo Hills Mission for a routine Medical Clinic. Balgo's away out into the Tanami Desert area of Western Australia, over near the Northern Territory border. Again, I was flying the Queen Air and we were returning to Derby. Anyhow, we'd climbed to cruising altitude and we were about

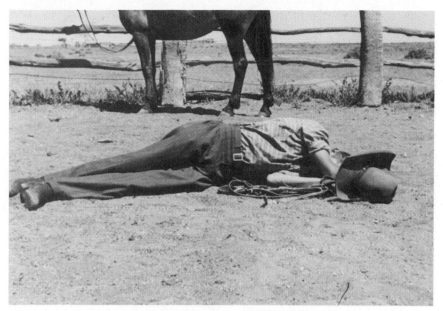

He'd been thrown and it seemed that the horse had broken practically
every bone in the poor old bugger's body—RFDS

halfway home when Derby Flight Service Unit called and asked me
to call the Flying Doctor on their discreet frequency, at the RFDS
base in Derby. I did that and on came our Base Director who said,
'Jan, we've got a bad one back at Lake Gregory. It's an injured
stockman. Have you got enough fuel to go back?'

'Yes, Jim,' I said, 'I've enough fuel for that.'

'Goodo,' he said, 'can you give us an ETA?'

So I gave Jim an ETA and I turned the Queen Air around and
headed to Lake Gregory to pick up this seriously injured stockie.

For those that don't know, Lake Gregory's right out in that
rotten bulldust country. You know the stuff I mean? It's very soft
and dirty, sandy soil. Terrible stuff. Anyhow, we duly landed and
we got the stretcher poles and the canvas and we set off in a flat-
bed truck, across country to where this injured stockie was. On
the way out we were told that a horse had thrown him, then it'd
rolled on him, then it'd got up and tap-danced all over him, before
galloping off into the bush. In the process the horse had pushed
the poor old bugger half underground into this bulldust and,

from their description, it seemed that the horse had broken practically every bone in his body.

By the time we arrived, the stockie was still lying there, sunken into this bulldust, and he was not looking too well, at all. In fact, the only sign of life was that he had a tiny, wee, thin roll-your-own weed drooping from his lips, from which rose the occasional wisp of smoke. So, no, things didn't seem too good.

But I must say, he looked like a tough old bugger. If I had to give a description of him, I'd liken him to a piece of old mulga. You know those old wizened mulga trees that've been stripped bare of leaves, where the wood's gone all grey and it's as hard as an old railway line. He was like that; the classic old stockman, as tough as you can make them.

Anyhow, as they were trying to gently slip the canvas under him, to lift him up out of the bulldust, I could see that the old feller was obviously in very great pain. And so, I guess, to give the poor old bastard a little bit of moral encouragement, I leaned across and gently said to him, 'How're you goin' mate?'

And I'll never forget it; he looked up at me with his watery, fading eyes, the excruciating pain etched into every crease of his weather-beaten face, and he took another tiny breath on his weed and he wheezed, 'Not too good, mate.'

Oh shit, the poor bastard. I just about wept at the situation. But he did survive. We put him on the back of the truck and drove him back to the Queen Air and we flew him to Derby Hospital and, eventually, he walked out of town and most probably went back to doing the only thing he knew how to do, stock work and riding horses.

Two Lumps

After I'd finished my Midwifery I went over to Western Australia with a girlfriend. We worked at Derby and we went out to Fitzroy Crossing and also to Halls Creek, sometimes. So that's when I really started to admire the work that the girls were doing in the Australian Inland Mission. The AIM, as it was known, was part of John Flynn's vision of a Mantle of Safety, which not only included the Royal Flying Doctor Service but also linked into the on-ground health and spiritual services.

Then, when I came home from Western Australia, I contacted the AIM and I finished up working at Cape York, up on the tip of the Cape York Peninsula, for two years. I was a bit wet behind the ears when I first went up there, but it was an amazing adventure for a young woman, and a very educational one as well. And when you're stuck out there, in such an isolated place like that and you strike a real tough problem well, I can tell you, the sound of that Flying Doctor Service King Air aeroplane coming in to land, you know, it was music for the soul.

So that's where this story takes place; up at Cape York, on a big Aboriginal Reserve.

I was the Nursing Sister at the little hospital there that was run by the Australian Inland Mission. That also included a hostel for school children. Basically, a lot of the work I was doing was what the average mother would do at home; you know, cleaning up cuts and scratches and things like that. Still, you had to keep a pretty close eye on things because you couldn't, say, give the Aborigines the whole course of antibiotics at once because they'd either take them all at once or share them around with everyone else. So you had to have them come back a couple of times a day to take their antibiotics.

*Medical session in progress—*Neil McDougall

And I must say, most of it wasn't too stressful. But, of course, you had to be able to cope with whatever came in and, having that doctor on the end of the radio, when you really needed help, was a godsend. At the Mission, we had a schedule chat with the Flying Doctor from the Cairns RFDS base, once or twice a day, on the radio. How it worked was that the doctor conducted a medical session and, if you had a problem, you discussed it over the radio with him and he worked out what he thought was wrong, then advised you as to what medication to take out of the RFDS medical chest. Of course, something that was very important was that, when you were talking to the doctor you had to be anatomically correct or else it could well lead to a wrong diagnosis.

At that time, David Cook was the main doctor for the RFDS at Cairns. I'm not exactly sure just how many other doctors there were, but whenever one of them went on holidays or whatever, Doctor Tim O'Leary used to take over. I think by then, Tim had been elevated to being an administrative person. But he still much preferred getting out and about rather than sitting in an office.

Tim was an excellent doctor and had my utmost admiration as a diagnostician. He was also a real character, so, when he was on the radio everybody used to listen in because of his great entertainment value. Mind you, those very same people secretly dreaded being the person on the receiving end of some of Tim's wit.

And that leads into this story.

It was around Christmas time—the wet season—so there was a lot of humidity around and a bit of thunder activity. All this was playing havoc with radio communications and, when that happened, you had to have somebody relay the messages on, because the radio signals weren't strong enough to get through to Cairns. So I was actually relaying messages and a call came through from the CSIRO research station at Somerset, which was just a little south of Cape York. It was from this young fellow who was working up there for a few months. He'd been out in the field and he'd developed a problem so he'd radioed in for a diagnosis from, as it just so happened, Doctor Tim O'Leary.

As usual, when you first got on the radio, you gave the doctor your personal details like your name, age, sex and so forth. Of course, I'm relaying messages backwards and forwards over the radio and, of course, all those who could were glued to their radios as well, because they knew that when Tim was on the line, there'd be some good entertainment.

So this young fellow gave Tim all his personal details, then Tim asked, 'And what seems to be the problem, son?'

'I felt a pain between my legs doctor so I put my hand down the front of my trousers and I discovered two large lumps, doctor.'

'So, you've got two lumps between your legs, son.'

'Yes, doctor.'

'Are you sure that there's two of them, son?'

There was a brief silence followed by the young fellow saying, 'Yes doctor, I'm sure that there's two lumps between my legs.'

And Tim, being the wily old Irishman that he was, replied, 'And how old did you say you were, son?'

'Twenty-three, doctor.'

And Tim's voice comes back over the radio with a poorly disguised laugh, 'Well, son,' he said, 'all I can say is that if you've got to be twenty-three years old and you've only just found out that you've got two lumps between your legs then, you have my very deepest sympathy.'

And you know, there was dead silence—a pregnant pause, you could say—much to the embarrassment of this young fellow. Then after everybody had settled down, questions and answers flew backwards and forwards and, in fact, as it turned out, this young chap had an infected wound on his foot, which, in turn, had caused the swelling of the glands in his groin. So that's what I mean about having to be anatomically correct when you were talking to the Flying Doctor, Tim O'Leary in particular.

Victorian Connections

Just because you live in a state like Victoria, with its small land area and very little outback, it's no reason to assume that you don't have the need for the Royal Flying Doctor Service, and I'll tell you why.

It was New Year's Eve 1994, very early, at about two o'clock in the morning when we got the telephone call from my youngest son, Ian, who lived in Western Australia, to say that my other son, Neil, had had this accident on Rottnest Island.

It's quite a long story really, but Neil was on Rottnest holidaying with his family. In fact, I'd spoken with him just the day before, on his mobile, and he was saying just what a great time they were all having. But Neil's wife had gone back to the mainland to keep an appointment that day and Neil had stayed there, on Rottnest, with their children. Neil, his wife and their children had a cabin, and some, practically, lifelong friends were also there, staying in another cabin, with their children. Neil had spent that day with his close friends and all the children had been playing games and whatnot. Then by night, all the children were tired so they went to bed in Neil's friend's cabin and, as Neil rode off on a bicycle to go back to his own cabin, they said, 'We'll meet you on the beach tomorrow.'

On Rottnest Island they only have pushbikes. There's no motor traffic on the island apart from the official stuff like a few buses and what have you. So that's what Neil was riding, a pushbike.

It was a downhill ride from Neil's friend's cabin and we simply don't know what happened. Neil could've hit a quokka [small wallaby], because they move around at night, or maybe the front wheel could've gone into a hole, because the place wasn't lit. Well, it is lit now, but it wasn't then. The police also ruled out foul play because his wallet and everything was still in his pocket when he was found.

So, we don't actually know what caused Neil to have the accident, but he went straight over the handlebars and fell on his head. The bike wasn't even damaged. This was before helmets were compulsory. After that they did make helmets compulsory. But he fell on his head, which rendered him unconscious, and the strange thing was, there wasn't even a mark on him, so he wasn't injured in any other way.

Luckily, a nursing sister and her husband were walking back from the town and that's when they found Neil, lying unconscious. Of course, they didn't know at that time if it could've been the result of foul play. But if they hadn't found Neil he might well have laid there until daylight and he could've died. The nursing sister could tell that there was a real problem, so she got her husband to ride back into town, on Neil's bike, to get help from the police and a doctor, which he did, and also an ambulance drove out to as near as they could, to pick up Neil.

Rather than wait until morning, the Flying Doctor was called and they took Neil straight to Jandakot Airport. Then, I suppose, he was transported by ambulance from there to Sir Charles Gairdner Hospital, where he was put on life support. And that's when we got the call.

Anyhow, my eldest son, who was with me at the time, he and I flew from Victoria to Western Australia on the first plane we could get, and my two daughters followed on a later flight.

But the brain injury was too great. Neil was kept alive until we all arrived, but he never regained consciousness. Then two days later, after all the various tests were done, he was pronounced brain dead. By that time the whole family was there. But one thing that I am thankful for is that, if it wasn't for the Flying Doctor Service, Neil would never have reached the hospital alive and we would have never have reached his side in time.

Neil had just turned forty, the previous October, and I'd been over for his birthday party and he was as fit as a fiddle; a fine physical specimen. But people were not all that conscious of organ donation back then. It wasn't publicised as it is now, so I asked, 'Did Neil sign his licence as an organ donor?'

And the answer was, 'No'.

I said, 'Well, I feel that he should be an organ donor.'

And there were a couple of 'Ums and ahs.'

I said, 'He's going to be cremated, isn't he? What good is his body going to be? You're not going to preserve it, if it's cremated.'

Of course, the organ donor people were there at the hospital, as were Neil's doctors, and Neil's doctors said, 'We want you to understand that we're always here for the patient and we don't have any connection with the organ donor people, so it must be your decision.'

Then we found out that Neil also had an unusual blood group and I said to the doctor, 'How's that possible? My husband and I had perfectly ordinary blood groups and I know that Neil's my son and I know my husband was his father.'

'Well,' the doctor said, 'that's quite possible. It's not unusual.'

So finally the family came around to my way of thinking as regards to organ donation. And there was, in fact, a heart patient—a family man—with that same blood group, who was waiting and then there were two kidney people, and Neil's bone tissue was also used. But they don't take any organs that aren't being waited for. His liver wasn't taken. The only organs that were required at the time were the ones they took.

And that was all made possible because of the speed with which Neil had been transferred to Perth by the Flying Doctor Service— that his organs were then available to be donated to people awaiting transplants. That, at least, gives us some comfort. And, oddly enough, Neil's organs were flown back to the eastern states; back to where he was born. So that was a strange one. But it was quite a remarkable thing and I do believe it helps the healing process—it really does—to know that the body is being used, and is made possible, to save someone else's life.

In actual fact, I had a wonderful letter sent through the organ donor people. You don't have any direct contact with the people who have received organs, but this lovely letter arrived and it said that this particular person—I don't even know if it was a man or a woman—was looking at two legs, of the same length, for the first time in their life. And after a little more rehabilitation they were hoping to walk perfectly normally, for the first time in their life. And that was such a wonderful letter to receive. What's more, Neil's two children have grown up into the most delightful people; extremely well adjusted and we all keep in close touch.

So that was one story. Now, there's a second part to our close Victorian connection with the RFDS and it was that, our grand-daughter, Melissa—the daughter of my oldest son—was living on the central coast of Western Australia, at Carnarvon. Her husband was actually teaching there and, in 2001, six years after Neil's accident, Melissa was riding a friend's horse and the horse slipped. It came down with her on it, and her leg was crushed under the horse. The only way Melissa could get back for help was to get back up on the horse, which she managed to do with great difficulty.

As it turned out, Melissa's leg was very badly broken and it needed a lot of work on it, as did her ankle. A rod was put in and all sorts of things, so she was literally screwed up. But the thing was, she kept on being terribly sick. I mean really, really sick and the doctors said, 'Well, you don't get sick with a broken leg.'

An ultrasound proved that Melissa, unbeknownst to herself, was six weeks pregnant, which was why she was being so sick. So then they stopped all her treatment immediately because, being pregnant, she couldn't have any more X-rays.

But it's 900 kilometres from where she was at Carnarvon to the Royal Perth Hospital and the Royal Flying Doctor Service flew her up and down on numerous occasions and, as you'll know, they never charge. They were quite wonderful, and she flew up and down with her leg in plaster for a lot of the time she was pregnant.

Actually, she spent a lot of time on those crutches because her leg was so crooked she couldn't walk properly. She had a terrible time. But now, I've got a beautiful great-grandson. I go to Western Australia as often as possible, especially for birthdays, Christmas and weddings. And that's just one of my great-grandchildren. I've got another three in Melbourne.

And so that's why I, for one, Lady Ena Macpherson, am such a staunch supporter of the RFDS.

Water, Water, Everywhere But …

Lionel: It was in about 2000 when all this happened. If we did the trip now we'd go later because I remember it was wintertime and it was freezing in the mornings and it was very wet. So I think it must've been around April or maybe a little bit earlier when we first set off from Nhill. There was just the three of us: Bill Day, Rex Bunge and myself—Lionel Ferris—and we only took one vehicle. The idea was to get up to Halls Creek, in the Kimberley region of Western Australia, then do the Canning Stock Route, which was something we'd talked about for quite a while.

Now, I'm just trying to think which way we went to get to Halls Creek because we were nearly a fortnight getting onto the stock route and another fortnight coming down. A lot of people go the other way, but we didn't. We started at the northern end and came back in the opposite direction, if you get what I mean. But Bill Day's got a fair account of it in his diary so you'd better let him fill in the gaps.

Bill: Well, before we start, you've sort of really got to know Lionel to appreciate what he's all about. He's a fellow that consistently down-plays things. He's unassuming to the extreme. In other words, what anybody else thinks is an important story, he just brushes it off as if it's an everyday occurrence, or at least he tries to. Then he's also got one of those really dry, wry, senses of humour. Like he used to be a helper on some of our outback tours and, on those trips, one of the first things we'd do was to get everyone together and let them introduce themselves by telling something about their life, and Lionel used to always rock them by saying that he left school at the age of thirteen because, by then, he was old enough to realise that it was severely interfering with his education.

So that's Lionel, and he's got lots of sayings like that. But he's a wizard musician—he can just about play anything—and yeah, he's probably told you he's a bachelor. And he's a collector and, believe me, if Noah kept two of everything, I reckon, Lionel's gone one step better because I'd say he's got just about three of everything, and in all sorts of conditions. You just really need to meet him one day.

But yeah, that trip was quite an experience for him, I'm sure.

Okay, so we headed off from Nhill in western Victoria. There was only the one vehicle and three of us; myself, another chap by the name of Rex Bunge and Lionel. We went up through the Gawler Ranges, across the Stuart Highway, over the Oodnadatta Track to Oodnadatta, right up through Dalhousie Springs, then out to Andado Station. Andado's Molly Clarke's station. It's an extremely remote property out on the north-western edge of the Simpson Desert. Old Molly's the owner of the place. She's a bit over eighty now and she still lives out there. Then, from Andado we went back into Alice Springs for supplies and spent a couple of days there, then we crossed the Tanami Desert to Wolfe Creek, up to Halls Creek.

At Halls Creek we refuelled and so forth before we started off down the Canning Stock Route, and we were probably about four

Yeah, that trip was quite an experience—Bill Day

or five wells down when we heard that the stock route had been closed due to the wet weather. And boy-o-boy, was it wet. But we just kept plugging on because we'd heard that some people were still coming the other way. I mean, it wasn't totally impassable or anything like that and we weren't chopping the hell out of the place because most of the rain was down the bottom end, which we still had to get to, of course.

Then, not far from the bottom end, Lionel first started to show signs of getting, you know, something wrong with him. Yeah, just a bit of stress. And then, when he finally sort of said that he couldn't pass any urine I thought, Hello, we've got troubles here because basically he had urine retention.

Lionel: Of course, had I known I was going to have all the trouble, well, I wouldn't have gone out into such an isolated area in the first place. But everything seemed to be working fine. Then as we went down the stock route I started having just a bit of trouble with my prostate. At first I didn't say anything because I thought it might spoil things for everyone. But then, on the last part of the journey down the Canning, we were actually camping on the station property and that's where it came on.

Still, I wasn't too bad for a while. You know, I'd go for a walk about every hour or so and that seemed to keep me going. But before too long I had to walk more often and then it got to the stage where I couldn't really walk at all and I just had to lay there. I couldn't drink or eat anything either, not that I felt like it, anyway, mind you. But I had no idea you could get so crook with something as simple as that.

So then, it sort of knocked me for six really, and that's when Bill and Rex decided they'd better get help. The trouble was, of course, we were still a long way from anywhere and so the first thing we had to think about was whether we'd go back or continue on. Anyway, I wasn't too keen on retracing our steps so we opted to go on.

Bill: It was in the evening when Lionel sort of realised he had trouble. Then the next morning I got on the RFDS radio to the Flying Doctor base at Meekatharra and they advised us to go to Wiluna where there was a doctor and a hospital.

So that's where we headed and because of the state of the track we did it with great difficulty. I tell you, I've never seen water running up hill, but it very nearly was, and it was still raining. Anyhow, we basically travelled non-stop to Wiluna and we got Lionel to the doctor there and they fitted a catheter to him, which relieved him greatly. And then, after the doctor removed the catheter, we thought, Alright, well, he'll be okay now.

Still and all, the doctor suggested that we stay in Wiluna for two or three days just to keep an eye on things, which we did. Well, because of the wet conditions nobody was allowed out of town anyway so we had to stay there. In fact, it was so bad that the town had run out of fuel because no one could get in to supply them, and we were about the only ones that had any.

Lionel: Well, they finally got me to Wiluna and I went to see the doctor and he fitted me with a catheter until he thought he had me right. And I thought I was right, also. Everything seemed to be working as it should.

Bill: Lionel was quite convinced that he was fine by then, too. And after the doctor had given him the okay, we went to the coppers and they said, 'Righto, well, you're the only ones in town who's got fuel—if you want to go, you can.'

By then the track was okay, so we took off and headed south and we stayed at Leonora overnight. It was still raining but Lionel seemed to be going well so we said, 'Righto, we'll start out going home along the Anne Beadell Highway.'

So we told the coppers at Leonora where we were going and they said, 'Well, okay, but there's already been somebody stuck out there so, you know, be careful and let us know when you get through.'

'Okay,' we said and so we went out east of Leonora to a little mining village—I can't think of the name of the place now. Then about a day and a half later Lionel's problem returned, only, this time, it was far more serious. Anyhow, Rex and I had a bit of a talk about the whole thing and we decided that we really had an emergency situation on our hands. So we called up the RFDS again and I'm not exactly sure which base station we got in contact with. Kalgoorlie would've been the closest place but it mightn't have necessarily been the right time of the day for radio communications. Somehow I have an idea we couldn't get in contact with either Meekatharra or Kalgoorlie on the low frequency so we used either 6890 and we got in contact with Port Augusta or it might've been 6950 and we got on to Alice Springs. I can't remember which.

Anyway, they said, 'Where's the nearest airstrip?'

It was probably mid-afternoon by then, so we had to make a decision as to whether we'd go up to Neale Junction and north to Warburton or down south to Rawlinna, which is on the east-west railway line. Well, we had a bit of a think and we decided that if Lionel was really crook, then Rawlinna was at least heading on our way home.

Now, seeing that the radio conditions where we were at that time were not really good because of the bad weather and the lightning and so forth we arranged with the RFDS that we'd phone them when we got to Rawlinna. And so we set out toward Rawlinna and, I tell you, the rain just got heavier and heavier.

Lionel: The weather had come in by then and we had to go through some pretty heavy downpours and, with so much rain, it formed huge waterholes all along the track. But, fortunately, it was solid underneath. I was pretty crook by then and so I was lying down in the back of the vehicle, a Nissan Patrol, and, oh, it was very rocky. In fact, one of the blokes likened it to driving over an everlasting cemetery because it seemed as if we were going over rocks the size of tombstones.

So, yes, it was terribly rough, particularly for me in my condition, and also, of course, you couldn't see what was ahead of you, on the track, because there was so much water. Not only that, but another problem was that there were other tracks branching off the one we were on which confused the issue. Anyhow, luckily, Rex had brought his GPS—Global Positioning System—along and so we tracked ourselves with that, just in case we got lost. So we'd be going along and Rex would say, 'Take the track on the right.'

And sometimes Bill would say, 'Are you sure?'

And Rex would say, 'Yes, I think so.'

So it was a good job that Rex had that GPS because even though by now it was at night, we couldn't have navigated by the stars anyway, you see, because it was so overcast with all the rain.

Bill: Believe me, it was quite an eventful trip, in extremely difficult conditions, driving at night, through water, while trying to follow the track. To keep ourselves alert Rex and I took it in turns, driving two hours each. As for the state of the track; well, in the sandhill country it was alright but once we got out onto the actual Nullarbor Plain it got worse from the point of view that any shallow depression was covered with water. So where there was water racing across the track, before we attempted to drive through it, we had to get out and wade across to see how deep it was. And believe me, in the early hours of the morning it was freezing cold. What's more, you didn't know whether you were going to drop into a washaway or what.

Then we came across a huge stretch of water. It must've been at least a kilometre wide. So we tackled that and I can remember, at one stage, the headlights and the driving lights of the Nissan were completely under the water and we had just this dull brown glow in front of us. Anyway, when we finally came out the other side, we decided we'd call it quits for a while and have a bit of a spell. All this time, of course, Lionel had been trying to lie down in the back and, believe me, he was really crook. Anyhow he agreed and he said, 'Yeah, have a spell and try and get some sleep.'

So we did try to get some sleep, but we were under strict instructions that if Lionel got, you know, really, really bad, he'd better just wake us up and we'd get going again. And that's exactly what happened because we were in our swags for not less than an hour when he said, 'Look, I really don't like to do this, but we've gotta get a move on.'

Anyway, we got going again and the track was still difficult to locate because there were sheets of water everywhere. But we pushed on under very, very adverse conditions and the only way we could really navigate was to use a bit of a line with Rex's GPS.

So I can tell you, it was a pretty welcoming sight when we first saw the lights of Rawlinna, from about 25 kilometres out, because, until then, basically, we didn't know exactly where we were.

Lionel: I suppose the rain had finished by the time we got near Rawlinna, but there was still a fair amount of surface water about. We arrived in town about an hour before daylight and it was in the middle of winter, so it was a bit chilly. I remember there being a lot of light at Rawlinna. There was quite a large building, like a cafeteria or something, and that was still lit up. Then there was another building near the railway line that looked like people might be in, and another house further down. But there wasn't a soul in sight. Really, at that time of the morning it looked to be more or less like a ghost town.

Bill: We got into Rawlinna in the wee hours of the morning. It was just sort of that twilight time before sunrise and, at a rough guess, I'd say the temperature was about minus three or four degrees, at least. It hadn't rained for about two or three hours and all the puddles were frozen over.

Anyhow, because I'd been to Rawlinna before, I knew where the telephone box was. So I got on the phone and that's where I made the biggest mistake ever. I didn't actually have the RFDS phone number so I thought, Well, the logical thing to do is to ring 000.

Now, I don't know exactly where 000 rang, but I imagine it was Perth. And to use a very common expression, that's where the shit hit the fan—absolutely—because I just couldn't get on to anybody with any sense. The first bloke thought it was a hoax call. Well I took that as an insult and I gave him a serve over that one. Boy-o-boy, did I see red. Next I got onto somebody who told me that he didn't know where Rawlinna was because he couldn't find it on his computer screen. So I tried to tell him where it was. I mean, I could've easily lost my cool but I realised the urgency of the situation. Then eventually, that person put me onto the ambulance people at Kalgoorlie. God knows why he put me onto the ambulance people, but he did, and the bloke that was on duty there, in Kalgoorlie, was an English fellow who'd only been in Australia for a fortnight, so the whole procedure started again.

'Where the hell's this Rawlinna?' he asked.

So I tried to explain to him where Rawlinna was then I said, 'Look, we're here, there's an airstrip here and we really need the Flying Doctor urgently.'

'Oh, no,' he said, 'I'll send out an ambulance. How far from Kalgoorlie is this place called Rawlinna?'

I said, 'It's probably 500 or 600 kilometres.'

'Oh, we could be there in a couple of hours.'

'More like half a day, mate,' I said. 'It's at least five hours and possibly more.'

'That'll be okay,' he said, 'we can get an ambulance straight out to him.'

Anyhow, I finally convinced him that it was a waste of time coming out in an ambulance. So then he put me onto the police station and the police realised that, yeah, well, this was quite an urgent problem and they'd better do something about it. So they told me to hold the line and the next thing I was talking to the RFDS and, boy-o-boy, what a relief that was because, by this stage, I'd say it would've taken at least an hour, or possibly more, just to get onto them. And I can assure you, by then, my feet were frozen up to the knees because, you know how much protection you've got from the weather in one of those telephone boxes. To use another common expression, bugger all!

Lionel: The telephone box was right beside the railway line, at the railway station, and Bill seemed to be taking forever in the telephone box, so it was well and truly daylight by then. He seemed to be having some sort of trouble or other but then, apparently, once he got in touch with the Flying Doctor Service, things really started to happen then. After the call we didn't spend much more time in the town because we went straight out to check the airstrip, to make sure it was safe for the plane to land.

Bill: Anyway, we had to do a check on the airstrip and that got a little bit confused as well because the RFDS told me that if I could drive up and down the airstrip at 85 kilometres an hour, in complete safety, that it'd be okay for them to land.

So I said, 'Righto, I'll do that and, if I can't do the safety drive, I'll give you a ring back and let you know.'

Well, we drove up and down the strip and there was no problem so I didn't bother to ring them back. But, what they should've said, or what I should've said was that I'd ring them back and advise them one way or the other as to the safety of the airstrip. But anyway that didn't happen so then there was another hold-up because they were waiting for me to ring back.

Then eventually, the RFDS must've rang a woman in at Rawlinna because she came out and she did the same as we did and she drove up and down the strip to check it. Then she disappeared and she must've rang them again because, the next thing, she came back out and she said, 'The Flying Doctor's on its way.'

Anyway, we lit a fire at the end of the airstrip so that they could get an idea as to which way the wind was blowing and then we sat there and waited in the cold around the fire until we heard an aircraft. By then, I'd say it was probably about half past eight or nine o'clock and, oh, you should've seen the look of relief on Lionel's face when he heard that sound in the sky.

Lionel: It was a gravelly sort of an airstrip but quite good, apparently. You know, the plane came down and it sailed along fairly well. Then I had to wait until it had slowed down enough to turn around to come back and stop near where we were. It was quite a big plane; a two-engine job. I've forgotten what type it was but it was quite an impressive sort of aircraft and it was all decked out like a hospital. There was a couch there to lay on and every nook and cranny had something in it, so I guess that they had everything they needed. Of course, they'd get some pretty awful cases to deal with at times so they've got to have enough room to airlift, at least, a couple of passengers back to hospital.

But when they saw me, they realised that I would've been in a lot of pain and, really, to be honest, I was feeling absolutely, terribly sick. So when I got inside the plane they put a catheter straight in, right up my penis. I don't remember the pain being that bad. Perhaps I was already in so much pain that I didn't really care any more. Anyhow, after they put the catheter in I started to get relief almost immediately. But the catheter was quite an ingenious affair; it was just a long tube that went from up in my penis, out into a bag, which had a tap on the end of it, and you just kept emptying the bag.

Actually, I thought I might've been sick for quite some time afterwards because they told Bill that, by then, the urine would've been starting to bank back from my kidneys and so forth. But I was fine, really. In fact, I was feeling pretty good by then.

Bill: Anyway, the RFDS aircraft landed and I could see Lionel struggling up the steps into the plane. The doctor was an English doctor who hadn't been out here all that long. I think he was sort of getting experience through the Flying Doctor Service. But anyway, he must've done a good job because within ten minutes Lionel came back out of the plane with a huge smile on his face. Oh, in fact, he just about ran down the steps. It was just absolutely unreal. So as soon as they, you know, put the catheter in and drained his bladder he was feeling a hundred per cent.

Another thing—and this hasn't anything to do with Lionel and his problem—in the meantime, while all this was going on, Rex and I had been talking to the pilot, whose name was one you'd never forget: Robert E Lee. And, I tell you, he reckoned he'd had plenty of comments about that. But it turned out that he knew my next-door neighbour, back home in Nhill. She'd been a Nursing Sister with the RFDS in Kalgoorlie. So it's a small world, isn't it?

Lionel: The Flying Doctor hung around until it was obvious I was getting relief and then they took off and Bill, Rex and I, we just continued on our trip. Actually, I think we might've even gained a bit of time because Bill and Rex had been, virtually, driving both day and night, though you wouldn't want to do that if you didn't really have to. So we didn't alter our plans much other than we went south to the Cocklebiddy Caves and camped there that night and I was well enough to go down into the caves by the following day. So it's pretty amazing what they can do. Then we just carried on home.

Bill: So yeah, the whole show sort of finished there. Anyway, after they put the catheter in, the RFDS people shot through, then. And so Lionel had the catheter and away we went, heading for home. But we popped in to do a bit of caving on the way at a place called Cocklebiddy. And I can tell you, that's another nightmare trip from Rawlinna across to Cocklebiddy.

Anyway, we met a bloke just north of Cocklebiddy. He was the owner or manager or something of a station there called Arubiddy and, because it was getting late in the day and we couldn't find anywhere to camp, we sort of hoped that he might say, 'Oh, come up and camp at the homestead.'

But he didn't. All he said was, 'There's a reserve down by the caves where you can camp. You might be lucky because there's a South Australian caving expedition down there; a cave group, diving.'

So we went down there and camped in the scrub with the caving expedition and the next morning they invited us to use their ladder and their line, down to the water level in the caves. And so we went down there for about an hour and a half, and Lionel was real impressed with that. In fact, he reckoned it was the highlight of the trip, really.

But that was just typical of Lionel's sense of humour. And believe me, he has got a sense of humour. Because on the way home, across the Nullarbor—needless to say we had our swags so we'd just camp in them alongside the road—but Lionel reckoned that he had one over Rex and I because when we'd had too much to drink, Rex and I would be up and down out of our swags all night going for a leak. But, with the catheter in, Lionel didn't have to worry about that because he could just roll over and have a leak while he was still in his swag. And he thought that was great. He reckoned he was going to get one of those catheters put in as a permanent fixture.

Well Prepared

Both my husband, Peter, and I are members of the Q3 District of Lions, up here in Queensland. Lions is a service club that raises money for various charities and helps out wherever it can. It's a great organisation. You'll find them all throughout Australia.

Anyway, several years ago it was the habit of the District Governor of Q3 to get us all together and we'd do what we called A Lion's Safari. See, any of us who wanted to take some time, we'd all pile into a bus and off we'd go and visit the Western Region of Lions Clubs. And it was on one of these—an eight-day trip—that this particular incident happened.

They're a real social event these Lion's Safaris, they are. It's a very friendly atmosphere. We go around to many of the western towns and meet some really lovely people and, of course, we're always shown the various sites of all the places we visit. So we set off from Brisbane, on this eight-day trip, and we hit Charleville and, of course, we were taken out and shown the sights of the district. I remember we visited the Distance Education facilities there, and that was fascinating.

Then, of course, we went off to the Royal Flying Doctor base and we were shown around there, which was also extremely interesting. Oh, they showed us everything. We were even taken out to the aircraft hangar. Anyhow, there we were, strolling around the Flying Doctor hangar when we noticed the plane they used. And one particular member of our Lions Club—we'll call him Charlie—well, he was particularly interested in aeroplanes and things.

He's really a lovely man, that's why I didn't want to mention his real name. But this Charlie, as I've called him, he wanted to know everything about the Flying Doctor's aeroplane and its operations, so he started asking lots and lots of questions. You know, you get those sorts of people on these tours, don't you?

Anyway, Charlie was asking about this and that, and that and this and, really, by that stage, as I said to my husband, Peter, 'Peter,' I said, 'I'm getting quite hungry.' And it looked like the others were getting quite peckish as well. But, that didn't seem to register on Charlie because he kept on firing questions like, 'What altitude does it fly at?' and 'How fast does it go?', 'What's it's flying range?' and all those technical sorts of things.

So after he asked a lot of questions about the aircraft he then walked around it, for a closer inspection. 'Heavens it's small,' Charlie remarked, which it was. Then, at Charlie's request, they let us look inside the plane, and that really got his interest going. He asked about all the nobs and dials, and he examined this and that. 'Dear me,' he remarked, 'there's not much room inside, is there?'

'No, not really,' said the person who was showing us around. 'There's only enough room for the pilot, the doctor, the nurse and the stretcher for the patient.'

'Very interesting,' answered Charlie before he fired off another volley of questions.

Anyway, the visit to the Flying Doctor base finally ended, which, as I said was very interesting, and we went to lunch. From memory, lunch was at the Lions Den. Of course, as with wherever we went, we were well catered for, so it was a beautiful meal, actually, and greatly anticipated by this stage, I can tell you.

So, there we were, enjoying our lunch, when Charlie got up for some reason or other and he suddenly collapsed over the table and, well, he couldn't move. Now, you always expect the worst in a situation like that, don't you? And in actual fact, it did look quite serious because nobody knew what the problem was.

'No, no, I'm alright,' Charlie kept saying. 'It's just the hip.'

But the thing was, he couldn't move. So we called the ambulance and the next thing we know an ambulance is screaming down and they come into the Lion's Den to see to Charlie.

'Yes,' the ambulance people said, 'it's certainly his hip.'

Apparently, he'd previously had a hip operation, but it had a habit of popping out of its socket without any warning. And, well,

Touring the RFDS base at Charleville—Judy Heindorff

if you're on a bus trip and you can't walk, well, you just can't carry on, can you? But of course, Charlie had to get home somehow, and we're a thousand-odd kilometres, or whatever it is, from Charleville back to Brisbane, aren't we?

So, the ambulance loaded Charlie up and took him to hospital. And it was only a matter of getting the hip back in but, the particular surgery, or whatever it was, to get the hip back into the socket could only be done in a Brisbane hospital. So the next day—and here's the irony of this story—the next day the Flying Doctor Service flew him back to Brisbane in the very same aeroplane that he'd taken so much interest in the day before.

As my husband, Peter, said, 'After asking all those questions about the plane and so forth, he was certainly well prepared to experience just what the Flying Doctor does, wasn't he?'

And, oh yes, they fixed him up in Brisbane. In actual fact, a nice end to the story is that a couple of days later we got the message that he was being sent home from hospital.

Where are You?

No matter how experienced you are as a pilot, sometimes you can get a bit caught out. The first time happened, back a few years ago, when I was flying for Aero-medical. That's before it was absorbed into the Royal Flying Doctor Service. Anyhow, Air Ambulance used to fly into a place called Kadina, which is a little town over on the Yorke Peninsula, in South Australia. But, with Kadina being located where it was and having a dirt strip, it was always very difficult to distinguish the actual airstrip from the land around it; you know, with the colour of the earth and everything.

This wasn't an emergency or anything, but, anyhow, the volunteer ambulance crew were on the ground at the Kadina airstrip with the patient, waiting for me to arrive. We were in radio contact so they could hear the aircraft coming in, but I was having difficulty finding the strip and I just needed a little time to get my bearings. What happens in a case like that is, us pilots would tell the ground crew that we were doing 'one zero minute's air work' in the area. Of course, all the other pilots had been in the same situation, so when they'd hear that someone was doing air work they'd have a great laugh. But the ambulance crew, nor the general public, weren't to know that air work was just an excuse to stall for time while you located the strip, because the last thing you want to admit to, as a pilot, is that you're lost.

So I'd just started trying to locate the strip and the woman from the volunteer Ambulance crew must've seen the plane up in the air and so she came back over the radio and said, 'Air Ambulance. Air Ambulance, are you lost?'

Well, I mean, when something like that is broadcast over the radio network then every Tom, Dick, Harry and Mary knows that you're lost. So I came back and, in a very embarrassed manner,

I replied with, 'Oh, I'm just having a little bit of difficulty in finding this strip.'

Then the ever-helpful woman from the Ambulance crew comes back on again and she says, 'Air Ambulance, Air Ambulance, we're just over here.'

Which wasn't much help at all because, if you're in an aircraft and you're hundreds of feet or so above the ground and you can't even find the airstrip, how in the hell are you going to see someone waving at you to let you know that they're 'just over here'? Where's over here? So yes, that was a little embarrassing for me and it also made me realise that while these ambulance volunteers really do try their best, sometimes they just don't get it.

Another one, I suppose, that could cause confusion is the term to 'hold position'. I was coming down from Port Pirie to Adelaide one time and a similar sort of confusion over terminology happened en route. Now, when you're out and about, you often get diversions, and I was probably about a hundred kilometres north of Adelaide—just a bit north of Port Wakefield—and I got a call that I had a Code One out of Renmark, which is over near the

He's up there somewhere—RFDS

Victorian border, in the Riverland area of South Australia. A Code One's an urgent response.

Anyhow, I was just about to call up Traffic Control to alter my flight plan and request a diversion to Renmark, when a second phone call came into the RFDS base saying that they had another Code One out at Wudinna. Wudinna's west of Adelaide, over on the Eyre Peninsula. That meant we now had two Code Ones, but they were in opposite directions. Of course, this caused a real dilemma back at base and so, until they decided who was to go where, they called me back and said, 'Please hold your position over Port Wakefield while we decide which place we're going to send you to.'

And of course, being in an aircraft, the Flight Nurse just started laughing, because by saying—'Please hold your position'—it almost came across like they wanted us to stop the aeroplane, dead still, in midair and hold it there until they'd decided where to send us. In reality, of course, what we were doing was holding our position by flying around in circles which, I may add, then had Air Traffic Control wondering what the hell was going on with this plane going around and around, circling over Port Wakefield.

Now, I'll tell you this last one, though we'd better not mention any names. But this particular pilot had just moved from Port Augusta down to Adelaide. He was an excellent pilot and was always very efficient. You know, he was one of those guys whose motto may've been along the lines of: let's get the job done as quickly and efficiently as possible so that the patient can receive treatment as soon as possible.

Anyhow, this pilot was in the King Air and he was asked to go to Keith, in the south-east of South Australia, to pick up a patient. Again, I must stress that it wasn't an urgent flight. But from the air, a lot of these small towns look very much the same and they also have very similar-looking airstrips.

So the pilot flew down to Keith but, actually, he mistakenly landed a few miles short at another place called Tintinara. So he landed at Tintinara instead of Keith. And I suppose you'd have to say that, because of his efficient manner, this particular pilot could get a little bit impatient at times. So when he landed at Tintinara and there's no ambulance in sight, he gets on the radio and says, 'Where's this bloody ambulance. We're here and you're not.'

And the ambulance crew comes back and they say, 'Where are you? We're at the airstrip, waiting.'

So he came back and said, 'Well, I'm here and you're not.'

'Well, we're here and you're not,' they replied.

Then he thought he'd better take a pause and have a bit of a think about things. And that's when he worked out that he'd landed at Tintinara instead of Keith.

'Won't be long,' he said.

Wouldn't be Alive

My name is Alex Hargans and I had my ninety-third birthday two weeks ago. These days I'm aching a bit with osteoporosis but I'm still going to have a new hip put in in a few months time and the doctor told me that I'll be the oldest person he's ever performed that sort of operation on. So there you go.

But what I want to talk about is that, in the previous Flying Doctor's book, there was a story titled 'A Piece of Piss'. It was all about a big head-on accident, involving an elderly couple, out on the dirt road between Halls Creek and Fitzroy Crossing, up in the Kimberley region of Western Australia. I believe it was told by a friend of Penny Ende's, who's the nursing wife of the Flying Doctor pilot who attended that accident. The pilot's name was Jan Ende. Well, that story was about me and my wife, Edna, and I'd like to tell my side of things because, to this day, I truly believe that if it hadn't been for the flying skills of Jan Ende, the RFDS pilot, I wouldn't be alive.

Okay then, here we go. Well, back in 1973, the wife, Edna, and I decided that we'd like to go on a big outback trip in my fairly new V8 Fairmont. So we left our home, here in Bathurst, which is in the central east of New South Wales, and we headed up into south-western Queensland, to Charleville, then on to the Stockman's Hall of Fame at Longreach, before getting on to the Barkly Highway, which came out just above Tennant Creek. That's where you'll find the memorial to John Flynn, these days.

From there we headed north along the Stuart Highway to Darwin. We fossicked around there for a while then we drove back down to Katherine and took the Victoria Highway across into northern Western Australia before heading south, down the Great Northern Highway to Halls Creek.

Mind you, I don't know why they call them highways because

they're not up to scratch as far as highways go. Back then, most of them weren't much more than poorly graded, corrugated, gravel roads, with lots of potholes which were overflowing with that very fine dusty dirt they describe as bulldust. I might add that they're not too wide either so when you come across one of those huge cattle tucks, or road trains as they're known, you've got to be extremely careful, as I was to find out.

Anyhow, our aim was to go and have a look at the tourist resort place of Broome, over on the west coast, then return to Halls Creek and go across the Tanami Track to Alice Springs, then back home again to Bathurst.

Well, we were on our way to Broome and we'd pulled up for petrol at Halls Creek and I was talking to the owner of the place there and he said, 'Do you mind if I give you a bit of free advice?'

'I don't mind at all,' I said. 'I'm always interested in a bit of free advice.'

'Well,' he said, 'from here on a lot of road trains use this road and there's also a lot of bulldust and these fellers know the track like the back of their hand so they don't slow down in the bulldust and there's been a few accidents lately involving people from the east coast who stop and wait for the dust to clear before they move on. And while they've stopped they've been hit by someone coming up from behind them. So my advice to you is,' he said, 'whatever you do, don't stop. If you come across one of these road trains just slow down a bit, but don't stop.'

'Okay,' I said. 'Thanks for that.'

And so we headed off towards Fitzroy Crossing. Then along the way we saw one of the big road trains coming toward us and it was drafting up a huge cloud of bulldust. So I switched on my headlights and I slowed down and kept well over to my left, off near the edge of the road.

Well, the bloke at the petrol station had been right because the bulldust that the road train kicked up was so thick I could only see about two car lengths in front of me.

Anyway, just as the prime mover had almost passed us, I caught this flash of a nickel-plated bumper bar coming straight

*It's a dangerous drive along those poorly graded dirt roads with all the corrugations and bulldust—*The Hansford Collection

at me, overtaking the road train in all the dust. It turned out to be a feller driving an old Holden and we found out later that he was towing a great big trailer with no brakes on. He also didn't have his headlights on. My estimate would be that he must've been doing at least 100 kilometres per hour and we were probably doing about forty. So the closing time was pretty brief.

Even so, I think I managed to get my foot on the brake. Though that didn't do much good because, when we collided, the engine of the Fairmont got knocked back under the seat and my right hip got displaced about 6 inches. Most of the damage was done to the driver's side of my vehicle, so I was pinned in the car. I couldn't move at all. I had the dash up under my chin, with one knee threaded up through the steering wheel. Still, I managed to say to Edna, 'Could you get out and undo the bolts underneath the seat so that I can get the seat back?'

And even though, due to the impact of the seatbelt, Edna had a number of broken ribs, she still managed to get out of the car on her side, the passenger's side. Anyway, she went and had a bit of a look around, then she came back and said, 'Look, the back of the car's broken and the tyres are flat, and it's on the ground.'

Now, because his truck had kicked up so much bulldust, the driver hadn't seen a thing and so he'd kept on driving. So there I was, stuck there, out on this pretty lonely stretch of road and, I can assure you, it was very painful.

Another thing that really, really frightened me was that I always carried my spare petrol on the roof-rack of the Fairmont, in a couple of those spitfire wind tanks. And when the collision occurred, the roof rack kept going and petrol went everywhere. So all the while I was trapped inside the car, and I couldn't move, there was this strong smell of petrol around the place. And my immediate thought was that: if somebody decides to light a fag to steady their nerves, then I'm well and truly done for.

So I said to Edna, 'Go and see the people in the other car and tell them not to strike a match.'

And Edna went over to speak to them, but I think the driver of the old Holden had a fractured skull and a ruptured spleen or something so he wasn't too interested in lighting up a fag at that stage. And the two women that were with him, they both had broken arms, so even if they wanted a fag—they couldn't light a match because they couldn't use their arms.

Then after a little while a drilling rig team came along. I forget how many vehicles they were travelling in but they were in a bit of a convoy and they stopped and chucked a big hook through where the windscreen used to be and they pulled the dash away from me. Then finally, they got my knee out from under the steering wheel and dragged me out through the back window of the Fairmont.

The next thing, a PMG [Postmaster General] bloke came along and he had a two-way radio, so he got onto that and he sent out a call. Now, I may be a little bit wrong here but I think that the Manager of Christmas Creek Station heard this call and then he came out with a tall antenna on the back of his utility and it was he that actually called the Flying Doctor base in Derby. And naturally the RFDS said they'd fly out as soon as humanly possible.

And the rest of the story is pretty much as it was written up in 'A Piece of Piss'. You know, about how the drilling rig people and the PMG bloke, along with the Manager from Christmas Creek Station, they blocked off a section of the road and everyone who stopped got out of their vehicles and helped knock down the anthills and clear the stones and stuff off a straight section of the road so that the RFDS plane could land.

Then Jan Ende flew out with the doctor and a flight nurse and he managed to put down the Queen Air aeroplane on that rough bit of straight road. And then came the other real scary bit with our dodgy escape out of there. Because, in reality, the bit of road Jan had to take-off along was far too short for the type of aeroplane he was flying, particularly with its increased passenger weight. So he really had to gun the Queen Air to get it back in the air again and he just made it because, in doing so, the propellers shredded the shrubbery as he inched the plane off the ground.

Both the vehicles were written off, of course, and I never saw my fairly new V8 Fairmont again. Anyhow, Jan and I have kept in touch ever since the accident. Incidentally, he's coming over in August, so I'll probably see him again then.

I've since lost my mate, Edna. I lost her about three years ago now and had she lived for another couple of months, we would've been married for sixty-nine years. And, you know, life's pretty lonely without Edna—real lonely, in fact. And we never had a row, not over all that time. Never a row, and we did everything together, everything that is, apart from the five years and sixty-five days I was serving in the Air Force during the war.

But there's a little bit of a twist to the story about that accident and it's one that I haven't really mentioned too much before. It's got to do with the generosity of humanity. Because, see, Edna and I, we were married back in 1934, in the Depression era. We had a very basic wedding, at the Methodist Manse in Bathurst, with just a couple of witnesses. There were no bridal bouquets or any of that sort of stuff, just a vow and a kiss and that sealed it for life. We were married, and that was it.

As you might know, things were very bad in 1934, you know, with the Depression going on. Unemployment was rife and so times were tough. Actually, I remember when Edna used to go shopping with just sixpence in her purse—yes, just sixpence— and she'd buy threepence worth of soup bones and threepence worth of soup vegetables, and she'd make up a huge pot of soup and we'd try and string that out.

Anyhow, the way the dole worked in those days was that if you weren't resident in a town, you could only get the dole once. So the people that were on the dole had to line up outside the police station and get interrogated by the cops. You know, they'd ask, 'Why did you lose your last job?' and 'Where was your last job?' All that sort of stuff, and some of them were quite strict about it. And so, about lunchtime, fellers who were down and out would come around and they'd say to Edna, 'Misses, I'll cut you a barrow load of wood in exchange fer a feed.'

And Edna, being Edna, would always reply with, 'Oh, there's no need for you to cut wood for us, but you're welcome to stay for a feed.'

'Oh, thank you, Misses,' they'd say. 'Thank you very much.'

When that happened, Edna would just add an extra cup of water into the soup pot so there was enough to go around.

So that was away back, during the Depression era, in the 1930s. Then in 1973, after we had the accident out on the Halls Creek to Fitzroy Crossing road, whilst Edna and I were recovering in the Derby Hospital—and I must say that they treated us extremely well up there—I got a letter from one of the down-and-out blokes that'd visited us a few times during the Depression. And in the letter he wrote, 'I don't know how you're fixed for money, but I read about your accident. I remember your kindness to me, the meals that I had at your place and I'm enclosing $20, just in case you're a bit short.'

So, wasn't that fantastic? And he was a Scotchman, too.

Final Flight

There's one really memorable trip that sticks in my mind. That was back on 9 February 1981 and I guess it turned out to be one of the main reasons why I gave flying up, in the end.

Of course, I'd been flying for a long time before then. Actually, I first joined the RFDS as a Flight Nurse back in 1976. That was up here, in Derby. Then after two years of constant flying, I just wanted a break and go overseas for three months with some friends. I already had six weeks' holiday due to me, then I wanted to add to that another six weeks' leave without pay. Anyhow, the Health Department, in Perth, who administered all those sorts of things— and from a long, long way down south, I may add—well, they just said, 'You can't do that. We won't give you leave without pay.'

So, then I resigned and I decided to take a whole year off. And when I was finishing up, the lady down in Perth who did the interviewing and the hiring of people for the Health Department, she said, 'Don't worry, when you come back, just give me a call and I'm sure we can do something for you.'

'Okay, thanks,' I said and off I went and had a wonderful year of travel.

Then when I returned from overseas I went to stay in my parents' house at Mareeba, in far north Queensland, and it was a desperate case of, 'Well, seeing I've got no money left, I'd better get a job.'

So, I wrote to the lady in Perth telling her that I was back in Australia and was enquiring about another position. I also explained that I wasn't available for about three or four weeks because my parents had gone on holidays and I'd promised to look after their house and garden. Next thing I know, a telegram arrives from Perth saying, 'Come immediately. We've got a position available at the Port Hedland RFDS base.'

Then I had to telegram back to say, 'Look, as I stated in my letter, I'm not available. I can't do anything for another three weeks.'

Anyhow, so then I thought they'd naturally go ahead and give the position to someone else. But when my parents returned home, the position was still available so I went to Port Hedland. But I didn't like it that much because Hedland was all emergency stuff. They didn't fly clinics out of Hedland whereas they did out of Derby and it was the clinic work—the people-contact—that I used to enjoy so much. I mean, you know, the emergency stuff was also in Derby and you had to do it, but I didn't thrive on it, if you understand what I mean. Anyhow, I did four months in Port Hedland and then, when a position came vacant up at Derby, I jumped at it. So yeah, in all I'd done my first two years with the RFDS in Derby, took a year off, and then I started up there again in 1979. And I was very pleased about that.

But the constant flying does tend to wear you down after a while, and it was a couple of years later, on 9 February 1981, when we got the call from Balgo Aboriginal Community. By then we'd increased our RFDS fleet in Derby. We now had two pilots and two aeroplanes—a Queen Air and a Beechcraft Baron—though, mind you, we still had just the two flight nurses. But that's the way it went in those days, and so I was one of the flight nurses.

Anyway, the other flight nurse plus a doctor and one of the pilots had already been down at Balgo in the Queen Air aeroplane earlier that day, running a clinic. And while they were there the doctor had attended to a young Aboriginal girl—a nine-year-old—who'd apparently shown some tablets to her mother and said, 'I've just eaten some of these.'

The little girl was a bit slow, you know, retarded. I guess that these days they'd say she was 'disabled'. So the doctor gave the girl some medicine to make her vomit, which she did and, sure enough, the tablets came out. She was still a little bit drowsy, but the doctor thought, 'Well, at least she's got it all out of her system. She should be okay, now.'

Then after they'd finished the clinic at Balgo, they jumped back into the Queen Air and headed back to Derby. But unbeknown to everybody, the little girl had also fed some of the tablets to a four-year-old boy. I forget now, but I think it might've been her baby brother. Now, the four-year-old had gone to bed earlier that afternoon and when his mum had tried to wake him around five o'clock, he wouldn't stir. He was right out of it, and that's when we got the call in at our Derby base.

By this stage, the Queen Air that had been out at Balgo was about due back in Derby. So, with the Queen Air being faster than our second aircraft, the Beechcraft Baron, they said, 'Well, as soon as the Queen Air arrives we'll refuel it and send it straight back out there again to pick up this deeply unconscious little boy.'

So the pilot, myself and a doctor—a paediatrician—arrived at the Derby airstrip ready to go to Balgo. The Queen Air landed and, while they were refuelling it, the two pilots exchanged conversation about the weather. Being February it was wet season so, you know, there was a lot of lightning about and storms and it was pretty blowy and very wet. But from all reports, apparently, at that stage, Balgo, itself, was okay.

Anyway, we took off into this driving rain. It was horizontal rain. Very bad weather. Terrible. We were being buffeted all around the place. But we kept on going and going, and after a while, to me, it seemed that we were taking much longer than expected. Normally, it used to take us around two-and-a-half-hours to get out to Balgo in the Beechcraft Baron and here we were in the Queen Air, a faster aircraft, and we'd already been in the air for that long.

Now the pilot we had with us was one of our older pilots. Mind you, he was also a very excellent pilot. He'd flown in Vietnam and places like that, so he'd had a lot of experience. Anyway, we kept flying and flying and I was thinking, Gosh, it's taking a long time.

So in the end, I went up front and I said to the pilot, 'Where are we? Surely we should nearly be there by now.'

'I know we should. It's out there somewhere,' he said, 'but I can't see the lights.' Normally, when Balgo knew we were coming at night, they'd put on their big basketball court lights. 'Perhaps we can't see them because the rain's so heavy between us and them,' the pilot added.

'Oh, okay,' I said and I went and sat back down.

Then, sure enough, much to my relief the lights of Balgo finally came into view. And oddly enough, while it was still raining where we were, when we got over Balgo, there was no rain at all. None at all. Though, mind you, there was still a savage wind.

Anyway, the pilot managed that alright and we landed safely and were met at the airstrip. Then the doctor and I, we were taken straight into the Balgo Clinic to stabilise the child, the little boy. First thing was to put up a drip in case we needed to give him IV drugs. I think the doctor's main concern was that, because the boy was unconscious, he might fit—you know, have a seizure—and the doctor just wanted to have a line in, just in case.

So we sorted out the little four-year-old boy. Then the doctor took a look at the nine-year-old girl and because she was still very drowsy he decided that it'd be better if we took both the children back to Derby with us. We had two stretchers so we laid the children down on those in the Queen Air. We placed the little boy—who was our main concern—with his head to the door of the aeroplane just in case the doctor needed to intubate him; you know, to breathe for him if he should stop breathing, which is always a danger when you've had an overdose of drugs. But the little boy seemed to be alright. We had the drip up and he was breathing by himself, though he was still right out to it. So the paediatrician's sitting over there. I'm here, the baby boy's just over there and then the older one, the girl, she was right behind me on her stretcher, and she was alright. You could rouse her but she was still very dopey.

By the time we'd got them both settled in the Queen Air the rain had started to come in again and there was also still a very strong wind blowing. But we took off alright, it was about nine o'clock at night, and I'm busy down the back, you know, taking obs and everything on the children.

Then we were only about 15 or 20 minutes out of Balgo, on our way back to Derby, and, you know, when you've flown a lot you tend to get accustomed to the monotonous drone of the engine. Well we'd levelled out at about 6000 feet and I heard this funny noise in one of the engines. I don't know how to describe it except that it was, like, it just wasn't normal. Anyhow I'm still busy with the children but when I hear this odd noise I look up at the pilot and there he is, he's sitting there in the cockpit, with these little half glasses on and he's peering over them at his controls.

So I said to the paediatrician, 'I think there's something wrong with that engine. Can you hear it?'

'No,' he said, 'I can't.'

But you know, as I said, when you fly a lot, you just know these things. Anyhow, because I wasn't backward in coming forward, and I wanted to know what was happening, I went up to the pilot and I tapped him on the shoulder and I said, 'What's wrong?'

And he was a really slow talker. 'Oh,' he drawled, 'I'm having trouble with the port engine.' He said, 'It's running a bit hot.'

Still and all, he didn't really seem all that worried so I just said something like, 'Oh, okay,' then I went back and sat down.

'What's up?' the doctor asked.

'The pilot's having trouble with one of the engines.'

And just as I said it, I was gripped by that fleeting fear of, 'Hey, we could be in big, big trouble here. Someone's got to know about this because if we go down away out here in the Kimberley, nobody will even know what's happened.'

Anyhow there was a radio at the back of the co-pilot's seat, which the nurse could use, so I used that to try and get in touch with Balgo. But there was no answer there. Then there's the red button—the emergency button—it's the same one the station people use in an emergency to get in contact with their nearest RFDS base. By this stage the pilot was talking to someone over his radio, but with all the racket going on with the wind and the rain and everything—I wasn't sure whether he was alerting anyone or not. But we were really limping, so I thought, well, this is an emergency.

So I pressed the emergency button and the wife of the Base Manager at Derby come over the radio and I said, 'You know how we just had to go to Balgo and pick up these two children.'

'Yes.'

'Well,' I said, 'we're on our way back to Derby and we've run into difficulty. We're having trouble with one of the engines in the Queen Air and I just think you ought to know.'

And the wife of the Base Manager said, 'Thanks very much for that information. We'll stand by if you need us.'

Then just as I'd replaced the radio, the pilot turned around to me and said, 'I'm going to have to close the port engine down.'

Well, from then on we were just so worried that something very serious was about to happen. And it was so dark outside the Queen Air that I couldn't see a thing, and I'm thinking, here we are in this big plane, which is now about to start flying on just the one engine, it's pitch black outside, it's raining, it's extremely windy, and if we're only travelling on one engine then it'll take at least two hours to get back to Derby.

We were still flying at 6000 feet at that stage, but when the pilot shut the engine down I took a look over his shoulder and I could see the altimeter in free-fall. From 6000 feet it dropped down to 5000 feet and there he was, the pilot, trying to steady the thing. Then it fell from 5000 feet down to 4000 feet, down to 3000 feet, and we eventually pulled up at 2000 feet. From experience, I knew that the lowest safe flying level was 1000 feet and that was because of the mountains that were around us—the 'jump-ups', as they were known.

Then it suddenly hit me, how will we ever make it?

So I'm desperately trying to work out just how long it was going to take us to get back to Derby, on one engine and in these horrific conditions. Now, my maths was never that good but whatever way I tried to figure it out, the result always ended up as being an extremely frightening prospect, indeed. An impossible equation. And, you know, it was one of those times when your whole life sort of flashes before you and I came to the conclusion, well, like, I'm not quite ready to go just yet.

And it was about then that the pilot turned around and said, 'I think we'll try and get back to Balgo. It's not as far.'

'Oh,' I replied, 'what a good idea.'

So he turned the Queen Air around and we started to head back to Balgo. But by that stage we were already twenty minutes out and I knew that they only left the basketball court lights and the airstrip lights on for twenty minutes after a plane left. And that meant, by the time we got back there, all the lights would be out and we wouldn't be able to find the place. So I tried to raise Balgo again on the radio to tell them, you know, 'Hey, switch the lights back on. We're in big trouble here and we have to come back.'

But again, there wasn't an answer. So I continued trying and trying to get on to Balgo and still, nothing, nothing, nothing. Then I realised that the staff in the clinic there would've probably been so pleased to have see the two children fly out that they would've said, 'Oh well, they're safe now so, with it being such a rotten night, we may as well just pack up and go home and go to bed.'

Then, for the first time that night, luck was with us because as we got closer to Balgo we could just make out the lights from the basketball court. Thankfully, someone must've forgotten to switch them off. What's more, when we got closer, the airstrip lights were still on. And, well, I just couldn't believe it.

Still, there remained the huge problem of trying to land the Queen Air on just the one engine, and in these terrible conditions. It was sheeting rain and you know how, when the pilots prepare to land, they fly across the airstrip then go around to line up so that the airstrip's right there in front of them. Well our pilot went around once, then twice, then three times and so on until he reached his eighth attempt and he still couldn't line up the airstrip to his satisfaction. He'd either lose sight of the airstrip lights in the pelting rain or the driving wind would blow the plane too far this way or too far that way, and by now I'm thinking, We're never going to make it.

But the people from Balgo must've heard our plane flying around because, as we passed over again we saw some cars coming out to the airport. They hadn't got our message. No message at all. Nobody knew. They just heard the drone of our Queen Air so they thought they'd better come and see what was going on. You know, when the RFDS plane has been your lifeline for so long, it's such a distinctive sound. You never forget it.

Now, back in those days, Balgo used to own Kingfisher Air and they had a plane sitting on the airstrip. So their pilot got in his aircraft and he was able to speak to our pilot. 'What's your problem?' he asked.

'Well,' replied our pilot, 'we've only got one engine. We're being blown around all over the place and I can't see the approach to the airstrip because of the driving rain.'

Then our pilot asked if they could park two cars with their headlights on at the approach to the airstrip so, at least, he could see where he was supposed to come down. So they did that and we were eventually able to land. And, oh, we were just so grateful when we finally touched down, just so relieved. Actually, we were all in a heap—a complete mess—absolutely spent.

But, you know, the wind was so bad that the windsock on their strip was blowing horizontal. So you really had to give it to our pilot. I mean, to keep his cool through all that and to make the right decisions, and get us all there in one piece. Well, as I said, you really had to give it to him.

So, we then unloaded the two little kids and the Balgo Hospital staff had to get up out of their beds and look after them overnight. We also stayed at Balgo that night, of course. Then the next day the RFDS sent out the little Beechcraft Baron and we brought the little boy back to Derby with us, in that. From memory, I think he'd started to regain consciousness by then. But we didn't take the older girl. She was okay by then. So yeah, they survived, no problem.

But something really scary; first thing on that following morning, before the Beechcraft Baron arrived to take us back to Derby, our pilot went out to try and start up the Queen Air and— you wouldn't believe it—but neither of the two engines would start. Not even the one that we flew in on would work. They'd both gone. And afterwards, when they had the investigation about it, apparently they found out that the driving rain had somehow gone in under the cowl—you know, the hooding around the engine—and it ended up wetting the magnetos, which put the engines out. And so that was the cause. That's what they said.

So, you know, if we would've continued on towards Derby, well, who knows what might've happened. And that's the experience that made me think, Well, it must be about time to hang up your wings. You've been at it for a fair while now and I think somebody's trying to tell you something.

And not long after that I finished up with the RFDS. Actually, what also helped make the decision easier was that I got married. 'Well,' I said, 'I've also got someone else to consider now.'

So that was it for me. There was no more flying.

Farewell—RFDS